Cassell Busi

FRANCE

Second Edition

Karsta Neuhaus and Margret Haltern

In association with
The British Chambers of Commerce

CASSELL

Cassell
Wellington House, 125 Strand
London WC2R 0BB, England

215 Park Avenue South
New York, NY 10003
USA

© ILT Verlag 1992
Salzborn 9
4630 Bochum 5
Germany

ILT-Verlag are grateful to Martine Brunel
for her translation.

First published 1992 by ILT Verlag
Revised edition first published in the UK in 1992 by Cassell
Second revised edition first published 1995

British Library Cataloguing-in-Publication Data
A catalogue record for this book is available from the
British Library.

ISBN 0–304–33116–3

Typeset by Litho Link Ltd, Welshpool, Powys, Wales
Printed and bound in Great Britain by Biddles Ltd, Guildford and
King's Lynn

CONTENTS

PART II

INTRODUCTION

The realization of the Single European Market on 1 January 1993 has increased competition among British firms for foreign markets. This means contacting potential business partners abroad initially by phone, fax, and letter, and then following up with talks and negotiations face to face. The ability to speak to business people in their own language has a major role in determining the success or otherwise of these undertakings.

Conventional phrasebooks are not specifically designed to meet these complex needs. *Cassell Business Companions: France* meets this challenge by providing a wide range of practical information in an easily accessible format, creating a guide which is both an invaluable aid to learning and an indispensable reference source. The *Cassell Business Companions* are specifically tailored to meet the needs of small and medium-sized companies.

Part I sets out the essential technical vocabulary and standard phrases for use in different aspects of business with French companies: advertising; buying and selling; insurance; accounting; personnel; contracts, etc.

This section is not intended as a substitute for technical dictionaries, but rather as a useful aide-mémoire for the practised negotiator. It will be especially useful for those companies which do not have access to translation services or trained interpreters. The vocabulary lists are complemented by formulation aids and model letters which enable the user to communicate in both the spoken and written word with accuracy and confidence.

A unique dimension to this book is the provision of many useful addresses which are an invaluable source of information for those conducting business abroad. Contact details for official or institutional agencies are given alongside the relevant vocabulary (with translations where appropriate).

Part II sets out the general language requirements and information on customs, travel, hotels and banks, etc. for anyone intending to visit France. A special section on small talk lists those expressions which so often prove essential in establishing initial contact and in the successful fostering of a business relationship. Helpful tips on French customs are also provided.

Part III comprises a generous compendium of data, including a glossary of French job titles, common abbreviations, useful key addresses for further research, as well as information on the Single European Market.

The **Appendix** incorporates a bilingual glossary of technical terms, with their phonetic transcriptions. A comprehensive index facilitates the use of this wide-ranging guide to the essentials of doing business in French.

The authors would like to point out that there is often no precise translation of technical terms and phrases, but that every effort has been made to provide translations which convey the closest meaning possible. Every care has also been taken to ensure that the addresses and telephone numbers given are accurate, but these are subject to change, particularly phone numbers.

Finally, good luck, and we hope that you will enjoy using this guide.

Karsta Neuhaus and Margret Haltern
Bochum

Notes on Signs, Symbols and Abbreviations Used in the Text

▼ Formulation aids for spoken and written contexts

✉ Model letters

■ Information on France and its inhabitants

▶ Possible reactions from listeners

→ Useful UK addresses

m masculine noun

f feminine noun

pl plural noun

PART I

1

Market	Le Marché
common market	le marché commun
to compete	faire concurrence
competition	la concurrence
competitor	le concurrent
distribution network	le réseau de distribution
domestic market	le marché intérieur
highly competitive market	un marché avec une haute concurrence
market analysis	l'analyse du marché
market research	l'étude de marché
market situation	la situation du marché
market survey	l'étude de marché
marketing	la vente, la commercialisation
monopoly	la position de monopole
price maintenance	le prix imposé, l'imposition des prix
questionnaire	le questionnaire
sales potential	le potentiel de ventes, les débouchés
sales territory	le secteur de vente
single European market	le marché européen
trend	la tendance

Our products sell well.
Nos produits se vendent très bien.

We are putting our products on the market.
Nous mettons nos produits en vente.

We are launching a new product.
Nous lançons un nouveau produit sur le marché.

French Chamber of Commerce
  and Industry in the UK
Knightsbridge House
197 Knightsbridge
London SW7 1RB

Tel: 0171–225 5250
Telex: 269 132 FRACOM
Fax: 0171–225 5557

3

The addresses of market research agencies in France can be obtained from:

Association Nationale du Marketing pour la Recherche sur le Développement des Marchés
(National Association for Marketing and Market Research) (ADETEM)
221 rue la Fayette
75010 Paris
Tel: (1) 40 38 97 10
Fax: (1) 40 38 05 08

Centre d'Études du Commerce et de Distribution
(Research Centre on Commerce and Distribution) (CECOD)
19 rue de Calais
75009 Paris
Tel: (1) 40 69 37 00
Fax: (1) 47 20 61 28

Association Européenne pour les Études d'Opinion et de Marketing (ESOMAR)
(European Association for Marketing and Opinion Polls)
J.J. Viottastraat 29
1071 Amsterdam
The Netherlands
Tel: 010 31 20 664 2141

Agence Nationale de Valorisation de la Recherche (ANVAR)
(National Agency for the Promotion of Research)
43 rue Caumartin
75009 Paris Cedex 09
Tel: (1) 40 17 83 00
Fax: (1) 42 66 02 20

Information on trade agencies can be obtained from:

Fédération Nationale des Agents Commerciaux

(National Federation of Commercial Agents)
23 rue de Rome
75008 Paris
Tel: (1) 42 93 61 24
Télex: 230 29823
Fax: (1) 40 17 83 19

The services of commercial agents are advertised in *Info*, a
publication of the French Chamber of Commerce and Industry in
the UK under the section, 'Opportunités d'Affaires'.

Institut National de la Statistique et des
Études Économiques (INSEE)
(National Institute of Statistics and
Economic Studies)
18 boulevard Adolphe Pinard
75675 Paris Cedex 14
Tel: (1) 41 17 50 50
Fax: (1) 41 17 66 66

Centre de Documentation Économique
(Centre for Economic Documentation)
Chambre de Commerce et d'Industrie de
Paris
27 avenue de Friedland
75382 Paris Cedex 08

La Documentation Française
(Documentation on France)
29/31 quai Voltaire
75007 Paris
Tel: (1) 40 15 70 00

DELPHES: Banque de Données
d'Information Économique
(Databank for Economic Information)
Chambre de Commerce et d'Industrie de
Paris
27 avenue de Friedland
75382 Paris Cedex 08

See Part III, 11 for a list of some of the French Chambers of Commerce and Industry.

→1 Useful UK addresses can be found in Part III, 10.

2

Advertising	La Publicité
advertisement	l'annonce publicitaire
advertising consultant	le conseiller publicitaire
advertising gimmick, free gift	le cadeau publicitaire
brochure, leaflet	la brochure
business reply card	la carte-réponse
catalogue	le catalogue
circular	la circulaire
commercial	le film/le spot publicitaire
demonstration	la démonstration
display material	le matériel de démonstration
follow-up letter	la lettre publicitaire de relance
free sample	l'échantillon
handbill	le tract
in-depth knowledge of the trade	connaissances approfondies dans un domaine
instructions, leaflet, pamphlet	la notice
mail-shot, mail circular	l'envoi postal collectif
poster	l'affiche
prospectus, catalogue	le prospectus, le catalogue
public relations	les relations publiques
publicity agency	l'agence publicitaire
publicity campaign	la campagne publicitaire
publicity expenditure	les frais de publicité
sales/promotional letter	la lettre publicitaire
sales promotion	la promotion de vente
show room	la salle d'exposition
training courses for salespersons	les cours de formation pour vendeurs
trial sample	l'échantillon d'essai

▼
We specialize in . . .
Nous sommes spécialisés dans . . .

We trade/deal in . . .
Nous vendons . . .

We are well-known distributors.
Nous sommes très connus comme société de distribution.

We are market leaders in the domestic market.
Nous sommes le numéro un sur le marché intérieur.

We are manufacturers of . . .
Nous sommes fabricants de . . .

The new technology which we sell is very reliable.
Nous vendons une nouvelle technologie sûre.

We are retailers/wholesalers/importers/exporters in the . . . trade.
Nous sommes détaillants/grossistes/importateurs/exportateurs dans la branche . . .

We know the market well.
Nous disposons de très bonnes connaissances sur le marché.

We are a small/medium-sized firm.
Nous sommes une petite/moyenne entreprise.

We are an international company in the . . . sector with annual sales of . . . and a range of well-established speciality products, many of which are market leaders.
Nous sommes une entreprise internationale, travaillant dans le secteur . . ., avec un chiffre de vente annuel de . . . et une gamme de produits spécialisés bien lancés sur le marché dont la plupart sont en tête des ventes.

I'm in advertising.
Je travaille dans la publicité.

For promotional purposes.
A des fins publicitaires.

Book tip:

Agences Conseils
(*Consulting agencies*)
(List of 1700 advertising firms)
Published by:

> Media
> 554 rue d'Amsterdam
> 75008 Paris
> Tel: (1) 42 85 50 00

Useful addresses:

> Fédération Française des Relations
>   Publiques
> (French Federation of Public Relations)
> 6 rue Oswaldo Cruz
> 75016 Paris
> Tel: (1) 45 27 18 70

> Fédération Nationale de la Publicité
> (National Federation for Advertising)
> 40 boulevard Malesherbes
> 75008 Paris
> Tel: (1) 47 42 18 35

→**2** Useful UK addresses can be found in Part III, 10.

3

Fair, Exhibition	La Foire, Le Salon
application	l'inscription
conditions of participation	les conditions de participation
exhibit	l'objet exposé, la pièce d'exposition
exhibition centre	le parc des expositions

exhibition regulations	**le règlement de la foire**
exhibitor	**l'exposant**
fair management	**la direction de la foire/du salon**
fair pass	**la carte de la foire**
floor plan	**le plan de la foire**
floor space	**la surface d'exposition**
hall plan	**le plan des halls d'exposition**
hostess	**l'hôtesse**
industrial fair	**la foire industrielle**
list of exhibitors	**la liste des exposants**
official catalogue	**le catalogue de l'exposition**
organizer (of a fair)	**l'organisateur de la foire**
specialized fair	**la foire spécialisée, le salon spécialisé**
stand rental	**la redevance pour le stand**
stand, stall, booth	**le stand**
trade fair	**la foire commerciale**
visitor at a fair	**le visiteur**
to apply for space	**s'inscrire (à une foire)**
to book exhibition space	**louer une surface d'exposition**
to dismantle a stand	**démonter un stand**
to exhibit, to show	**exposer**
to open a fair	**ouvrir une foire**
to organize a fair	**organiser une foire**
to participate in a fair	**participer à une foire**
to put up a stand	**monter un stand**
to visit a fair	**visiter une foire**

I work for . . .
Je travaille chez . . .

We make . . . and are interested in . . .
Nous produisons . . . et sommes intéressés à . . .

This is our latest model.
C'est notre tout dernier modèle.

We've got some of our latest models here on our stand.
Ici, à notre stand, nous avons quelques-uns de nos tout derniers modèles.

We are launching our product at this exhibition.
Nous lançons notre produit sur cette foire.

We are introducing our product.
Nous présentons notre produit.

I'm sure there's a lot we can offer you.
Je suis sûr que nous avons un tas de choses à vous proposer.

Most customers appreciate the quality of our products.
L'ensemble de nos clients apprécient la qualité de nos produits.

The most important trade fair organizations are:

**Fédération Française des Salons Spécialisés
(French Federation of Trade Fairs)
22 avenue Franklin Roosevelt
75008 Paris
Tel: (1) 42 25 05 80
Fax: (1) 42 56 45 77**

**Comité Français des Expositions
(French Committee of Exhibitions)
22 avenue Franklin Roosevelt
75008 Paris
Tel: (1) 40 76 45 00
Télex: 644578 F**

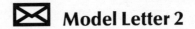 **Model Letter 2**

4

Conferences and Meetings | Conférences et Réunions

agenda	l'ordre du jour
chairperson	le président/la présidente
unanimous(ly)	unanime, à l'unanimité
to attend a conference	prendre part à une conférence
to bring forward a motion	présenter une demande/une requête
to carry a motion	adopter une résolution
to clarify a position	exposer clairement son point de vue
to close the meeting	clore une réunion
to constitute a quorum	atteindre le quorum
to decide on a motion	décider d'une requête
to go into details	aller dans les détails
to keep the minutes	rédiger le compte rendu
to open the meeting	ouvrir une séance
to outline	donner une vue d'ensemble
to reject a motion	rejeter une demande
to vote for/against	voter pour/contre

Some useful phrases:

Frankly, . . .	Franchement, . . .
I am convinced that . . .	Je suis convaincu que . . .
I don't think so	Je ne crois pas
I quite agree	Je suis de votre avis
I think so	Je crois que oui
I'm afraid I couldn't go along with that	Je ne partage pas cet avis
I'm afraid I don't agree	Je ne suis pas de votre avis
In my experience	D'après mon expérience

May I bring up the question of . . .	Est-ce que je peux soulever le problème de . . .
On the contrary	Au contraire
On the one hand, . . . on the other hand	D'une part, . . . d'autre part
That's an important point	C'est un point important
The main problem is . . .	Le problème principal, c'est . . .
The pros and cons	Le pour et le contre
This sort of thing is in my line	C'est de mon ressort
To start with . . .	Au début . . .
To sum up, I can say that	En conclusion, je peux dire . . .
Well, it depends	Ça dépend
What do you think?	Que pensez-vous?
What's your opinion?	Quel est votre avis?

If you need help with translation you will find the following helpful:

Société Nationale des Traducteurs
(National Association of Translators)
(Provides addresses of translation services)
11 rue Navarin
75009 Paris
Tel: (1) 48 78 43 32

Chambre Nationale des Entreprises de Traduction
(National Chamber of Translating Services)
34 bis rue Vignon
75009 Paris
Tel: (1) 47 42 84 14
Fax: (1) 47 42 84 98

The French place great importance on the use of the French language in discussions and negotiations, so as to avoid the need to employ expensive translators and interpreters.

Book Tip:

Salles de Réunion. Guide des salles de réunion adhérentes.
This guide to conference centres and congress halls is published
by the Paris Tourist Office and the Chamber of Commerce, Paris.
It contains detailed information on capacity, technical equipment,
translation services, accommodation, restaurants, etc.

If you require secretarial services, the Chamber of Commerce and
Industry will be able to help you.

In Paris you can rent equipment from a number of firms, e.g.:
CNIT, ASPAC, Centres d'Affaires des Aéroports de Paris.

You can rent offices, as well as various related services (such as
message taking, mail reception and forwarding, fax and telex),
for periods varying from half a day to two years.

> **Centre de Communication et d'Echanges**
>   **(CNIT)**
> **(Centre for Communication and Exchanges)**
> **Club Sari Affaires**
> **CNIT BP 240**
> **92053 Paris La Défense**
> **Tel: (1) 46 92 12 12**
> **Télex: 616203 F**
> **Fax: (1) 46 92 24 00**
>
> **Centres d'Affaires des Aéroports de Paris**
> **(Business Centre at Paris Airports)**
> **Orly:**
> **Tel: (1) 49 75 12 33**
> **Fax: (1) 48 84 47 68**
> **Télex: 265 866**
> **Charles de Gaulle–Roissy:**
> **Tel: (1) 48 62 33 06**
> **Fax: (1) 48 62 47 86**
> **Télex: 233 347**

Franco-British Chamber of Commerce and Industry
7 rue Cimarosa
75116 Paris
Tel: (1) 45 05 13 08

→3 Useful UK addresses can be found in Part III, 10.

5

Product Descriptions

Description de Produit

a limited number of	un nombre limité de
a wide range of	un grand choix de
bulk goods	les marchandises en vrac
capital goods	les biens d'investissement
commodities, goods, merchandise	la marchandise, le produit, les marchandises, les produits
consumer goods	les biens de consommation
finished products	les produits finis
item, lot	le lot (de marchandises)
label	l'étiquette de marque
model, pattern, specimen	l'échantillon, le modèle, le spécimen
operating instructions	le mode d'emploi
pattern	l'échantillon
product liability	la responsabilité du fabricant ou de l'importateur (pour le produit)
quantity	la quantité
raw materials	les matières premières
sample	l'échantillon
sample collection	la collection d'échantillons
sample of no commercial value	l'échantillon sans valeur
semi-finished goods	les produits semi-finis
serial/mass production	la fabrication en série
shortage	le manque

single-part production	**la fabrication hors série**
special design	**la fabrication spéciale hors série**

Some classifications:

blend (coffee, tea)	**le mélange (café, thé)**
brand	**la marque**
grade	**la sorte, la catégorie**
quality	**la qualité**
– commercial quality	**– la qualité d'usage**
– fair average quality	**– la qualité moyenne**
– first-class quality	**– qualité de première classe**
– outstanding quality	**– qualité supérieure**
– poor quality	**– une mauvaise qualité**
– second-rate quality	**– le deuxième choix**
– standard quality	**– la qualité standard**
registered trade mark	**la marque déposée**
size	**la taille**

You inform your customer:

Our product . . .	Notre produit . . .
. . . conforms with French safety regulations	**correspond aux normes de sécurité françaises**
. . . is made to the highest technical standards	**. . . correspond aux normes techniques les plus avancées**
. . . is carefully manufactured	**. . . est fabriqué avec soin**
. . . is maintenance-free	**. . . ne nécessite pas d'entretien**
. . . is reliable	**. . . est sûr**
. . . can be fully adapted to/is fully compatible with all XY systems	**. . . est adaptable à tous les systèmes XY**
. . . is easy and safe	**. . . est simple et sauf**
. . . to handle, to operate	**. . . à manier**
. . . to assemble	**. . . à monter**
. . . to repair	**. . . à réparer**

This is what you might hear in French:

Est-ce qu'il y a une garantie sur cet appareil?
Does it come with a guarantee?

La garantie est de deux ans.
The guarantee lasts for two years.

La garantie est expirée.
The guarantee has run out.

Est-ce que c'est facile d'emploi?
Is it user-friendly?

Pourriez-vous m'expliquer s'il vous plaît, comment ça fonctionne?
Could you explain how it works, please?

Useful addresses:

Association Française de Normalisation
(AFNOR)
(French Association for Standardization)
Tour Europe
92080 Paris La Défense Cedex 7
Tel: (1) 42 91 55 55
Fax: (1) 42 91 56 56
Télex: 611 974

Association Française pour la Qualité
(AFCIQ)
(French Association for Quality Standards)
Tour Europe
92080 Paris La Défense Cedex 7
Tel: (1) 42 91 59 59

Union Fédérale des Consommateurs
(Consumers' Federation)
11 rue Guénot
75555 Paris Cedex 11
Tel: (1) 43 48 55 48

The registration of patents must be done through:

**Institut National de la Propriété
Industrielle (INPI)
(National Institute for Patent Rights)
26 bis rue de Saint Pétersbourg
75008 Paris
Tel: (1) 42 94 52 52**

6

Buying, Selling	**Acheter, Vendre**
accepted in the trade	d'usage dans le commerce, d'usage courant
buyer	l'acheteur
commission agent	le courtier, le commissionnaire
customer	le client
distribution network	le réseau de distribution
exporter	l'exportateur
franchised dealer	le concessionnaire, le commerçant en franchise
hire-purchase	l'achat à tempérament
importer	l'importateur
profit margin	la marge bénéficiaire
purchase	l'achat
purchasing power	le pouvoir d'achat
representative, agent	le représentant
representative on commission	le représentant à la commission/ au pourcentage
retailer	le détaillant
sales	les ventes
sales on commission	la vente à la commission
seller	le vendeur
subcontractor, middle man	le sous-traitant, l'intermédiaire
supplier	le fournisseur
trade	le commerce
trade customs	les usances commerciales
trade mark-up	la marge commerciale

trade relations	**les relations commerciales**
trader, merchant	**le marchand/le négociant**
turnover	**le chiffre d'affaires**
wholesaler	**le grossiste**
to bargain	**marchander**
to buy, to purchase	**acheter**
– to buy at best price	**– acheter au mieux**
– to buy secondhand	**– acheter d'occasion**
to find a ready market	**se vendre bien**
to lease	**louer à bail**
to rent	**louer**
to sell	**vendre**
– to sell at a loss	**– vendre à perte**
– to sell direct	**– vendre directement**
– to sell off	**– liquider**
to trade	**faire du commerce**
to trade in	**faire reprendre, donner en paiement**

▼
Sales are up by 10%.
Les ventes ont augmenté de 10%.

On a sale or return basis.
Vente avec droit de reprise.

The goods are out of stock.
Les marchandises sont épuisées.

You might hear the following in French:

La vente intérieure
domestic market sales

les exportations
export sales

augmentation/diminution du chiffre d'affaires
increase/decrease in sales

18

Centre Français du Commerce Extérieur (CFCE)
(French Centre for Foreign Trade)
10 avenue d'Iéna
75783 Paris Cedex 16
Tel: (1) 40 73 30 00
Télex: 611 934 CFCE F
Fax: (1) 40 73 39 79
Service Orientation: (1) 40 73 38 88

Ministère du Commerce Extérieur
(Ministry of Foreign Trade)
41 quai Branly
75007 Paris
Tel: (1) 45 50 71 11
Télex: 205885
Fax: (1) 45 51 99 61

Direction des Relations Économiques Extérieures (DREE)
(Department of Foreign Trade and Economic Relations)
139 rue de Bercy
75572 Paris
Tel: (1) 40 04 04 04
Télex: 214 463

SIMPLEXPORT/SIMPROFRANCE (Comité Français pour la Simplification des Procédures du Commerce International)
(French Committee for the Simplification of International Trade Procedures)
61 rue de l'Arcade
75008 Paris
Tel: (1) 42 93 03 02
Télex: 640 795

Société pour le Financement des Industries
   Exportatrices (SOFININDEX)
(Society for the Financing of Exporting
   Industries)
3 rue Scribe
75009 Paris
Tel: (1) 42 65 88 08

Union Française des Industries
   Exportatrices (UFIE)
(French Association of Exporting
   Industries)
24 place Dauphine
75001 Paris
Télex: 650 040
Fax: (1) 40 51 73 09
Databank via Minitel: 36 28 2001

Normes et Règlements Techniques pour
   l'Exportation (NOREX)
(Standards and Technical Regulations for
   Export)
Tour Europe
92080 Paris La Défense Cedex 7
Tel: (1) 42 91 59 36
Télex: 611974 F
Fax: (1) 42 91 56 56

→4 Useful UK addresses can be found in Part III, 10.

7

Inquiries, Offers, Prices	Demandes, Offres, Prix
buying conditions	les conditions d'achat
detailed information about	des informations détaillées sur
latest catalogue	le tout dernier catalogue

list of products	**la liste des produits**
price list	**la liste des prix**
references	**les références**
selection of samples	**un choix d'échantillons,**
	l'échantillonnage
selling conditions	**les conditions de vente**
specification	**la description détaillée**
terms	**les conditions**
to be interested in	**être intéressé par**
to inform	**informer**
to refer to	**s'adresser à**
estimate	**le devis**
offer, proposal	**l'offre**
– bid	**– l'offre (d'achat)**
– binding offer	**– une offre ferme**
– subject to confirmation offer	**– une offre sans engagement**
– quote	**– l'offre avec indication de prix**
– written offer	**– une offre écrite**
pro-forma invoice	**la facture fictive**
tender	**l'appel d'offre**
to accept an offer	**accepter une offre**
to make a firm offer	**offrir ferme**
to offer subject to confirmation	**offrir sans engagement**
to revoke an offer	**revenir sur une offre**
to submit an offer	**soumettre une offre**
all-in price	**le prix tout compris**
at half price	**à moitié prix**
buying price	**le prix d'achat**
competitive price	**le prix compétitif**
consumer price	**le prix à la consommation**
factory gate price	**le prix à la production**
fair price	**un prix raisonnable**
favourable price	**un prix avantageux**
fixed price	**le prix fixe**
list price	**le prix-catalogue**
lump sum	**la somme globale forfaitaire**
price increase	**l'augmentation de prix**

21

price reduction	**le rabais, la remise, la ristourne**
retail price	**le prix de détail**
selling price	**le prix de vente**
special price	**le prix spécial**
subscription cost	**le prix de souscription/ d'émission**
surcharge	**le supplément, la majoration**
unit price	**le prix unitaire/à l'unité**
wholesale price	**le prix de gros**
to adjust prices	**ajuster les prix**
to undercut	**vendre moins cher que, pratiquer le dumping**
to quote prices	**fixer les prix**
cash discount	**l'escompte au comptant**
discount	**la remise, l'escompte, la ristourne**
quantity discount	**le rabais d'achat en grande quantité**
special discount	**la remise spéciale**
trade discount	**le rabais négociant**

▼

We see from your advertisement in . . . that you are producers of . . .
Il ressort de votre annonce parue dans . . . que vous produisez . . .

We have heard of your products.
Nous avons entendu parler de vos produits.

Your name was given to us by . . .
Votre nom nous a été donné par . . .

We saw your stand at the Hanover Fair.
Nous avons visité votre stand à la foire de Lyon.

We would like to have further details about . . .
Nous aimerions avoir de plus amples renseignements sur . . .

We require for immediate delivery . . .
Nous avons besoin dans les plus brefs délais de . . .

We are in the market for . . ./ we require . . .
Nous avons besoin de . . .

Would you please quote your best price and terms of payment.
Pourriez-vous s'il vous plaît nous faire part de vos prix les plus avantageux et de vos conditions de vente.

Full information regarding export prices and discounts for regular orders would be appreciated.
Nous aimerions recevoir des informations détaillées sur vos prix à l'exportation et la remise que vous faites dans le cas de commandes régulières.

We are prepared to place a trial order.
Nous sommes prêts à passer une commande d'essai.

Please find enclosed our price list, as requested.
Comme vous l'avez demandé, veuillez trouver ci-joint une liste des prix.

We are sending you our illustrated catalogue under separate cover.
Nous vous envoyons sous pli séparé notre catalogue illustré.

We can make you a firm offer for . . .
Nous pouvons vous faire une offre ferme sur . . .

Our offer is firm subject to acceptance by . . .
Notre offre est ferme jusqu'au . . .

We give a trade discount of 20% on our catalogue prices.
Nous vous accordons le rabais négociant de 20% sur nos prix de catalogue.

Packing included.
Emballage compris.

The price quoted is fob London.
Ce prix s'entend FOB Londres.

Recommended price
Le prix indicatif

No extra charge
Pas de supplément

Prices are subject to change without notice
Sous réserve de modification de prix

Subject to prior sale
Sauf vente

Prices are subject to revision according to the following sliding scale:
Les prix sont soumis à une variation des prix conforme à la clause d'échelle mobile des prix:

We assure you that your order will be carried out to your complete satisfaction.
Nous vous certifions que votre commande sera exécutée à votre entière satisfaction.

 Model Letters 3 and 4

8

Order and Acknowledgement	Commande et Confirmation
acknowledgement of order	l'accusé de réception de la commande
advance order	la commande d'avance
initial order	la première commande
order	la commande, l'ordre
order book	le carnet de commandes
order form	le bon/bulletin de commande
order number	le numéro de la commande
orders on hand	les commandes en carnet
repeat order	la commande supplémentaire
to enter/book an order	noter une commande
to carry out an order	exécuter une commande

to place an order **passer une commande**
as per your order/in accordance **d'après votre commande**
 with your order

We thank you for your quote and have pleasure in placing an order for . . .
Nous vous remercions de votre offre et sommes heureux de vous passer une commande de . . .

Kindly supply the following goods at your earliest convenience.
Veuillez nous livrer les marchandises suivantes le plus vite possible.

The delivery dates stipulated in our order must be strictly adhered to.
Les délais de livraison que nous avons indiqueś dans notre commande doivent être strictement observés.

Your careful attention to our instructions would be appreciated.
Nous vous serions reconnaissants de bien vouloir respecter exactement nos directives.

This order is subject to our General Terms and Conditions.
Cette commande est soumise à nos conditions contractuelles générales.

Please confirm this order in due course.
Veuillez confirmer cette offre en temps voulu.

We acknowledge receipt of your order for . . .
Nous vous accusons réception de votre commande de . . .

The order will be carried out in accordance with your instructions.
Votre commande sera exécutée conformément à vos directives.

 **Model Letter 5**

9

Sales Contract	Le Contrat de Vente
agreement	la convention, l'accord
commercial settlement of a dispute	le règlement d'un litige
contract clause	la clause du contrat
contract of sale	le contrat de vente
contracting parties	les parties contractantes
deadlines	les dates limites, les délais
dispute	le litige
fulfilment of contract	l'exécution du contrat
guarantee, warrant	le contrat de garantie
hire-purchase	l'achat à crédit
maturity date of contract	la date d'échéance du contrat
penalties	les pénalités
period of contract	la durée du contrat
sale on trial	la vente à l'essai
sale or return	la vente avec droit de retour
seller's warranties	les garanties
terms of contract	les termes/les conditions du contrat
as per contract . . .	d'après le contrat d'achat/de vente . . .
the contract expires	le contrat expire
the contract is null and void	le contrat est nul et non avenu
to amend a contract	modifier un contrat
to cancel a contract	annuler un contrat
to certify a contract	certifier un contrat
to contract/to enter into a contract	conclure un contrat
to extend a contract	prolonger un contrat
to negotiate the conditions of a contract	débattre des conditions d'un contrat

We reserve title to the goods delivered pending payment in full.

Nous nous réservons la propriété des marchandises livrées jusqu'à paiement total.

In the event of litigation, the courts in Paris shall have exclusive jurisdiction.
Pour toute contestation, le tribunal de Paris est seul compétent.

This is what you might read in French:

Nous vous réservons un droit de préemption.
We will give you first option.

Nous prenons un pourcentage de 10%.
We work on 10%.

In property transactions intermediaries provide practical assistance for British business people.

The 'agent immobilier' specializes in property transactions.

The 'avocat conseil juridique' provides legal advice, drafts contracts, and represents clients in court.

The 'notaire' carries out all the formalities necessary for the purchase of residential and commercial property.

Contacts with French solicitors and specialist lawyers can be made through:

CFCE (Service de l'Information Juridique et Fiscale)
Tel: (1) 40 73 33 36/35 20 (50) between 9.30 am and 12.30 pm.

Association Nationale des Conseils Juridiques
(National Association of Legal Advisers)
23 avenue Mac-Mahon
75017 Paris
Tel: (1) 47 66 30 07

Commission Nationale des Conseils
  Juridiques
(National Commission of Legal Advisers)
67 rue du Rocher
75008 Paris
Tel: (1) 42 93 52 10

Chambre des Notaires
(Chamber of Legal Advisers)
12 avenue Victoria
75005 Paris
Tel: (1) 42 33 71 06

Conseil Supérieur du Notariat
31 rue du Général Foy
75008 Paris
Tel: (1) 42 93 06 45

10

Production

Production

after-sales/customer service	le service après-vente
assembly	le montage
assembly instructions	les instructions de montage
assembly line	la chaîne
direct labour	les salaires directs
engineering	la conception technique
industrial plant	l'usine, l'entreprise industrielle
industrial production	la production industrielle
industrial standard	la norme industrielle
machine shop/workshop	l'atelier
maintenance contract	le contrat d'entretien
mass production	la fabrication en série
one-off production	la fabrication individuelle hors série
output	le rendement
production	la production

production period	**le temps de production**
production programme	**le programme de production**
production schedule	**le plan de production**
quality assurance	**l'assurance de la qualité**
quality control	**le contrôle de la qualité**
quality system	**le système qualité**
service	**le service**
service manual	**la notice d'entretien**
subcontractor, supplier	**le sous-traitant**
tool	**l'outillage, l'outil**
workshop	**l'atelier**
to make, to produce, to manufacture	**produire, fabriquer**
to streamline (production)	**rationaliser, moderniser**

In accordance with the CEN/CENELEC Common Rules, all CEN members are bound to implement the International Standard ISO 9001: 1987 quality systems: the model for quality assurance in design/development, production, installation and servicing.

11

Storage   Le Stockage

stock	**le stock, les stocks disponibles**
stock clerk/warehouseman	**le magasinier**
stock control	**le contrôle des stocks**
stock rotation	**la rotation des stocks**
warehouse	**l'entrepôt**
– bonded warehouse	**– l'entrepôt en douane**
warehouse company	**la société d'entrepôts**
to have in stock	**avoir en stock**
to store, to stock	**stocker**
to take stock	**faire l'inventaire**

▼
Our stock is running short.
Nos stocks s'épuisent.

12

Packing and Marking	**Emballages et Marquage**
export packing	l'emballage d'exportation
package	le colis
packing	l'emballage
packing at cost price	l'emballage au prix de revient
packing list	la liste des emballages
seaworthy packing	l'emballage maritime
special packing	l'emballage spécial
wrapping	le papier d'emballage
gross weight	le poids brut
net weight	le poids net
tare	la tare
barrel	le tonneau
can, metal container	le bidon
cardboard box, carton	la boîte, le carton
case	la caisse
container	le container
crate	la caisse
pallet	la palette
returnable container	le container consigné
sack, bag	le sac
skid (rollers)	le chariot, le traîneau

Shipping marks:	**Le marquage sur emballage d'expédition:**
made in . . . /country of origin	fabriqué en . . . /le pays d'origine
marks	le sigle du destinataire
order no.	le numéro de la commande
package numbers	le numéro du colis
port of destination	le port de destination
weight and measurements	le poids et les dimensions

Caution marks:	**Inscriptions de prudence:**
Bottom	Bas

Flammable	**Inflammable**
Glass – Fragile	**Verre – Fragile**
Handle with Care	**Attention**
Keep Dry	**Protéger de l'Humidité**
Keep Cool	**Conserver au Frais**
Lift Here	**Soulever Ici**
Poison	**Poison**
Radioactive Substance	**Substance Radioactive**
Store Away from Heat	**Préserver de la Chaleur**
Top	**Haut**
Use No Hooks	**Ne Pas Employer de Crochet**

13

Transport and Delivery

Transport et Livraison

air cargo, air freight	**le fret aérien**
Bill of Lading (B/L)	**le connaissement**
– (non-negotiable) n.n. copy of BL	**– copie non négociable du connaissement**
bulk haulage	**le transport des marchandises en vrac**
carriage paid	**franco à domicile**
Community Transport Procedure	**le système d'expédition en commun**
consignee	**le destinataire**
consignment, shipment	**l'envoi**
consignor, shipper	**l'expéditeur**
country of destination	**le pays de destination**
date of shipment	**la date d'expédition**
deadline	**le délai, la date limite**
delivery note	**le bon de livraison**
dispatch department	**le service d'expédition**
dispatch note	**l'avis d'expédition**
forwarder, carrier	**le transporteur**
freight, cargo, carriage	**le fret, la cargaison**
freight/forwarding charges	**les frais de transport**

freight rate	le tarif des transports
– freight collect	– fret contre remboursement
– freight included	– frais de transport compris
long hauls	le transport à longue distance
lot	le lot
notifying address	l'adresse notifiée
piggyback (combined road and rail) service	le service de ferroutage/ le trafic combiné rail/route
place of destination	le lieu de destination
place of dispatch	le lieu d'expédition
roll-on/roll-off service	le service roulier
shipping documents	les documents d'expédition
– air waybill	– la lettre de transport aérien
– consignment note, waybill	– la lettre de voiture, la feuille de route
– duplicate consignment note	– le duplicata de la lettre de voiture
– railway consignment note	– la lettre de voiture ferroviaire
short hauls	le transport de marchandises à courte distance
suppliers, contractors	le fournisseur
supply contract	le contrat de livraison
transport	le transport
– air transport	– le transport aérien
– rail transport	– le transport par rail/ferroviaire
– road transport	– le transport routier
– water transport	– le transport par eau
transshipment, reloading	le transbordement
to deliver	livrer
to deliver within the specified time	livrer dans les délais de livraison
to dispatch, to send off	envoyer, expédier
to effect delivery	effectuer une livraison
to load, to unload	charger, décharger
to ship, to forward	expédier, transporter
to specify the delivery route	spécifier les voies d'acheminement
to supply, to furnish a customer with goods	livrer, fournir, approvisionner
in transit	en transit

via (Dover)	**voie (Douvres)**

The delivery can be effected, e.g.:

carriage paid	**franco à domicile**
ex warehouse	**pris à l'entrepôt**
freight pre-paid	**port payé**
freight forward	**fret dû**

Incoterms

International Commercial Terms are a set of international rules for the interpretation of trade terms, published as ICC Publication Number 460, 1990 edition, by:

> **ICC Publishing SA**
> **International Chamber of Commerce**
> **38 cours Albert 1er**
> **75008 Paris**

Incoterms 1990

EXW	Ex works (. . . named place)	**EXW**	**à l'Usine** **(. . . lieu convenu)**
FCA	Free carrier (. . . named place)	**FCA**	**Franco Transporteur** **(. . . lieu convenu)**
FAS	Free alongside ship (. . . named port of shipment)	**FAS**	**Franco le long du navire** **(. . . port d'embarquement convenu)**
FOB	Free on board (. . . named port of shipment)	**FOB**	**Franco bord** **(. . . port d'embarquement convenu)**
CFR	Cost and freight (. . . named port of destination)	**CFR**	**Coût et fret** **(. . . port de destination convenu)**

CIF	Cost, insurance and freight (. . . named port of destination)	CIF	Coût, assurance et fret (. . . port de destination convenu)
CPT	Carriage paid to (. . . named place of destination)	CPT	port payé jusqu'a (. . . lieu de destination convenu)
CIP	Carriage and insurance paid to (. . . named place of destination)	CIP	Port payé, assurance comprise, jusqu'à (. . . lieu de destination convenu)
DAF	Delivered at frontier (. . . named place)	DAF	Rendu frontière (. . . lieu convenu)
DES	Delivered ex ship (. . . named port of destination)	DES	Rendu ex ship (. . . port de destination convenu)
DEQ	Delivered ex quay (duty paid) (. . . named port of destination)	DEQ	Rendu à Quai (droits acquittés) (. . . port de destination convenu)
DDU	Delivered duty unpaid (. . . named place destination)	DDU	Rendu droits non acquittés (. . . lieu de destination convenu)
DDP	Delivered duty paid (. . . named place destination)	DDP	Rendu droits acquittés (. . . lieu de destination convenu)

▼
Delivery can be effected at the earliest possible date.
Votre livraison peut être effectuée aussi rapidement que possible.

Delivery immediately after receipt of order.
Livraison à exécuter immédiatement après réception de la commande.

We forwarded today by order and for account of . . .
Nous vous avons expédié aujourd'hui par ordre et pour le compte de . . .

We inform you that the goods have been dispatched by rail today.
Nous vous informons que les marchandises ont été expédiées aujourd'hui par train.

Union des Fédérations des Transports
Air France Cargo
(Federation of Transport Associations)
Orly, Télex: 200 666
63 avenue de Villiers, Roissy, Télex: 230 964
75017 Paris UTA Export, Tel: (1) 48 64 11 41
Tel: (1) 47 66 49 68 Télex: 230 271

Syndicat National des Agents et
Groupements de Fret Aérienne
(National Association of Agents and
Groups for Air Freight)
BP 10462
95708 Aéroport D 6
Tel: (1) 48 62 34 58
Fax: (1) 48 62 22 89

Direction Commerciale Fret-SNCF
(Head Office Freight-SNCF)
10 place de Budapest
BP 384
75436 Paris Cedex 09
Tel: (1) 42 85 60 00
Télex: 640 142

Fédération Nationale des Transporteurs
Routiers
(National Federation of Carriers)
6 rue Paul-Valéry
75116 Paris
Tel: (1) 45 53 92 88
Télex: 648 576

**Comité des Armateurs Fluviaux
(Committee of Shipowners (River))
8 rue Saint-Florentin
75001 Paris
Tel: (1) 42 60 36 18**

**Union des Fédérations des Transports
(Federation of Transport Associations)
63 avenue de Villiers
75017 Paris
Tel: (1) 47 66 49 68**

→**5**   Useful UK addresses can be found in Part III, 10.

14

Complaints	Réclamations
adjustment, settlement	le règlement des réclamations
circumstances beyond our control	des conditions imprévisibles
claim	la demande d'indemnisation
compensation	le dédommagement
complaint	la réclamation
defect	le défaut, l'imperfection
defective goods	une marchandise défectueuse
delay	le retard
fault	le défaut
faulty material	un matériau défectueux
hidden defect	un défaut caché
non-conformity with sample	la non-conformité à l'échantillon
poor quality	une mauvaise qualité
replacement	l'échange
substitute	le produit/la marchandise de remplacement
well-founded complaint	une plainte/réclamation justifiée/fondée

to allow a claim	**accepter une réclamation**
to compensate	**dédommager**
to complain about	**se plaindre de**
to demand compensation, claim damages	**réclamer un dédommagement**
to exchange the goods	**échanger une marchandise**
to grant an allowance	**accorder une réduction**
to refund	**rembourser**
to refuse a claim	**refuser une réclamation**
to take the goods back	**reprendre la marchandise**

When dealing with this subject verbally, you could begin as follows:

▼
I don't like to complain, but I have had a lot of trouble with . . .
Je n'ai pas l'habitude de me plaindre, mais j'ai eu un tas de problèmes avec . . .

I'm sorry, but I'm not at all satisfied with . . .
Je regrette, mais je ne suis pas du tout satisfait de . . .

I am very annoyed about . . .
Je suis très en colère au sujet de . . .

I'm not the sort of person who normally complains, but . . .
Je ne suis pas d'habitude de ceux qui se plaignent, mais . . .

I'm disappointed with . . .
Je suis déçu de . . .

I'm so sorry to hear . . .
Je suis désolé d'apprendre . . .

I'm very sorry about this, it's our fault.
Je le regrette beaucoup, mais c'est de notre faute.

I'll look into the matter immediately.
Je vais m'en occuper tout de suite.

I'll find out what happened.
Je vais essayer de trouver ce qui s'est passé.

37

Can I see the guarantee?
Est-ce que je peux voir le bon de garantie?

The following phrases are used for written complaints:

▼

We are sorry to inform you . . .
Nous sommes désolés de vous informer . . .

We are disappointed with the execution of our order.
Nous sommes déçus de l'exécution de notre ordre.

On checking the items we noticed . . .
Lors du contrôle des articles nous avons constaté . . .

The quality of the goods does not correspond with that of the sample.
La qualité des marchandises ne correspond pas à celle de l'échantillon.

The goods were damaged in transit.
La marchandise a été abîmée pendant le transport.

The damage seems to have been caused by inadequate packing.
Le dommage semble être dû à un emballage mal approprié.

We were promised delivery by the end of the month.
On nous a promis la livraison pour la fin du mois.

We are placing the defective goods at your disposal.
Nous tenons les marchandises défectueuses à votre disposition.

Please send us replacements for the damaged goods.
Veuillez nous envoyer des marchandises de remplacement pour les marchandises endommagées.

We must apologize for not having dispatched the goods in time.
Nous vous prions de bien vouloir nous excuser de ne pas avoir envoyé les marchandises à temps.

We regret not having carried out your order properly.
Nous sommes désolés de ne pas avoir exécuté correctement votre ordre.

A new consignment has been sent off to you today.
Une nouvelle livraison vous a été expédiée ce matin.

Please return the goods at our expense.
Renvoyez-nous s.v.p. les marchandises à nos frais.

We will take all possible steps to ensure that such a mistake does not occur again.
Nous allons faire tout notre possible, pour qu'une telle erreur ne se reproduise pas.

Please accept our apologies for the trouble caused.
Nous vous prions de nous excuser pour les ennuis causés.

We regret to inform you that we cannot assume any liability.
Nous sommes désolés de devoir vous informer que nous ne pouvons pas nous porter garant.

 Model letters 6, 7 and 8

15

Insurance	Assurance
beneficiary	**le bénéficiaire**
claim	**la déclaration de sinistre**
cover	**la couverture**
credit insurance	**l'assurance-crédit**
damage	**le dommage**
insurance	**l'assurance**
insurance certificate	**le certificat d'assurance**
insurance company	**la compagnie d'assurances**
insurance policy	**la police d'assurance**
insurance against loss on the exchange rate	**l'assurance sur les pertes au change**
liability	**la responsabilité**
policy holder	**l'assuré**

premium	**la prime**
third-party insurance	**l'assurance de responsabilité civile**
transportation insurance	**l'assurance contre les risques du transport**
underwriter	**assureur, le souscripteur de risques**
to cover a risk	**couvrir un risque**
to settle a claim	**régler une déclaration de sinistre**
to take out insurance	**contracter une assurance**
to underwrite a risk	**assurer un risque**

International insurance is frequently taken out under the terms of Institute Cargo Clauses, e.g.:

Clause A   full cover/all risks (**tous risques**)
Clause B   stranding cover (**en cas d'échouer**)

There are more than 550 insurance companies in France, all of them supervised by:

> **Direction Générale des Assurances (DGA)**
> **54 rue de Châteaudun**
> **75009 Paris**
> **Tel: (1) 42 81 91 55**

It is worth enlisting the services of a tied agent or insurance broker who can offer advice on the various types of policy and companies.

> **Fédération Française des Sociétés d'Assurances**
> **(French Federation of Insurance Companies)**
> **26 boulevard Haussmann**
> **75311 Paris Cedex 09**
> **Tel: (1) 42 47 90 00**
> **Fax: (1) 42 47 93 11**
> **Télex: 640 477**

SEREBRAT (Groupe des Assurances
  Nationales)
(Group of National Insurances)
9 rue Le Peletier
75009 Paris
Tel: (1) 42 47 78 00
Fax: (1) 42 47 79 00

Compagnie Française d'Assurance pour le
  Commerce Extérieur (COFACE)
(French Company for Export Insurance)
12 Cours Michelet
92065 Paris La Défense Cedex 51
Tel: (1) 49 02 20 00
Fax: (1) 40 90 06 71

Centre de Documentation et d'Information
  de l'Assurance (CDIA)
(Centre for Insurance Documentation and
  Information)
Public enquiries to:
2 rue de la Chaussée d'Antin
75009 Paris
Tel: (1) 42 46 13 13

Groupement Assurance Transports des
  Exportateurs Français
(Group of Transport Insurances for French
  Exporters)
1–3 rue Caumartin
75009 Paris
Tel: (1) 47 42 26 86

→6   Useful UK addresses can be found in Part III, 10.

16

Invoicing and Payment	**Facturation et Paiement**
advance payment	le paiement d'avance
commercial invoice	la facture commerciale
consular invoice	la facture consulaire
date of invoice	la date de la facture
down-payment	l'acompte
invoice	la facture
invoice amount	le montant de la facture
invoice number	le numéro de la facture
item	l'article, le poste, l'item d'un compte
part payment	le paiement partiel
payment of the balance	le règlement du solde
payment on account	l'acompte
payment, settlement	le paiement, le règlement
remittance	le versement
statement of account	le relevé de compte
terms of payment	les conditions de paiement
total (sum) amounting to £/FF	la somme totale (d'un montant) de £/FF
as per invoice	d'après la facture
brought forward (b/f)	le report
E & OE (errors and omission excepted)	sous réserve d'erreur/sauf erreur

Some usual terms of payment:

3% discount for cash	**3% mois de date**
3 months' credit	**payable à 3 mois**
2% off for payment within 10 days (10 days 2%)	**2% d'escompte pour paiement dans les 10 jours**
30 days net	**comptant net dans les 30 jours**
cash with order (CWO)	**paiement à la commande**

cash on delivery (COD)	**paiement comptant à la livraison**
cash against documents (CAD)	**paiement comptant contre documents**
documents against payment (D/P)	**documents contre paiement**
documents against acceptance (D/A)	**documents contre acceptation**
payment against bank guarantee	**paiement contre garantie bancaire**
payment by acceptance	**paiement par traite acceptée**
payment by cheque	**le règlement par chèque**
payment by irrevocable confirmed documentary letter of credit (L/C)	**paiement par accréditif documentaire irrévocable et confirmé**
payment by sight draft	**paiement par traite à vue**
payment on receipt of goods (ROG)	**paiement à la réception de la marchandise**

The Accreditif Documentaire (Documentary Letter of Credit) has an important role in exports: as a method of payment it protects both buyer and seller. Payment under a confirmed irrevocable L/C is the safest method of payment in foreign trade.

Normally, the following shipping documents have to be presented under the terms of the credit:

freight/consignment note	**la lettre de voiture**
commercial invoice	**la facture commerciale**
Bill of Lading/air waybill	**le connaissement/la lettre de transport aérien (LTA)**
certificate of origin	**le certificat d'origine**
insurance certificate	**le certificat d'assurance**

The International Chamber of Commerce, Paris, has published sets of rules governing documentary credits. The guidelines, *Uniform Customs and Practice for Documentary Credits, 1983 Revision*, are

43

used by the banks and banking associations of virtually every country and territory in the world.

to balance an account	**solder, équilibrer un compte**
to charge	**faire payer, débiter, compter**
to credit	**porter au crédit d'un compte**
to draw a cheque	**tirer un chèque**
to invoice, to bill	**facturer**
to pay, to make payment	**payer, régler**
to effect payment	**effectuer un paiement**
to pay on the due date	**payer à la date d'échéance**
to pay cash	**payer comptant**
to pay in advance	**payer d'avance**
to pay under reserve	**payer sous réserve**
to remit	**verser, virer**
to transfer	**transférer, virer**
without charge	**non facturé**

▼

Please remit the sum of £ . . .
Veuillez virer la somme de £ . . .

I have an account with XY Bank.
J'ai un compte à la banque XY.

We transferred £ . . . to your account yesterday.
Nous avons viré hier £ . . . sur votre compte.

The amount of £ . . . will be paid to your account with XY Bank.
La somme de £ . . . sera versée sur votre compte à la banque XY.

We have drawn a cheque for FF . . . on XY Bank.
Nous avons viré à la banque XY un chèque d'un montant de FF . . .

We have accepted your draft and will honour it at maturity/when it is due.
Nous avons accepté votre traite et nous l'honorerons à la date d'échéance.

Please credit this amount to our account.
Nous vous prions de porter cette somme au crédit de notre compte

We enclose a cheque covering your invoice no . . .
Pour le règlement de votre facture no . . . nous vous joignons un chèque.

Please send us an official receipt.
Nous vous prions de nous accuser réception du chèque.

> **Association Française des Banques
> (French Association of Banks)
> 18 rue La Fayette
> 75009 Paris
> Tel: (1) 42 46 92 59
> Télex: 660 282**

See also Part II, 5.

 Model letters 9 and 10

17

Outstanding Accounts	Créances
additional period of time	le délai supplémentaire
amount overdue	l'arriéré
arrears	les arriérés
assignment of a debt	la cession d'une créance
bill overdue	l'effect en souffrance, la traite non honorée
collection agency	l'agence d'encaissement
debt, claim	la créance
– bad debt	– la créance irrécouvrable
– doubtful debt	– la créance douteuse
default interest	les intérêts de retard/moratoires
due date	la date d'échéance/l'échéance

dunning/reminder letter	**la lettre de rappel**
extension	**la prolongation (d'un crédit)**
factoring	**l'affacturage**
outstanding accounts	**les créances à recouvrir**
overdue	**arriéré, impassé, en retard**
payee	**le bénéficiaire**
period of limitation	**le délai de prescription**
prolongation	**la prolongation**
recourse	**le recours**
security	**la garantie, le nantissement**
transfer of title for the purpose of securing a debt	**la remise d'un bien en propriété à titre de garantie**
to bounce (a cheque)	**être sans provision, être refusé pour non-provision**
to control	**contrôler**
to demand payment	**exiger le paiement**
to fall due	**tomber à échéance**
to grant an extension	**accorder un ajournement/une prorogation d'échéance**
to object to something	**protester**
to overdraw an account	**mettre un compte à découvert**
to prolong, to extend	**prolonger**
to remind somebody of something	**rappeler quelque chose à quelqu'un**
business reputation	**la renommée, la notoriété**
credit inquiry	**la demande de renseignements commerciaux**
estimated annual turnover	**le chiffre d'affaires estimé**
financial standing	**la situation financière**
honest	**honnête, intègre**
reliability	**le sérieux, l'honnêteté**
solvency	**la solvabilité**
strictly confidential	**strictement confidentiel**
without obligation	**sans engagement**

▼

Looking through our books we note that a balance of . . . is still
outstanding.

A la lecture de nos livres de compte nous avons constaté qu'un solde de . . . restait ouvert.

May we remind you that your payment has been overdue since 31 July?
Permettez-nous de vous rappeler que votre paiement est à échéance depuis le 31 juillet.

Our invoice of . . . is still unpaid.
Notre facture du . . . n'est pas encore réglée.

Your account is overdrawn/in the red.
Votre compte est à découvert/non soldé.

Please send your cheque by . . .
Nous vous prions de bien vouloir envoyer votre chèque jusqu'au . . .

Messrs . . . have given us your name as a trade reference.
L'entreprise . . . nous a fait part de votre nom.

Do you think it would be justifiable to allow them credit of up to . . . ?
Est-ce qu'un crédit d'un montant de . . . est possible?

They have always met their financial obligations promptly.
Cette entreprise a toujours payé ponctuellement.

This information is given in strictest confidence and without any obligation on our part.
Nous vous donnons ces renseignements à titre strictement confidentiel et sans aucune garantie de notre part.

> **Chambre Syndicale Nationale
> Professionelle des Agences de
> Renseignements Commerciaux et de
> Recouvrement de Créances
> (National Association of Agencies for
> Trade References and Credit Enquiries)
> 17 rue de Joinville
> 94130 Nogent sur Marne
> Tel: (1) 48 75 19 85**

A copy of **Comment vous renseigner sur vos clients et partenaires commerciaux?** (*How to obtain information on your clients and business partners*) is available from: Chambre de Commerce et d'Industrie de Paris.

 **Model letters 11, 12, 13 and 14**

18

Bankruptcy, Liquidation	La Faillite
affidavit	la déclaration sur l'honneur/ l'affidavit
attachment (seizure of goods)	la saisie
bankruptcy, liquidation	la faillite
composition	le concordat
compromise	le compromis
compulsory sale	la vente obligatoire/forcée
creditor	le créancier
debtor	le débiteur
dispute	le litige, le conflit, le différend
insolvency	l'insolvabilité
lawsuit, litigation	le procès, les poursuites judiciaires
lawyer	le conseiller juridique, l'avocat
official receiver (OR)	le syndic de la faillite
receiving order	la décision d'ouverture de faillite
reservation of title	la réserve de propriété
solicitor	le conseiller juridique
trustee	le syndic de la faillite
to bring an action against . . .	porter plainte contre . . .

| to file for bankruptcy | **déclarer faillite, déposer le bilan** |
| to go bankrupt | **faire faillite** |

Contacts with French legal advisers can be made through:

> **CFCE (Service de l'Information Juridique et Fiscale)**
> **Tel: (1) 40 73 33 36/35 20 (s.o.) between 9.30 am–12.30 pm.**
>
> **Association Nationale des Conseils Juridiques**
> **(National Association of Legal Advisers)**
> **23 avenue Mac-Mahon**
> **75017 Paris**
> **Tel: (1) 47 66 30 07**
>
> **Ordre des Avocats à la Cour de Paris Palais de Justice**
> **(Order of the Lawyers at the Court of Paris)**
> **4 boulevard du Palais**
> **75001 Paris**
> **Tel: (1) 46 34 12 34**

→7 Useful UK addresses can be found in Part III, 10.

19

Accounting	**La Comptabilité**
account	**le compte**
accountant, bookkeeper	**le comptable**
accounting, bookkeeping	**la comptabilité**
amortization instalment	**la tranche d'amortissement**
annual financial statement	**le bilan annuel (de fin d'année)**
auditing	**la vérification des comptes**
balance	**le solde, la balance**
book value	**la valeur comptable**

budgetary accounting	**le planning budgétaire**
call money	**l'argent au jour le jour**
cash flow	**le cash-flow**
credit note	**l'avis de crédit**
debit note	**l'avis de bordereau/de débit**
entry	**l'entrée**
expenditure	**les dépenses**
inventory	**l'inventaire**
ledger	**le grand livre**
liquidity	**la liquidité**
mortgage	**l'hypothèque**
order book	**le carnet de commandes**
overdraft credit	**le crédit dépassé, le découvert de compte**
percentage	**le pourcentage**
profitability	**la rentabilité**
receipts	**les rentrées, les recettes**
(trading) result	**le résultat**
short/medium/long-term credit	**le crédit à court/moyen/long terme**
statistics	**les statistiques**
valuation	**l'évaluation**
voucher	**la pièce justificative, le reçu, la quittance**
yield	**le rendement, le rapport**
to book	**comptabiliser, passer en écriture**
to calculate	**calculer**
to cancel	**annuler, extourner**
to carry forward (the balance)	**reporter (le solde)**
to certify	**certifier**
to close an account	**fermer, arrêter un compte**
to open an account	**ouvrir un compte**

**Fédération Nationale des Experts
  Comptables de France
(National Federation of French
  Bookkeepers)
7 boulevard des Capucines
75002 Paris
Tel: (1) 47 42 08 60**

20

The Balance Sheet — Le Bilan

accruals	**les charges à payer**
assets	**l'actif**
balance sheet	**le bilan**
chartered accountant	**l'expert comptable**
current assets	**l'actif réalisable**
finished products/goods	**les produits finis**
fixed assets	**l'actif immobilisé**
inventories	**les stocks**
legal reserves	**les réserves légales**
liabilities	**les dettes, le passif**
liquid funds	**les valeurs disponibles**
loan	**le prêt, le crédit**
notes payable	**les dettes représentées par des effets de commerce**
raw materials	**les matières premières**
receivables	**les créances**
share	**l'action**
trade payables	**les dettes sur achats et prestation de service**
work in progress	**le produit en cours de fabrication**

If you have any queries about preparing accounts or a balance sheet you can contact the Fédération Nationale des Experts Comptables de France. (The address is given above.)

See the Appendix for the layout of the balance sheet (Structure de Bilan) according to Accounting and Reporting Legislation, Adoption of the 4th, 7th and 8th EC Directives.

21

Statement of Earnings	Compte de Pertes et Profits
administration expenses	**les frais d'administration**
after-tax profit	**le bénéfice après impôt**
compound interest	**les intérêts composés**
depreciations	**les amortissements**
dividend	**le dividende**
gross profit	**le bénéfice brut**
interests	**les intérêts**
operating expenses and income	**les frais et le produit d'exploitation**
pre-tax profit	**le bénéfice avant impôt**
profit and loss account	**le compte profits et pertes**
rate of interest	**le taux d'intérêt**
sales	**le chiffre d'affaires**
to write off	amortir

See the Appendix for the layout of the Profit and Loss Account (Compte de pertes et profits) according to Accounting and Reporting Legislation, Adoption of the 4th, 7th and 8th EC Directives.

22

The Annual Report	Le Rapport Annuel
annual general meeting of the shareholders	**l'assemblée générale ordinaire/ l'assemblée annuelle**
annual report	**le rapport annuel**
bookings	**la rentrée des commandes**
business development	**le développement des affaires**
capital structure	**la structure des capitaux**
development (of a product)	**l'activité de développement**
economic position	**la situation économique**

expected growth	**le développement prévu**
indebtedness	**l'endettement**
investment	**l'investissement**
production	**la production**
research	**le travail de recherche**
return, yield	**le rapport, le rendement**
revenues	**les recettes**
subsidy	**la subvention**
year under review	**l'année sous revue**

23

Costs and their Calculation

Coûts et Calculation

all-in costs	**le coût total**
at cost	**au prix de revient/au prix coûtant**
at your/our expense	**à vos/nos frais**
business licence tax	**la taxe professionnelle**
calculation	**le calcul (du prix de revient)**
capital gains tax	**l'impôt sur les plus-values en capital**
corporation tax	**l'impôt sur les sociétés**
cost free/free of charge	**gratuit, exempt de frais**
cost price	**le prix de revient**
cost-covering	**qui couvre les frais**
costs	**les coûts, les frais**
direct material	**le matériel de fabrication**
direct wages	**les salaires directs**
expenditure, expenses	**les dépenses**
extras	**les frais supplémentaires**
fixed costs	**les frais fixes, les charges fixes**
income tax	**l'impôt sur le revenu**
inheritance tax	**les droits de succession, l'impôt sur les successions**
liable for tax	**imposable**
local taxes, rates	**les impôts locaux**

marginal costs	**le coût marginal**
no hidden extras	**sans frais supplémentaires cachés**
overhead charges	**le coefficient de frais généraux**
overhead costs	**les frais indirects/les frais généraux**
production costs	**les frais/le coût de production**
property tax	**l'impôt foncier**
refund of costs	**le remboursement des frais**
royalty	**la redevance de brevet**
selling expenses	**les frais de vente**
surtax	**l'impôt supplémentaire**
tax	**l'impôt, la taxe**
tax allowance	**l'abattement/le dégrèvement fiscal**
tax consultant	**le conseiller fiscal**
tax exemption	**l'abattement à la base, l'exonération fiscale**
tax-favoured	**dégrèvé**
tax-free	**libre d'impôt**
turnover tax	**la taxe sur le chiffre d'affaires**
unit cost	**le coût unitaire**
VAT (Value Added Tax)	**la TVA (taxe à valeur ajoutée)**
variable costs	**les frais variables**
wage tax	**l'impôt sur le salaire**
wealth tax	**l'impôt sur la fortune**
zero-rated	**exempt de TVA**

Value-Added Tax in EC countries

	Lower %	*Standard %*	*Higher %*
Belgium	6 and 17	19	25 and 33
Denmark	—	22	—
Germany	7	14	—
France	5.5 and 7	18.6	33.3
Greece	6	18	36
Great Britain	0	17.5	—
The Netherlands	5	19	—

Ireland	0 and 10	23	—
Italy	2 and 9	18	38
Luxembourg	3 and 6	12	—
Portugal	0 and 8	17	30
Spain	6	12	33

Contacts with French tax consulting firms can be established through:

> **Institut Français des Conseils Fiscaux**
> **(French Institute of Tax Consultants)**
> **9 rue Richepanse**
> **75008 Paris**
> **Tel: (1) 42 60 10 18**

> **Société Accréditée de Représentation**
> **Fiscale**
> **(Society of Fiscal Representation)**
> **2 rue des Petits-Pères**
> **75002 Paris**
> **Tel: (1) 42 86 00 18**

If you have any questions on tax matters please contact:

> **CFCE (Service de l'Information Juridique et**
> **Fiscale)**
> **(Department for legal and tax queries)**
> **Tel: (1) 40 73 35 20 between 9.30 am and**
> **12.30 pm.**

24

Personnel Matters	**Affaires de Personnel**
application	**la candidature**
apprentice	**l'apprenti**
boss	**le chef, le patron**

chairman/chairwoman	le directeur général/la directrice générale
clerk	l'employé(e) de commerce
contract of employment	le contrat de travail
curriculum vitae	le curriculum vitae
dismissal	le licenciement
education, training	la formation
employee	l'employé(e), le salarié
employer	l'employeur, le patron
executive	le cadre, le cadre supérieur
expert	l'expert
financial controller	le chef du service financier
flexible working hours/ flexi-time	l'horaire à la carte
foreign-language secretary	le/la secrétaire bilingue/trilingue
foreman	le contre-maître, l'agent de maîtrise
fringe benefits	avantages en nature ou en espèces (qui ne sont pas intégrés dans le salaire de base; avantages de fonction)
full-time worker	la main-d'œuvre à plein temps
interview	l'entretien
job	l'emploi
management	la direction de l'entreprise
manager	le directeur, la directrice, le chef d'entreprise
managing director	le directeur général
master (craftsman)	l'artisan
on-the-job training	la formation sur le terrain/la formation professionelle
part-time workers	la main-d'œuvre à temps partiel
pension fund	la caisse de retraite
personal assistant	la secrétaire de direction
personnel manager	le chef du personnel
plant manager	le directeur de l'usine
probation period	la période d'essaie
professional experience	l'expérience professionnelle
profit sharing	la participation aux bénéfices
promotion	la promotion
proxy	le fondé de procuration commerciale

purchasing manager, chief buyer	**le responsable des achats**
qualification	**la qualification**
questionnaire	**le questionnaire**
references	**les références**
rise	**l'augmentation de salaire**
salary	**le salaire**
sales manager	**le chef des ventes**
school leaving certificate	**le diplôme de fin de scolarité**
secretary (to XY)	**le/la secrétaire (de XY)**
shift work	**le travail en équipes/par postes**
skilled worker	**l'ouvrier/l'ouvrière spécialisé(e)**
superior	**le chef, le supérieur (hiérarchique)**
temporary staff	**le personnel intérimaire**
testimonial	**le certificat de travail**
trade union	**le syndicat**
trainee	**le/la stagiaire**
typist	**la dactylo(graphe)**
unemployment	**le chômage**
unskilled worker	**le/la manœuvre**
vacancy, opening	**la vacance, l'offre d'emploi**
vocational training	**la formation professionnelle**
wage(s)	**le salaire**
worker participation (in decision-making)	**la cogestion**
workforce, staff, personnel	**le personnel, les effectifs**
working hours	**la durée du travail**
works council member	**le délégué du comité d'entreprise**
to apply for	**solliciter un emploi, poser sa candidature**
to attend an evening course	**suivre des cours du soir**
to employ, to engage, to take on	**embaucher**
to give in one's notice (of intention to leave)	**donner sa démission**
to give notice (of redundancy, dismissal)	**licencier**
to manage	**diriger**

57

to serve an apprenticeship	**faire un apprentissage**
to train, to instruct	**former/donner une formation professionnelle**
to work overtime	**faire des heures supplémentaires**

In an interview you may be asked:

Pourriez-vous me parler un peu de vous et de votre formation professionnelle?
Will you tell me something about yourself and your educational background?

Quelles langues étrangères connaissez-vous?
What foreign languages have you learned/studied?

Savez-vous travailler sur ordinateur?
Are you computer-literate?

Pourquoi voulez-vous changer de travail?
Why do you want to leave your present job?

Quand pouvez-vous commencer?
When can you start working for us?

Quelle position occupez-vous dans votre entreprise?
What job do you hold in your present company?

member of the board	**membre du conseil de direction**
managing director	**directeur général**
manager/head of . . .	**directeur**
holder of procuration/power of attorney	**fondé de pouvoir**
department manager/head	**chef de service**
person in charge of . . .	**le responsable de**

▼
With reference to your advertisement in yesterday's . . . I would like to apply for the position of . . . in your company.
Me référant à votre annonce parue dans le journal . . . d'hier, j'aimerais poser ma candidature pour la place de . . . dans votre entreprise.

I am familiar with export and import procedures.
J'ai de bonnes connaissances d'exportation et importation.

I am very interested in working in France because . . .
Je suis tréx intéressé(e) à l'idée de travailler en France, parce que . . .

I have a good working knowledge of French.
J'ai de bonnes connaissances du français.

I enclose a CV with details of my practical training and experience.
Je vous joins un curriculum vitae avec quelques renseignements supplémentaires sur mon expérience et ma formation professionnelle.

Please find enclosed copies of testimonials by . . .
Veuillez trouver ci-joint mes certificats de travail.

My present position is subject to three months' notice.
J'ai un préavis de trois mois.

> **Conseil National du Patronat Français**
> **(National Employers' Association)**
> **31 avenue Pierre 1er de Serbie**
> **75116 Paris**
> **Tel: (1) 40 69 44 44**
> **Télex: 620 814**
> **Fax: (1) 47 23 47 32**
>
> **ANPE Agence Nationale pour l'Emploi**
> **(National Agency for Job Availabilities)**
> **2 cité Charles-Godon**
> **75009 Paris**
> **Tel: (1) 42 81 47 90**
>
> **Ministère du Travail, de l'Emploi et de la**
> **   Formation Professionnelle**
> **(Employment Ministry)**
> **1 place de Fontenoy**
> **75007 Paris**
> **Tel: (1) 40 56 60 60**

CANAM Caisse National d'Assurance
Maladie
(National Health Insurance)
Centre Paris Pleyel
Tour Quest
93521 Saint Denis Cedex 1
Tel: (1) 49 33 38 00

 Model Letter 15

25

Applying for a Job

25.1 Useful phrases

Covering letter:

I have read your advertisement in . . . and would like to apply for the position of . . .

I am replying to the above advertisement

I am interested in this position

I am writing to enquire whether you have a vacancy for a window dresser

La lettre de candidature:

J'ai lu votre annonce parue dans . . . et je désire poser ma candidature pour l'emploi de . . .

Je réponds à l'annonce citée en reference

Cet emploi m'interesse

Je vous écris pour savoir si vous auriez un emploi de libre pour un étalagiste

Personal details:

I was born on . . .
I am . . . years old
I am single
I am married

Données personnelles:

Je suis né(e) le . . .
j'ai . . . ans
je suis célibataire
je suis marié(e)

Education:

From 1977 to 1988 I attended . . . School

secondary school

grammar school
comprehensive school

I passed the General Certificate of Education (A levels) in 1990

In 1992 I took a degree in . . .

I studied economics at . . . University

Formation scolaire:

J'ai fréquenté l'école . . . de 1977 à 1988

collège d'enseignement générale

lycée

En 1990 j'ai obtenu le baccalauréat

En 1992 j'ai obtenu mon diplôme de . . .

J'ai fait des études d'economie à l'université de . . .

Career history:

From 1982 to 1987 I worked as . . . for . . .

In this field I have been able to gain valuable experience

At present I am employed as . . . for . . .

For the past years I have been responsible for . . .

As you can see from my CV, I have many years of experience

I would like to change my job

Expérience professionnelle:

De 1982 à 1987 j'ai travaillé comme . . . chez . . .

Dans ce domaine j'ai pu acquérir des connaissances précieuses

En ce moment je travaille en tant que . . . chez . . .

ces dernières années j'ètais responsable de . . .

Comme mon curriculum vitae ci-joint vous le montrera, je possède une longe expérience

J'aimerais changer de travail

Enclosures:

please find enclosed
the CV,
certified copies of the school leaving certificates (A-level) and my degree

Pièces jointes:

voulez trouver ci-joint
un curriculum vitae
les copies certifiées de mon baccalauréat et de mes diplômes

61

Concluding phrases:	**Phrases de politesse:**
I would be grateful for a positive answer	Je serais heureux(se) de recevoir une réponse positive de votre part
I would be grateful if you would invite me to come for an interview	Je serais reconnaissant(e) de m'accorder un entretien
Yours sincerely,	Je vous prie d'agréer, Madame/ Messieurs/Mesdames à l'assurance de mes salutations distinguées

25.2 Looking for a Job

In France ANPE has the monopoly for job placement in general:

> **Agence Nationale pour l'Emploi**
> **(National Agency for Job Availabilities)**
> **2 cité Charles-Godon**
> **75009 Paris**
> **Tel: (1) 42 81 47 90**

There are 730 branches of ANPE to which foreigners looking for jobs may apply direct. It is, however, very important that they should have a good knowledge of the French language. Applicants can also use the MINITEL services of ANPE, e.g. ULYSSES, which offers 3000 vacancies daily.

Graduates from the UK wanting to work in France will find that the chances of employment vary according to the subjects studied. Arts students, for example, will have fewer possibilities for employment than they would at home.

APEC is a private job-placement organization which foreigners seeking work can join:

> **Association pour l'Emploi des Cadres**
> **(Association for the Employment of**
> **Foreigners)**

It is especially intended for graduates. The journal *Courrier Cadres* contains 1000 advertisements.

There are many private employment agencies in France which are listed in:

Le guide des chasseurs de têtes et des cabinets de recrutement

Dunod

You also have, of course, the possibility of answering job advertisements in French newspapers. In this case, the following newspapers and magazines may be of assistance to you:

Daily national newspapers, e.g.:

Le Figaro
Libération
Le Monde
France Soir
Le Parisien

Regional newspapers, e.g.:

Midi-Libre
Sud-Ouest
Nice Matin

Magazines, e.g.:

L'Expansion
Le Point
Campus
Le Moci
Entreprises et Carrières
Le Moniteur

25.3 Applying for a job

In France, the papers accompanying the application consist of a covering letter and a CV. References and certificates are not enclosed.

The accompanying letter should be short (not more than one page) and written by computer – as also the CV. Sometimes a handwritten application is requested in the advertisement. This is necessary if the firm wants a graphalogical analysis.

Suggestions for information to include in a CV may be found in Appendix 1.

 Model Letter 15

25.4 Useful addresses

Agence Nationale pour
l'Emploi (ANPE)
69, rue Pigalle
75009 Paris
Tel: (1) 48 78 37 82
Fax: (1) 48 74 42 53

Association pour l'Emploi
des Cadres (APEC)
51 boulevard Brune
75689 Paris Cedex 14
Tel: (1) 40 52 20 00

Centre Info
Tour Europe Cedex 07
92080 Paris la Défense
Tel: (1) 47 78 13 50

Ministère du Travail, de l'Emploi
et de la Formation
Professionelle
1 pl Fontenoy
75007 Paris
Tel: (1) 40 56 60 00

The British Council
10 Spring Gardens
London SW1A 2BN
Tel: 0171 930 8466

Central Bureau for Educational
  Visits and Exchanges
Seymour Mews House
Seymour Mews
London W1H 9PE
Tel: 0171 486 5101

25.5 Book tips

Le Guide des entreprises qui recrutent
L'Etudiant

Guide des chasseurs de têtes et des cabinets de recrutement
Dunod

Comment trouver une situation
Les Editions d'Organisation

90 fiches pour trouver un emploi
Les Editions d'Organisation

Le Nouveau CV
Editions de Veechi

Getting a job in Europe
Northcote House Publishers Ltd
Plymouth

Working in . . . France
Overseas Placing Unit

Working Abroad
Kogan Page

The Directory of Jobs and Careers Abroad
Vacation Work

26

Data Processing	Le Traitement de l'Informatique
application software	le logiciel d'application
back-up	la sauvegarde
blank, space	le blanc
bootstrap	l'amorce
buffer	le tampon
CA	AO
cable connection	le branchement
central processing unit (CPU)	l'unité centrale
communication line	la passerelle
cursor	le curseur
databank	la banque de données
data acquisition	la saisie (de données)
data transfer	le transfert de données
density	la densité
digital	numérique
direct memory access	l'accès direct
disk	la disquette, le disque
disk operating system (DOS)	le système d'exploitation disque
disk storage	la mémoire à disque
display, screen, VDU	l'écran
drive (disk)	le lecteur
electronic data processing	l'informatique
to erase	effacer
floppy disk	le disque souple, la disquette
flowchart	l'organigramme

hard disk	**le disque dur**
input	**l'entrée**
interactive	**conversationnel**
interface	**l'interface**
keyboard	**le pupitre, le clavier**
label	**l'étiquette**
listing	**l'état, listing**
magnetic head	**la tête magnétique**
magnetic tape unit	**le dérouleur**
manual	**le manuel**
mask, picture	**le masque**
master file	**le fichier permanent**
memory	**la mémoire**
memory protection	**la protection de la mémoire**
mouse	**la souris**
network	**le réseau**
office automation	**la bureautique**
operating system	**le système d'exploitation**
output	**la sortie**
package	**le progiciel**
paper feed	**l'avance, la réserve de papier**
password, keyword	**le mot de passe, le mot réservé**
plotter	**la table traçante**
plug compatible	**compatible de prise**
power supply	**l'alimentation en energie électrique**
printer	**l'imprimante**
private line	**la ligne permanente**
programming language	**le langage (de programmation)**
random-access memory (RAM)	**la mémoire vive, RAM**
read-only memory (ROM)	**la mémoire morte, ROM**
scanner	**scanner, numériseur d'images**
screen, monitor	**l'écran, le moniteur**
service	**le service (de maintenance)**
shift key	**la touche de changement de mode**
software	**le logiciel**
software house	**SSII**
source program	**le programme source**
specifications	**le cahier des charges**
spreadsheet	**le tableau**

subroutine	**le sousprogramme**
tape drive unit	**l'unité de la bande magnétique**
teleprocessing	**téléprocessing**
transmission channel	**la voie de transmission**
update	**la mise à jour**
utility software	**l'utilitaire**
word processing	**le traitement de texte**
working storage	**la mémoire de travail**

▼

Is the computer IBM compatible?
Est-ce que l'ordinateur exécute des logiciels IBM compatibles?

Can I use 3½ or 5¼ inch disks?
Est-ce que je peux utiliser des disques 3½ ou 5¼ pouces?

Can I run colour and graphics software on the PC?
Est-ce que je peux utiliser des logiciels couleurs ou graphiques sur cet ordinateur?

Are there single or twin disk drives?
Est-ce que l'ordinateur possède un ou deux lecteurs à disquettes?

Can I use any IBM compatible monochrome or colour monitor?
Est-ce que je peux utiliser n'importe quel moniteur monochrome ou couleur IBM compatible?

Can I choose foreground or background colours?
Est-ce que je peux choisir les couleurs du premier plan ou de l'arrière plan?

Can I use any type of PC monitor provided it has a standard 9-pin 'D' connector?
Est-ce que je peux utiliser n'importe quel moniteur à condition qu'il possède une fiche 'D' à 9 broches?

Can I use the modem for commercial information services?
Est-ce que je peux utiliser un modem pour des services d'information commerciaux?

Does the computer include a built-in modem?
Est-ce que l'ordinateur possède un modem de communication intégré?

Does the keyboard have all the special function keys?
Est-ce que le clavier possède toutes les fonctions spéciales?

Does the price include manual, word processor and software?
Est-ce que le manuel, le traitement de texte, les disquettes de logiciel sont inclus au prix?

27

Co-operation and Business Partnerships	Coopération et Participations
acquisition	l'achat
agent, representative	le représentant
branch	la succursale
commission	la commission
consortium	le consortium
franchise	la franchise
general agency	l'agence (la représentation) générale
group, concern	le groupe
head office, headquarters	le siège social
joint venture	la co-entreprise
legally protected	protégé juridiquement
letter of intent	la lettre d'intention
merger	la fusion, la concentration
parent company, holding company	la société mère
patented	breveté
registered office	le siège social
royalties	la redevance de brevet
sole proprietorship	l'entreprise individuelle
subject to payment of royalties	sous droit de licence
subsidiary	la filiale

take-over	**le rachat/la reprise d'une entreprise**
under patent law	**sous le droit des brevets**
venture capital	**capital spéculatif, capital-risques**
to acquire a licence	**acquérir une licence**
to apply for a patent	**déposer un brevet**
to do business	**faire des affaires**
to entrust a firm with the agency	**confier les droits de représentation à une entreprise**
to establish, to found	**fonder**
to exploit a patent	**exploiter un brevet**
to grant sole selling rights	**accorder le droit de vente exclusive**
to join a firm	**entrer dans une entreprise**
to manufacture under licence	**fabriquer sous licence**
to merge	**fusionner**
to run a business	**exploiter une affaire**
to sell as sole agent	**vendre/diffuser en tant que représentant exclusif**
to sell goods on commission	**vendre à la commission**
to set up a business	**se mettre à son compte**

▼

We are looking for representatives to sell our products.
Nous recherchons des représentants pour la vente de nos produits.

Please state the terms on which you are willing to act as our representative.
Veuillez nous communiquer vos conditions auxquelles vous seriez disposé de travailler pour nous en tant que représentant.

You will be paid 3% commission on all sales.
Nous vous payons une commission de 3% sur toutes vos ventes.

Some types of firms:

Entreprise Individuelle (one-person business)
 – Personally liable for all debts incurred by the business
 – No minimum capital required

70

SARL (Société à Responsabilité Limitée) (Limited liability company)
– Minimum capital of FF 50,000 required
– Minimum of 2 shareholders required (maximum 50)
– Shareholders' liability is limited to the amount of capital they have invested

EURL (Enterprise Unipersonelle à Responsabilité Limitée) (Limited liability one-person business)
– Limited liability principle of the SARL is applicable
– Minimum capital of FF 50,000 is required

SNC (Société en Nom Collectif) (General partnership)
– No minimum capital required
– 2 or more partners (with status of traders), unlimited liability for all company debts

SA (Société Anonyme) (Public limited companies)
– Minimum capital of FF 250,000 required
– At least 7 shareholders, whose liability is limited to amount of capital they have invested.
– The SA is entitled to issue bonds and sell stocks to private investors
– The SA must have a board of directors with at least 3 members, or a managing or supervisory committee, an annual general shareholders' meeting and the accounts must be audited

For details of setting up a business in France please apply to the Information Desk of the Chamber of Commerce, Paris.

Every business in France has to be registered. Most towns have a Commercial and Company Registry (Registre du Commerce et des Sociétés) attached to the local Commercial Court (Tribunal de Commerce). The local Chamber of Commerce has a centre for business formalities and should be a first port of call.

When acquiring a commercial property in France there are some transactions to be made:
– acquisition of the business itself (fonds de commerce), including the 'clientèle' or goodwill

– acquisition of the property (les murs)
– the premises may also be leased and the tenant (the owner of the business) and the landlord (the owner of the premises) will both be subject to regulations defined as 'le bail commercial' (commercial lease).

When looking for commercial premises you are strongly advised to use the services of an estate agent.

> FNAIM Fédération Nationale des Agents Immobiliers et Mandataires en Vente de Fonds de Commerce
> (National Federation of Estate Agents)
> 129 rue du Faubourg Saint-Honoré
> 75008 Paris
> Tel: (1) 42 25 24 26

If you do not wish to lease or purchase commercial premises, you can use the services of agencies which rent office space (sociétés de domiciliation) or you can consult specialist magazines such as *ICF* (*Indicateur de Commerce de France*), *Les Annonces*, *PIC* (*Professions–Informations–Commerces*), etc.

A list of such agencies is available from the Chamber of Commerce, Paris.

If you are going to enter the French market and need support you can refer to:

> Chambre de Commerce Internationale
> (International Chamber of Commerce)
> 38 cours Albert 1er
> 75008 Paris
> Tel: (1) 45 62 34 56
> Fax: (1) 42 25 86 63

> Assemblée Permanente des Chambres de Commerce et d'Industrie (ACFCI)
> (Assembly of Chambers of Industry and Commerce)
> 45 avenue d'Iéna
> 75116 Paris Cedex 16
> Tel: (1) 40 69 37 00

Télex: 610 396
Fax: (1) 47 20 61 28

Union des Chambres de Commerce et
d'Industrie Françaises à l'Étranger
(UCCIFE)
(Federation of French Chambers of
Industry and Commerce Abroad)
2 rue de Viarmes
75001 Paris
Tel: (1) 45 08 39 10
Télex: 230823 F
Fax: (1) 45 08 38 51

Assemblée Permanente des Chambres de
Métiers
(Assembly of Chambers of Trades)
12 avenue Marceau
75008 Paris
Tel: (1) 47 23 61 55

Centre Français du Commerce Extérieur
(CFCE)
(French Centre of Foreign Trade)
10 avenue d'Iéna
75783 Paris Cedex 16
Tel. (1) 40 73 30 00
Télex: 611 934 CFCE F
Fax: (1) 40 73 39 79
Service Orientation (1) 40 73 38 88

Crédit d'Équipement des Petites et
Moyennes Entreprises (CEPME)
(Credit Facilities for Small and
Medium-sized Firms)
14 rue du 4-Septembre
75007 Paris
Tel: (1) 42 98 80 00
Télex: 211 633
Fax: (1) 42 98 80 97

Chambre Syndicale des Sociétés de
  Développement Régional (SDR)
(Association of Companies for Regional
  Development)
40 rue Jean-Jaurès
93170 Bagnolet
Tel: (1) 49 72 31 01

Agence Nationale pour la Création
  d'Entreprises (ANCE)
(National Agency for the Establishment of
  Businesses)
142 rue du Bac
75007 Paris
Tel: (1) 45 49 58 58
Télex: 250043
Minitel 3615 Chances

DATAR
(Délégation à l'Aménagement du
  Territoire et à l'Action Régionale)
(Industrial Development Board)
1 avenue Charles Flauquet
75700 Paris
Tel: (1) 40 65 12 34
    (1) 47 83 61 20
Télex: 200970
Fax: (1) 43 06 99 01

DATAR in the UK:
French Industrial Development Board
21–24 Grosvenor Place
London SW1X 7HU
Tel: 0171-235 5148

Registre du Commerce
(Companies Registration Office)
1 quai de Corse
75181 Paris Cedex 04
Tel: (1) 43 29 12 60

Fédération Française du Franchisage
(French Franchise Federation)
9 boulevard des Italiens
75002 Paris
Tel: (1) 42 60 00 22
Fax: (1) 42 60 03 11
Minitel 3616 FFF

Annuaire de la Franchise
(Franchising Year Book) published by:
CECOD
19 rue de Calais
75009 Paris
Tel: (1) 42 80 43 94

European Franchise Federation
Home Tune House
Guildford Road
Effingham
Surrey KT24 5QS

Further information on the Single European Market can be found in Part III, 7.

→8   Useful UK addresses can be found in Part III, 10.

28

Business Letters	La Lettre Commerciale
address	l'adresse
date	la date
care of (c/o)	c/o, aux bons soins de (abs)
enclosure	la pièce jointe
for the attention of	à l'attention de
printed letterhead	l'en-tête imprimé

(our/your) reference	**(notre/votre) référence**
signature	**la signature**

See the Appendix for a standard layout of a French business letter.

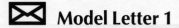 # Model Letter 1

PART II

1

1 First Contacts

1.1 Greeting someone and saying goodbye

Good morning	**Bonjour, monsieur/madame/ messieurs-dames**
Good afternoon	**Bonjour, monsieur/ . . . / . . .**
Good evening	**Bonsoir**
Good night	**Bonne nuit**
Hello	**Salut**
Are you Mrs Brunel by any chance?	**Seriez-vous par hasard Madame Brunel?/Vous êtes Madame Brunel?**
▶ Yes, that's me	▶ **Oui, c'est moi**
Nice to meet you/How nice to see you	**Je suis content(e) de vous voir**
Did you have a good journey/ trip?	**Vous avez fait bon voyage?**
How was your flight?	**Votre vol s'est bien passé?**
How long are you planning to stay?	**Vous voulez rester combien de temps?**
Are you enjoying your stay?	**Vous vous plaisez ici?**
How are you? ▶ Fine, thanks and you?	**Comment allez-vous?** ▶ **Bien, merci et vous?**
▶ Not too bad, thanks	▶ **Pas mal, merci**

If you are not feeling well, you can respond to the question, **'Comment allez-vous?'** by saying **'Pas trop bien'**.

Goodbye/bye-bye	**Au revoir, madame/monsieur**
Cheerio	**Salut**

Have a good trip	**Bon voyage**
See you soon	**A bientôt**
See you later	**A tout à l'heure**
See you tomorrow	**A demain**
Have a nice time	**Amusez-vous bien**
I'm afraid I must go now	**Malheureusement il faut que je parte**
Thank you very much for . . .	**Merci beaucoup pour . . .**
Thank you very much for making my stay so pleasant	**Merci beaucoup pour cet agréable séjour**
It was very nice	**Cela a été très bien**
I've enjoyed talking to you	**J'ai été très content(e) de parler avec vous**
It's been a useful meeting	**Notre rencontre a été très utile**
Pleased to have met you	**Je suis très content(e) d'avoir fait votre connaissance/Heureux(euse) d'avoir fait votre connaissance**
I'll give you a ring soon	**Je vous téléphone bientôt**
I'll be in touch	**Je vous appellerai**
Please give my regards to your wife	**Toutes mes salutations à votre femme/épouse**

1.2 Communication

Do you speak English?	**Vous parlez anglais?**
I don't speak much French	**Je ne parle qu'un peu français**
I'm afraid my French isn't very good	**Malheureusement je ne parle pas très bien français**
I'm English	**Je suis anglais(e)**
I don't understand	**Je n'ai pas compris**

Don't speak so fast, please	**Parlez plus lentement, s'il vous plaît**
Could you speak more slowly, please?	**Pourriez-vous parler un peu moins vite, s'il vous plaît?**
Could you repeat that, please?	**Pourriez-vous répéter, s'il vous plaît?**
I'm afraid I didn't quite understand	**Malheureusement je n'ai pas très bien compris**
I'm sorry, I can't follow you; could you write it down, please?	**Je ne peux pas vous suivre, pouvez vous me l'écrire, s'il vous plaît?**
Could you spell it, please?	**Vous pouvez épeler, s'il vous plaît?**
Could you translate that for me, please?	**Vous pouvez me le traduire, s'il vous plaît?**
What does it mean? ▶ Oh, I see	**Qu'est-ce que ça veut dire?** ▶ **Oh, je comprends**
How do you pronounce this word?	**Comment est-ce qu'on prononce ce mot?**
How do you say . . . in French?	**Qu'est-ce qu'on dit en français pour . . .?**

If you do not know the exact French equivalent to an English word and wish to paraphrase something, you can say:

It's a kind of . . ./sort of . . .	**C'est une espèce de . . . / c'est équivalent à . . .**

1.3 Introductions

My name's . . .	**Je m'appelle . . .**
May I introduce . . .	**Puis-je vous présenter . . .**
This is my wife my husband my son/daughter	**C'est ma femme mon mari mon fils/ma fille**

my (boy)friend/(girl)friend	**mon ami/mon amie**
my colleague	**mon collègue/ma collègue**
a colleague of mine	**un/une de mes collègues**
our chief engineer	**notre ingénieur en chef**

■ Please note:

The French always shake hands when they greet one another, and/ or they often kiss one another on the cheek several times (or into the air), depending on what part of the country they are from.

When saying 'Bonjour/Au revoir' you should always add Monsieur, Madame or Messieurs-Dames.

There is a difference between 'vous' and 'tu'. It is not usual to use 'tu' in the business world. 'Tu' is used among friends, often between students, and sometimes at work between colleagues of the same rank. You should leave it up to your business partner to decide.

In general the French like titles. It is not unusual to address a director of a company by saying 'Monsieur le Président', or a lawyer by saying 'Bonjour, maître'. It is, however, not common to address someone with a PhD as 'Docteur', if he or she is not a medical doctor.

The following are examples of various ways of introduction:

J'aimerais vous présenter Madame Gresillon.
▶ **Bonjour, Madame/Enchanté**

Permettez-moi de vous présenter Monsieur Clerin.
▶ **Bonjour, Monsieur. Je suis content(e) de faire votre connaissance.**

Vous connaissez déjà Madame Hody, ma secrétaire?
▶ **Quel plaisir de faire votre connaissance après nos nombreuses conversations téléphoniques.**

If you want to introduce yourself, you can say:

Bonjour, je suis Fred Herring.
▶ **Enchanté, je suis Raoul Dubois.**

1.4 Appointments and arranging to meet someone

I'm . . . /I'm from . . .	**Je suis . . . /je viens de . . .**
I work for . . .	**Je travaille chez . . .**
May I speak to . . .?	**Puis-je parler à . . .?**
I've got an appointment with . . .	**J'ai rendez-vous avec . . .**
Nice to meet you/Pleased to meet you	**Je suis très content(e) de faire votre connaissance**
Can we meet tomorrow morning?	**On peut se voir demain matin?**
When?	**Quand?**
What about 10 o'clock?	**A dix heures, ça va?**
At two o'clock	**A deux heures**
From two to three	**De deux à trois heures**
Between two and three	**Entre deux et trois heures**
In an hour's time	**Dans une heure**
Not before seven	**Pas avant sept heures**
Not after nine	**Pas après neuf heures**
Where shall we meet?	**On se retrouve où?**
I'll pick you up at the hotel	**J'irai vous chercher à votre hôtel**
Can I give you a lift?	**Je peux vous emmener en voiture?**
▶ Thank you, that's really not necessary	▶ **Merci, ce n'est vraiment pas la peine**
It's (too) late	**Il est (trop) tard**
It's (too) early	**Il est (trop) tôt**
I'm sorry I'm late	**Je suis désolé(e) d'être en retard**
Have you been waiting long?	**Vous attendez déjà depuis longtemps?**

What you might hear in French:

Qui voulez-vous voir?	Who would you like to speak to?
Vous avez rendez-vous avec qui?	With whom have you arranged an appointment?
Vous avez rendez-vous?	Have you got an appointment?
Vous vous appelez comment?	May I have your name, please?
Qui dois-je annoncer?	Who shall I say is here?
Bureau 493, quatrième étage à gauche	Room 493, 4th floor, on the left
Mme Jayot va venir vous chercher; veuillez attendre ici un moment, s'il vous plaît.	Mrs Jayot will pick you up in a minute; please wait here for a moment
Entrez!	Come in
Monsieur Fouchet vous attend	Monsieur Fouchet is expecting you.
Quel plaisir de vous voir!	How nice to see you!
Quel bonheur que vous ayez pu venir	I'm glad you could come
Puis-je vous aider à retirer votre manteau?	Let me take your coat
Veuillez vous asseoir	Won't you take a seat?
Puis-je vous offrir quelque chose à boire?	Can I get you something to drink?
Puis-je vous inviter à prendre un café?	Would you like a cup of coffee?
Vous fumez?/Une cigarette? ▶ **Non, merci, je ne fume pas**	Do you smoke?/Cigarette? ▶ No, thank you I don't smoke
Cela vous dérange, si je fume? ▶ **Non** ▶ **Je préfererais que vous ne fumiez pas**	Do you mind if I smoke? ▶ That's fine/Go ahead ▶ I'd rather you didn't

Vous avez du feu?
▶ **Oui, voilà**

Have you got a light?
▶ Here you are

Vous avez fait bon voyage?

Did you have a good journey?

Vous êtes ici déjà depuis quand?
▶ **Depuis deux jours**

How long have you been here?

▶ For two days

C'est votre premier voyage à Grenoble?
▶ **Nous sommes déjà venu(e)s ici il y a deux ans**

Is this your first trip to Grenoble?

▶ We came here two years ago

Vous vous plaisez ici?
▶ **Oui**

Do you like it here?
▶ Yes, I do

Où habitez-vous?
▶ **J'habite à l'hôtel . . .**

Where are you staying?
▶ I'm staying at the . . . Hotel

J'espère que votre hôtel est bien

I hope you're satisfied with your hotel.

Peut-être pourrions-nous déjeuner/dîner ensemble?

Perhaps we could have lunch/dinner together?

Vous avez le temps demain?
▶ **Oui, très bien, je suis libre**
▶ **Oui, je viendrai avec plaisir**

Are you free tomorrow?
▶ Yes, that's fine, I'm free then
▶ Yes, I'd love to come

Voulez-vous que nous mangions ensemble la semaine prochaine?
▶ **Oui, volontiers**

Would you like to go for a meal next week?

▶ Yes, I'd love to

J'aimerais vous montrer le service
▶ **C'est très gentil à vous**

I'd like to show you round the department
▶ That's very kind of you

Je pourrais vous faire visiter un peu la ville

I could show you something of the town

Que pensez-vous de lundi?
▶ **Très bien**
▶ **Faites-moi voir . . .**
▶ **Je vous confirmerai notre rendez-vous par écrit**

What about Monday?
▶ That's fine
▶ Let me see . . .
▶ I'll confirm that date in writing

▶ Je vais essayer d'arranger ça   ▶ I'll try and make it

▶ Je ne peux malheureusement pas   ▶ Sorry, I can't

▶ Je ne peux malheureusement pas me libérer, j'ai déjà quelque chose   ▶ Sorry, I can't make it; I have a prior engagement

A plus tard/à dimanche   See you later/see you on Sunday

■ Please note:

As in English, answering a question with a mere 'Yes' or 'No' does not sound very communicative, so here are a few suggestions:

Vous vous plaisez ici?
▶ **Oui, beaucoup**

On va dîner ensemble, ce soir?
▶ **Oui, avec plaisir**

Vous êtes libre cet soir?
▶ **Non, je regrette**

Several ways of answering in the affirmative and in the negative:

Yes, of course	**Mais oui, bien sûr**
With pleasure	**Avec plaisir**
Perhaps	**Peut-être**
I'm afraid not	**J'ai bien peur que non**
Certainly not	**En aucun cas**

On the other hand, it is important to know that the French are more direct than the English, and a simple 'non' in conversation is not considered impolite.

1.5 Asking and telling the time

What's the time, please?   **Quelle heure est-il?**

It's about/exactly . . .   **Il est à peu près/exactement . . .**

two o'clock	**deux heures**
a quarter past twelve (at lunch time)	**midi et quart**
a quarter past twelve (at midnight)	**minuit et quart**
ten past twelve	**midi dix**
half past twelve	**midi et demie**
twenty to one	**une heure moins vingt**
a quarter to one	**une heure moins le quart**

■ Please note:

The 24-hour clock is used when you refer to timetables, but not in general everyday conversations.

Remember, there is a time difference between Britain and France (one hour).

Il est trois heures

Il est midi vingt

Il est dix heures et quart

Il est une heure moins le quart

Il est quinze heures
trente-cinq

Il est quatre heures
moins vingt-cinq

Il est neuf heures
et demie

General expressions of time:

during the day	**dans la journée**
in the morning	**le matin**
at noon	**le midi**
in the evening	**le soir**
at night	**la nuit**
at midnight	**à minuit**
today/yesterday/tomorrow	**aujourd'hui/hier/demain**
the day before yesterday	**avant-hier**
the day after tomorrow	**après-demain**
daily	**tous les jours**
hourly	**toutes les heures**
at any time	**à tout moment**
this morning/tonight	**ce matin/ce soir**
last week	**la semaine dernière**
every week	**toutes les semaines**
two weeks ago/two years ago	**il y a deux semaines/deux ans**

in two days' time	**dans deux jours**
in two weeks/in a fortnight	**dans deux semaines/dans 15 jours**
for two days	**depuis deux jours**
from 8 o'clock onwards	**depuis huit heures**
1992	**mille neuf cent quatre-vingt-douze**

See Part III, 5 for a list of days of the week, months and public holidays.

The date:

What's the date today?	**Nous sommes le combien?**
Today's January the 25th	**Aujourd'hui nous sommes le vingt-cinq janvier**
On June the 26th of this year/last year/next year	**Le 26 juin (le vingt-six juin) de cette année/de l'année dernière/de l'année prochaine**
Until the first of January	**Jusqu'au premier janvier**
In your letter of May the 5th	**Dans votre lettre du 5 mai**
The letter was posted on the 30th of March	**La lettre a été envoyée le trente mars**
The 10th of this month	**le dix courant**
The 10th of last month	**le dix du mois dernier**

■ Please note:

There are a number of ways of writing the date in French:

written as:	spoken as:
15 April 1992	**le quinze avril dix neuf cent quatre-vingt-douze**

15/4/92	**le quinze quatre quatre-vingt-**
15.04.82	**douze**
1992	**dix neuf cent nonante-deux**
	(in Belgium and Switzerland)

Ordinal numbers are not used for stating the date, with two exceptions: the first of . . .

April 1st		**le premier avril**
	and	
April 11th		**le onze avril**

Months are written without capital letters.

Part III, 3 contains a list of ordinal numbers which will be useful when stating the date.

2

Everyday Topics

2.1 The weather

Talking about the weather is a popular way of getting into a conversation with someone. You may hear such sentences as:

C'est une belle journée/Belle journée	It's a beautiful day
Quelle belle journée aujourd'hui, n'est-ce pas?	Nice day today, isn't it?
Quel temps affreux aujourd'hui, non?	It's an awful day, isn't it?
Il va pleuvoir	It's going to rain
Le temps va rester au beau	It's going to stay fine
Quel temps fait-il en Angleterre?	What's the weather like in England?
Quel temps fera-t-il demain?	What's the weather going to be like tomorrow?

Il y a pas mal de brouillard	It's rather foggy
La température est au-dessus/en-dessous de zero degré	The temperature is above/below freezing point

Be careful not to talk too much on this topic, otherwise you will be thought of as a boring conversationalist.

In Part III, 4 you will find a conversion table for Fahrenheit and Celsius (centigrade) temperatures.

2.2 General questions

Where is . . ./ where are . . .?	**Où est-ce qu'il y a . . .?**
▶ There is . . ./there are . . .	▶ **Il y a . . .**
Is there . . ./are there . . .?	**Est-ce qu'il y a . . .?**
Who?	**Qui?**
What?	**Quoi?**
Which/What kind of . . .?	**Lequel?/Laquelle?**
Whose?	**A qui?/De qui?**
Where?	**Où?**
Where from?	**D'où?**
Where (to)?	**Où?**
When?	**Quand?**
For how long?	**Combien de temps?**
Since when?/How long?	**Depuis quand?**
Why?	**Pourquoi?**
How?	**Comment?**
Pardon?/I beg your pardon?	**Comment?**
What would you like?	**Qu'est-ce que vous voulez?/ Qu'est-ce que vous désirez?**
How much does it cost?	**Ça coûte combien?**

How much do I owe you?	**Je vous dois combien?**
Have you got . . .?	**Vous avez . . .?**
What does that mean?	**Ça s'appelle comment?**
What's that?	**Qu'est-ce que c'est?**
Who's that?	**Qui est-ce?/c'est qui?**
When do you open/close?	**Vous ouvrez/fermez quand?**
Excuse me, can you tell me where I can find . . .	**Pardon, Madame/Monsieur/ Mademoiselle, pourriez-vous me dire où il y a . . .**
. . . a department store?	**. . . un grand magasin?**
. . . a tourist information office?	**. . . le syndicat d'initiative?**
	. . . une agence du tourisme?
. . . a toilet?	**. . . les toilettes?**
How do I get to . . .?	**Pour aller à . . .?**
Where's the British Embassy, please?	**Où est l'ambassade d'Angleterre, s'il vous plaît?**

**Embassy of the United Kingdom
Great Britain and Northern Ireland
35 rue du Faubourg Saint-Honoré
75383 Paris Cedex 08
Tel: (1) 42 66 91 42
Télex: 650264
Fax: (1) 42 66 98 96**

■ Please note:

If you want to speak to a stranger in the street, it is more polite to begin sentences with 'Excusez-moi, Madame/Monsieur' or 'Pardon, Madame.'

Excuse me, can I park here?	**Excusez-moi, Monsieur, est-ce que je peux me garer ici?**
Excuse me, do you happen to know if there's a bank near here?	**Excusez-moi, Madame, savez-vous par hasard, s'il y a une banque près d'ici?**

There are different ways of asking questions in French:

Il est parti?
Est-ce qu'il est parti?

Vous l'avez vu où?
Où est-ce que vous l'avez vu?

2.3 Apologizing

I'm very sorry (about it)	**Je suis vraiment désolé(e)**
▶ It's all right	▶ **Ça ne fait rien**
▶ It was my fault	▶ **C'était (de) ma faute**
I'm afraid it's not possible	**Ce n'est malheureusement pas possible**
I (do) apologize	**Je (le) regrette vraiment**
I'm sorry to hear that	**Je suis désolé(e) d'entendre ça**
I'm sorry, I didn't notice	**Veuillez m'excuser, mais c'était une erreur**
My apologies for being late	**Je vous prie d'excuser mon retard**
Excuse my saying so, but . . .	**Cela m'est très désagréable, mais je dois vous dire que . . .**

2.4 Requesting and thanking

Can you do me a favour, please?	**Pourriez-vous me rendre un service?**
▶ Certainly	▶ **Bien sûr**
Excuse me, I wonder if you could help me?	**Pourriez-vous m'aider?**
I'm sorry to trouble you, but could you . . .?	**Excusez-moi de vous déranger, mais pourriez-vous . . .?**

May I?	**Vous permettez?**
▶ Yes, certainly/Go ahead	▶ **Mais oui, je vous en prie**
Do you mind if I open the window?	**Puis-je ouvrir la fenêtre, s'il vous plaît?**
May I ask you a question?	**Puis-je vous poser une question?**
Can I help you?	**Puis-je vous aider?**
▶ Can you tell me . . ., please?	▶ **Pourriez-vous me dire . . .?**
▶ Can you show me . . ., please?	▶ **Pourriez-vous me montrer . . .?**
▶ I need . . .	▶ **J'ai besoin de . . .**
▶ I'd rather . . ./I'd prefer . . .	▶ **Je préférerais . . .**
Please hurry up, it's urgent	**Dépêchez-vous s'il vous plaît, c'est urgent**
Pardon?/I beg your pardon?	**Comment?**
There/here you are	**Voilà**
Thank you	**Merci**
Thank you very much (indeed)	**Merci beaucoup**
Thank you for showing me round the factory/shop	**Je vous remercie de m'avoir fait voir l'usine/l'atelier**
It's been a useful meeting, thank you	**Notre entretien a été fructueux, je vous en remercie**
That's very kind of you, thank you	**Merci, c'est très gentil de votre part**
You've been very helpful/Thank you for all your help	**Vous m'avez vraiment été d'un grand secours**
▶ Don't mention it	▶ **De rien**
▶ My pleasure	▶ **Tout le plaisir a été pour moi**
	▶ **Ça a été un vrai plaisir**
▶ That's quite all right	▶ **Je vous en prie**
▶ You're welcome	▶ **Ce n'est rien**
Yes, please	**Oui, s'il vous plaît**
No, thank you	**Merci, non**

If you only say 'merci', it means 'no' to the French!

93

■ **Please note:**

It is always more polite to add 's'il vous plaît' when you ask for something. It is also more polite (and virtually always done) to add the word 'Madame', or 'Monsieur' or 'Mademoiselle' when addressing somebody.

When you address someone to make a request it is better to start your sentence with 'Pardon' or 'Excusez-moi', e.g.:
Pardon, Monsieur, pourriez vous me dire . . ., s'il vous plaît? (s.v.p.)

There are various ways of requesting something. To ask the time, for example, you could say:

Quelle heure est-il?
Il est quelle heure?
Vous avez l'heure?
Pouvez-vous me dire quelle heure il est?
Excusez-moi, pouvez-vous me dire quelle heure il est, s.v.p.?

If you want to send a thank-you letter for an invitation, you will find the model letters in the Appendix useful.

 Model letters 16, 17, 18 and 19

2.5 Personal data

What's your name, please?
▶ My name's . . .

Quel est votre nom?
▶ **Je m'appelle . . .**

When were you born?

Quelle est votre date de naissance?

▶ I was born on . . .
▶ **Je suis né(e) le . . .**

How old are you?
▶ I'm . . . years old
▶ I'm over . . ./under . . .

Vous avez quel âge?
▶ **J'ai . . . ans**
▶ **J'ai plus de . . ./moins de . . .**

Are you married?
▶ I'm married
▶ single/divorced
▶ a widower/widow

Vous êtes marié(e)?
▶ **Je suis marié(e)**
▶ **célibataire/divorcé(e)**
▶ **veuf/veuve**

Have you any children? | **Vous avez des enfants?**

Are you here on business? | **Vous êtes ici pour affaires?**
▶ Yes, I am | ▶ **Oui**

Where do you come from? | **D'où venez-vous?**

Which part of England do you come from? | **De quelle région de l'Angleterre venez-vous?**

Where do you live? | **Vous habitez où?**

Please fill in this form | **Voulez-vous remplir ce formulaire, s.v.p.**

What's your profession? | **Quel est votre profession?**

What do you do for a living? | **Qu'est-ce que vous faites dans la vie?**

May I ask you what you do? | **Je peux vous demander ce que vous faites?**
▶ I'm a businesswoman/ businessman | ▶ **Je suis femme/homme d'affaires**
▶ I'm responsible for/in charge of the export department | ▶ **Je suis responsable du service d'exportation**
▶ I'm head of research | ▶ **Je dirige le service des recherches**
▶ I'm head of the sales department | ▶ **Je suis chef des ventes**

What line of business are you in? | **Dans quelle branche travaillez-vous?**
▶ I'm in computers | ▶ **Je travaille dans l'informatique**

Who do you work for? | **Pour qui travaillez-vous?**
▶ I work for . . . | ▶ **Je travaille pour . . .**

I'm over here for the Trade Fair | **Je suis venu(e) pour le salon/la foire**

What kind of hobbies do you have? | **Quels sont vos hobbies?**

Do you like golf? | **Vous vous intéressez au golf?**

95

Do you do any sport?	**Vous faites du sport?**
Do you speak any foreign languages?	**Vous parlez des langues étrangères?**

See the Appendix for a standard layout of a curriculum vitae (model letter 15).

3

Travel

3.1 Customs and Immigration

import/export duty	**la taxe/le droit d'importation/ d'exportation**
entry	**l'entrée**
border	**la frontière**
customs/customs officer	**le service des douanes/le douanier**
duty/duty-free/dutiable	**le droit de douane/en franchise/à déclarer à la douane**
customs clearance	**le passage en douane**
customs control	**le contrôle douanier**
customs declaration	**la déclaration de douane**
customs declaration form	**le formulaire de déclaration de douane**
I'm travelling with my family	**Je voyage avec ma famille**
I'm here on business	**Je suis ici pour affaires**
I'm here on holiday	**Je suis en vacances**
I'm staying for three weeks	**Je vais rester trois semaines**
I've been here before	**Je suis déjà venu ici**
I'm not going to work in France	**Je ne vais pas travailler en France**
These are only personal belongings	**Ce ne sont que des affaires personnelles**

These are samples	**Ce sont des échantillons**
These are presents	**Ce sont des cadeaux**
This is my suitcase	**C'est ma valise**
This is not mine	**Ce n'est pas la mienne**
I've nothing to declare	**Je n'ai rien à déclarer**
I'm declaring this bottle of brandy	**Je dois déclarer cette bouteille de cognac**

At the border you might hear or read the following sentences in French:

Articles/marchandise à déclarer	Goods to declare
Rien à déclarer	Nothing to declare
Je peux voir votre passeport, s.v.p.?	Can I see your passport, please?
Vous papiers, s.v.p.	Your travel documents, please
Avez-vous rempli votre carte de débarquement?	Have you filled in your landing card?
Quel est l'objet de votre voyage?	What's the purpose of your visit?
▶ **Je suis ici pour affaires**	▶ I'm here on business
Combien de temps allez-vous rester?	How long are you going to stay?
Est-ce que c'est votre premier séjour en France?	Is this your first visit to France?
Ressortissants de la Communauté Européenne	Citizens of EC Countries
Alors, vous pouvez passer	You can go through, then
Avez-vous quelque chose à déclarer?	Have you got anything to declare?
Est-ce que c'est votre valise?	Is this your suitcase?
Ouvrez le coffre, s.v.p.	Open the boot, please
Qu'est-ce qu'il y a là-dedans?	What's in here?
Vous avez droit à 200 cigarettes	You're allowed 200 cigarettes

97

**Pour ça il faut payer des droits
de douane** You'll have to pay duty on this

■ Please note:

Details of customs regulations are beyond the scope of this
language guide. Should you have any questions concerning
customs you can write to the following:

> **HM Customs and Excise
> Dorset House
> Stamford Street
> London SE1 9PS**

You can also make inquiries at the London Chamber of Commerce
and Industry:

> **London Chamber of Commerce and
>   Industry
> 69 Cannon Street
> London EC4N 5AB
> Tel: 0171-248 444
> extension: 3008/9/10**

The Customs and Trade Procedures department provides helpful
information on the following areas: customs procedures/
documents/clearance/import controls/foreign/UK exports/
temporary movements.

The British Chamber of Commerce and Industry will, of course, also
be able to offer you further help:

> **British Chamber of Commerce and Industry
> 8 rue Cimarosa
> 75116 Paris
> Tel: (1) 45 05 13 08
> Télex: 614 806
> Fax: (1) 45 53 02 87**

> **Chambre de Commerce Française de
>   Grande Bretagne
> Knightsbridge House**

197 Knightsbridge
London SW7 1RB
Tel: 0171-225 5250

Direction Générale des Douanes et Droits
   Indirects
(Board of Customs and Excise)
8 rue de la Tour des Dames
75009 Paris
Tel: (1) 42 80 67 22
Télex: 220 200
Fax: (1) 40 04 25 57

Service des Réglementations du Commerce
   Extérieur – Centre Français du Commerce
   Extérieur – CFCE
(Department for Foreign Trade
   Regulations)
Tel: (1) 40 73 30 00

Service de Renseignements Douaniers
(Customs Information Service)
192 rue Saint-Honoré
75001 Paris
Tel: (1) 42 60 35 90

3.2 Planes

Can you help me, please?	**Pouvez-vous m'aider, s.v.p.?**
Where's the office of . . . Airline?	**Où se trouve le bureau de la compagnie . . .?**
I'd like to book a flight to Paris, please	**J'aimerais réserver un vol pour Paris**
A single/return flight	**Un vol aller/un vol aller-retour**
When's the next plane to . . .?	**Quand part le prochain avion pour . . .?**
I'd like to fly to . . .	**J'aimerais prendre l'avion pour . . .**

Can I fly directly from here?	**Est-ce qu'il y a un vol direct?**
Do I have to change planes?	**Est-ce qu'il faut changer?**
Is there a connection to . . .?	**Est-ce qu'il y a une correspondance pour . . .?**
Is there a stop-over?	**Est-ce qu'il y a une escale?**
Are there any seats available?	**Est-ce qu'il y a des places libres?**
Where can I confirm the return flight?	**Où dois-je confirmer le vol retour?**
I'd like a seat by the window	**J'aimerais avoir une place près de la fenêtre**
Non-smoking section	**La partie non-fumeur**
What is the flight number?	**Quel est le numéro du vol?**
When does the plane take off?	**Quand décolle l'avion?**
Will we arrive on time?	**Arriverons-nous à l'heure?**
How long will the flight be delayed?	**L'avion aura un retard de combien?**
Has the plane already landed?	**Est-ce que l'avion a déjà atterri?**
Will a meal be served during the flight?	**Est-ce qu'un repas sera servi au cours du vol?**
How much does my suitcase weigh?	**Combien pèse ma valise?**
What's the charge for excess luggage?	**Combien coûte l'excédent de bagages?**
I'll take this hand luggage with me	**Je prends ça comme bagages à main**
I feel sick. Could you bring me something for airsickness?	**J'ai mal au cœur. Avez-vous un médicament?**
My suitcase has got lost	**J'ai perdu ma valise**
My suitcase has been damaged	**Ma valise est endommagée**
Could you send this suitcase to the following address, please?	**Veuillez envoyer ma valise à l'adresse suivante . . .**

You might read or hear the following at French airports:

Aéroport	Airport
Arrivée des vols	Incoming Flights
Arrivée/Départ	Arrivals/Departures
Attachez vos Ceintures, s.v.p.	Fasten your Seatbelts, Please
Attention, s.v.p.	Attention Please
Bagages Encombrants	Bulky Luggage
Carte d'Accès (à bord)	Boarding Card
Classe Affaires	Business Class
Classe Touriste	Economy Class
Déclaration en Douane	Export Declaration
Départ	Take Off/Departure
Dernier Appel	Last Call
Enregistrement des Bagages	Baggage Check-in
Escale	Stop-over
Guichet des Renseignements	Information Desk
Heure Locale	Local Time
Ligne Aérienne	Airline
Livraison des Bagages	Baggage Claim
Location de Voitures	Car Hire
Marchandise en Franchise	Duty-Free
Porte d'Embarquement	Gate
Première Classe	First Class
Réservations	Reservations
Sortie de Secours	Emergency Exit
Valable	Valid
Vol Régulier	Scheduled Flight

Tous les passagers en transit sur le vol BA 123 sont priés de se rendre immédiatement à la porte d'embarquement numéro 5

All BA flight 123 transit passengers are now requested to proceed immediately to gate No 5

Dernier appel pour le vol BA 123 Londres–Paris, porte 52

Last call for British Airways flight 123 from London to Paris, gate 57.

Embarquement Immédiat

Immediate Boarding

Vous pouvez faire enregistrer vos bagages une heure avant	Check-in is one hour before departure
Avez-vous des bagages à main?	Have you got any hand luggage?
Je peux vous mettre sur la liste d'attente	I can put you on the waiting list
Le vol est reporté	The flight is delayed
Nous avons un retard de 40 minutes	We're 40 minutes late
Le vol a été supprimé	The flight has been cancelled

■ Please note:

There are many direct flights between the French-speaking countries of the Continent and the UK/Ireland:

Paris: Aberdeen, Birmingham, Bristol, Cardiff, Edinburgh, Glasgow, Jersey, London, Manchester, Southampton and Dublin

London: Bordeaux, Bruxelles, Genève, Lille, Luxembourg, Lyon, Marseille, Montpellier, Mulhouse/Basel, Nantes, Nice, Paris, Strasbourg, Toulouse

There are also direct flights from Birmingham and Manchester to Brussels, Geneva and Nice.

Some useful telephone numbers/addresses:

Air France	
Réservation centrale Paris	**(1) 45 35 61 61**
or Minitel	3615/3616 code AF
British Airways	
Reservation Centre London	0181–897 4000
Reservation Linkline	(0345) 222 111
(local call rate)	

Air France in the UK/Ireland:

Birmingham	International Airport	0121-782 4161
London	158 New Bond Street	0171-499 9511
Manchester	International Airport	0161-436 3800
Dublin	Dawson House, 29 Dawson Street	(1) 778 899

British Airways in France:

Paris	12 rue Castiglione	(1) 47 78 14 14
Bordeaux/Lyon/Marseille/Mulhouse/Nice/Toulouse Airports		
		05 125 125

Inland flights:

Air-Inter	Reservations and information	(1) 45 39 25 25

Airports:

Orly	(1) 49 75 15 15
Roissy–Charles de Gaulle	(1) 48 62 22 80

Air freight:

If you have any questions about air freight the following
numbers of the 'Messagerie' could be useful:

Air France Cargo Minitel	**3614 code AF Cargo**
Reservations Cargo	**(1) 4875 7314**
Position Colis	**(1) 4675 7085**
SODETAIR Collection from/delivery to premises	**(1) 4864 1665**

Arrivals, departures, transfers:

From the UK or Ireland you usually arrive in Paris at Roissy Airport,
Charles de Gaulle (CDG) and you also fly back from this airport.

Inland flights in France:

(Air-Inter) leave from Orly. Transfer from CDG by bus takes 55
minutes – unless you get stuck in an 'embouteillage' (traffic jam).

Transfer between Charles de Gaulle (CDG) and Paris:

	Frequency	*Travelling time*
RER, line B	15 minutes	20 minutes
RATP bus	30 minutes	40 minutes
Air France bus	20 minutes	35 minutes

Information on these connections can be obtained by calling (1) 43
23 87 75.

Inexpensive flights:

Travel agencies will provide information on ABC (Advance
Booking Charter) and APEX (Advance Purchase Excursion) flights,
which cost considerably less than normal flights. Tickets must be
bought three to four weeks before you intend to travel. However,
you cannot change your reservations on such flights.

When in France do not forget to get information on 'vols bleux' and 'vols blancs' (Air Inter): there are some considerable reductions for inland flights at certain times.

Centres d'Affaires des Aéroports de Paris (Business Centres at Paris Airports)

Orly:
Tel: (1) 49 75 12 33
Fax: (1) 48 84 47 68
Télex: 265 866

Charles de Gaulle–Roissy:
Tel: (1) 48 62 33 06
Fax: (1) 47 86 50 02
Télex: 233 347

3.3 Trains

Where's Marseille Central station?	**Où est la gare centrale de Marseille?**
Which bus goes to the station?	**Quel bus va à la gare?**
Take me to the station, please?	**Pouvez-vous me conduire à la gare, s.v.p.?**
At which counter can I get international tickets, please?	**A quel guichet est-ce que je peux acheter un billet international?**
What's the fare to . . .?	**Combien coûte le billet pour . . .?**
Are there any reductions?	**Est-ce qu'il y a des réductions?**
I'd like a ticket to . . .	**Je voudrais un billet pour . . .**
Two singles to Nantes, please	**Deux aller simples pour Nantes, s.v.p.**
Do I need a reservation?	**Est-ce qu'il faut que je réserve?**
Do I have to pay a supplement/ excess fare?	**Dois-je payer un supplément?**

How long is the return ticket valid?	**Le billet de retour est valable combien de temps?**
When's the next train to . . .?	**Quand part le prochain train pour . . .?**
When does the train arrive at . . .?	**Quand est-ce que le train arrive à . . .?**
When does the last train leave?	**A quelle heure part le dernier train?**
Which platform does the train leave from?	**Le train part de quel quai?**
Where do I have to change?	**Où est-ce que je dois changer?**
Is this the train for . . .?	**Est-ce que c'est le train pour . . .?**
Does the train stop at . . .?	**Est-ce que le train s'arrête à . . .?**
I've just missed my train will there be another one?	**Je viens de rater mon train, est-ce qu'il y en a un autre?**
Where will I find a porter?	**Où y a-t-il un porteur?**
Can you help me with my luggage, please?	**Pouvez-vous m'aider à porter mes bagages?**
Where can I check-in my luggage?	**Où est-ce que je peux faire enregistrer mes bagages?**
Excuse me, please	**Est-ce que je pourrais passer?**
Is this seat free/taken?	**Est-ce que cette place est libre/occupée?**
Is anybody sitting here?	**Il y a déjà quelqu'un ici?**
I'm afraid this is my seat	**C'est ma place**
Are there any free compartments in the sleeping car?	**Est-ce qu'il y a des compartiments de wagons-lits libres?**

Is this a non-smoking compartment?	**C'est un compartiment non-fumeurs?**
Whose suitcase is this?	**Cette valise est à qui?**
▶ It's mine	▶ **C'est la mienne**
Do you mind if I open/shut the window?	**Est-ce que je peux ouvrir/fermer la fenêtre?**
Would you mind keeping an eye on this, please?	**Pouvez-vous jetter un coup d'œil sur/surveiller ça?**
Where do I have to get off?	**Où dois-je descendre?**
Could you tell me when we're there, please?	**Pouvez-vous me dire s.v.p. quand nous y serons?**
Where can I get a taxi, please?	**Où est-ce que je peux avoir un taxi?**

At railway stations and on trains you may hear the following:

Un aller simple ou un aller-retour?	Single or return?
Première ou deuxième classe?	First or second class?
Quand partez-vous?	When do you want to leave?
Vous devez changer à . . .	You have to change at . . .
Le train part du quai numéro un	The train leaves from platform 1
Il y a un train toutes les heures	There's a train every hour
Le train a un retard de dix minutes	The train will be delayed by ten minutes
Le prochain train pour . . . a un retard	The next train for . . . is late
. . . à la suite d'une grève	. . . because of industrial action
Vos billets, s.v.p.	Tickets please/Any more tickets, please?

Montez en voiture	All aboard
Changez à Lyon	Change at Lyon
Les voyageurs en direction de Lyon changent ici	Change here for Lyon
Tout le monde descend	All change please
Ici/Là-bas	Here/Over there
Pour cela il faut payer un supplément	You'll have to pay a supplement
Le TGV qui vient d'entrer en gare à la voie 11, est en provenance de Lyon et repart à 12.15 heures en direction de Marseille	The TGV from Lyon arriving at platform 11 is the 12.15 for Marseille
Départ à 17 h 34	Scheduled time of departure 17.34
Prochain arrêt:	The next stop is . . .
Pour prendre le TGV il faut payer un supplément	For the TGV a supplement is required
Vous avez une correspondance à 10.45 pour Angers	There is a connection to Angers at 10.45
Départ 17 h 45, au même quai, voie d'en face	Time of departure 17.45, from the same platform, on the opposite side
Au quai 11, montez en voiture	All aboard on platform 11
Attention à la fermeture automatique.	Take care, the doors close automatically
Attention au départ	Please be careful as the trains is pulling out of the station

If you do not understand announcements over a public address system such as those given above you can ask:

Pouvez-vous me dire, s.v.p. ce qu'on vient de dire au haut-parleur?

(Can you tell me what was just announced over the PA?)

Agence de Voyages	Travel Agency
Arrivée/Départ	Arrivals/Departures
Chariot	Luggage Trolley
Chef de Gare	Station Master
Consigne	Left Luggage Office
Consignes	Left Luggage Lockers
Contrôleur	Guard/Ticket Collector
Couchettes	Couchettes
Dames	Ladies
Entrée	Entrance
Fumeurs/Non-Fumeurs	Smoker/Non-Smoker
Guichet	Ticket Office
Guichet des Renseignements	Information Desk
Horaire	Timetable
Les Dernières Voitures	Rear Coaches
Les Premières Voitures	Front Coaches
Libre	Vacant
Messieurs	Gentlemen
Occupé	Engaged
Quai	Platform
Rafraîchissements	Light Refreshments
SNCF (Société Nationale des Chemins de Fer)	French Railways
Salle d'Attente	Waiting Room
Sortie	Exit
Tableau d'Affichages	Platform Indicator
Toilettes	Lavatories
Wagon-Lit	Sleeping Car
Wagon-Restaurant	Restaurant Car
Accès aux Quais	To the Trains

■ Please note:

There are various kinds of trains in France:

TGV	High-speed train, first and second class; reservations necessary.
Euro City	International train, first and second class.
Inter City	Long-distance fast train operating between main cities in France; supplementary charge payable.
Rapide	Fast train
Express	Ordinary fast train
Autorail	Diesel rail car for short distances
Motorail (Trains auto accompagnés)	Motorails operate to Amiens, Boulogne, Calais, Dieppe, Lyon, Marseille, Avignon, Fréjus, Lille, Metz, Nancy, Nantes, Paris and Toulouse. A leaflet called 'SNCF – Plan d'accès aux gares' shows the stations where cars can be loaded.
Sleepers/Couchettes	These should be booked beforehand.

Ticket machines:

All tickets must be punched: for this purpose you will need to find a 'machine à composter', these are usually located on or close to platforms.

If you travel with a ticket that has not been punched it is considered invalid and you may be fined. This also applies when

you break your journey. The ticket punching machines are orange
in colour. You can read the following in French on them:

Accès au quai	Access to the platform
Au-delà de cette limite votre billet doit être validé	For travel beyond this barrier you must have a valid ticket.
Compostez-le	Punch it
Introduire chaque billet **– face imprimée dessous** **– sous la flèche verte**	Insert each ticket – printed side downwards – under the green arrow
Le glisser vers la gauche jusqu'au déclic	Slide it to the left as far as it will go

Tickets:

You can obtain a ticket at any of the SNCF ticket offices as well as
in the 50 'boutiques-SNCF'. You can pay for it by credit card
(American Express, Visa, Access, Eurocard, Mastercard, Carte
Bleue) at most of them.

You can also buy tickets and make reservations at a ticket machine
('Billeterie automatique') at 200 of the larger stations. You can
pay in cash, or, if more than 40 FF, by Visa, Eurocard, Mastercard or
Carte Bleue. If you buy your ticket on the train you will have to pay
an additional charge.

On a ticket machine ('Billeterie automatique') you will read the
following:

Billeterie automatique	Automatic ticket machine
Grandes lignes	Long-distance connections
Mode d'emploi	Instructions for use
Pour faire votre choix appuyez sur l'écran	To make your choice press the screen
Appuyez sur le pavé bleu à votre choix	Press the blue path of your choice
Une réservation	A reservation

Un billet	A ticket
Un supplément	Additional charge
Un abonnement de travail	Monthly season ticket
Où allez-vous?	Where are you going?
Annulation de la demande	Cancel

There are first and second class carriages on trains. First class carriages can be recognized by the yellow line on them. You will be given an on-the-spot fine if you travel in a first class carriage with a second class ticket.

Reductions:

Be sure to make enquiries about reductions at railway stations and travel agencies. The *Calendrier voyageurs* indicates at which time of the year you can travel at reduced rates ('période bleue') and which are the peak times ('période rouge') when you will have to pay an additional charge. This information is also provided in English.

The timetables displayed at French railway stations show trains marked in red on which an additional charge is payable when travelling at peak times. There are reductions for those marked in blue.

Stations in Paris:

Like London, Paris has several main stations. Make sure you find out beforehand which station you need to travel from:

Gare du Nord	north, to Lille, Calais, Dunkerque, London, Brussels, Cologne
Gare de l'Est	east, to Luxembourg, Strasbourg, Saarbrücken, Zürich
Gare de Lyon	south, south-east, to Lausanne, Bern, Modane, Lyon, Marseille, Nice, Béziers.
Gare d'Austerlitz	south, south-west, to Lyon, Marseille
Montparnasse	west, to Brest, Nantes, Bordeaux, Biarritz, Toulouse

St Lazare	North-west, to Dieppe, Le Havre, Caen, Cherbourg, Rouen

It is always better to check beforehand as departures and arrivals might be at other stations.

TGV Train à Grande Vitesse:

With a top speed of 300 km/h the TGV offers great comfort and a range of services to meet your needs. You can relax, eat and drink and make telephone calls. At the bar you will find a range of hot and cold snacks as well as drinks. At the bar shop you can buy cigarettes, newspapers, magazines and phonecards. You can make phone calls to places in Europe and even Japan and North America.

The TGV can take you to various parts of France, e.g.:

Paris to Nantes	1 hour 59 minutes
Paris to Bordeaux	2 hours 58 minutes
Paris to Toulouse	5 hours 10 minutes
Paris to Brest	3 hours 59 minutes
Paris to Lyon	2 hours 3 minutes
Paris to Marseille	4 hours 46 minutes

When travelling on the TGV you need two tickets: a travel ticket for the journey; and for the 'TGV Atlantique' a 'Resa 300' reservation which entitles you to a seat in the area of your choice ('espace'). The Resa 300 is only valid on the TGV train for which you have reserved a seat.

You have to punch ('composter') both your tickets for the TGV train in the orange machines ('composteurs') on the platforms.

Reservations:

There are various ways of reserving tickets/seats for the TGV:
1 By Minitel with the help of the codes 3615 SNCF or 36 26 50 50 (direct access)
2 By telephone: if you phone the station from which you intend

to travel you can book your tickets for the TGV up to two
months in advance; for peak travelling times (e.g. ski holidays)
up to six months in advance.
3 At ticket offices of 1500 railway stations and travel agents (up
to two months in advance).
4 New vending machines ('billeteries automatiques') from which
you can buy tickets and the Resa 300. Carte Bleue, Visa and
Eurocard are accepted.

Brochures:

The SNCF issue a number of leaflets, e.g.: *Guide du voyageur, TGV-
Atlantique, TGV-Sud-Est, TGV- Est,* in which you will find
comprehensive timetables and fare structures in addition to
explanations in English. There are also booklets available which
only list departure and arrival times ('horaires').

Useful addresses and telephone numbers:

French Travel Service
Francis House
Francis Street
London SW1P 1DE

French Travel Services
69 Boston Manor Road
Brentford
Middlesex TW8 9JQ

French Railways
178–179 Piccadilly
London W1V 0BA
Tel: 0171-409 1224

SNCF Railways	
Informations Générales	(1) 45 82 50 50
Réservation TGV	(1) 45 65 60 60
Minitel SNCF	3615 Code SNCF

Syndicat des Agents de Voyages
6 rue Villaret-de-Joyeuse
75017 Paris
Tel: (1) 42 67 61 20
Télex: 640 981
Fax: (1) 46 22 33 39

Information on the Channel Tunnel
Eurostar
(London–Paris passenger service)
Tel: (01233) 617575

Eurotunnel/Le Shuttle
(Folkestone–Calais car service)
Le Shuttle Customer Service Centre
PO Box 300
Cheriton Parc
Folkestone CT19 4QD
Tel: (0990) 353535

3.4 Ships, boats, ferries

When does the boat for Calais leave?	**Quand part le bac pour Calais?**
Where can I get tickets?	**Où est-ce que je peux acheter des billets?**
I'd like a single/double cabin	**Je voudrais une cabine pour une/deux personnes**
How long does the crossing take?	**Combien de temps dure la traversée?**
When do we land at Dover?	**A quelle heure arriverons-nous à Douvres?**
Is the sea rough?	**Est-ce que la mer est forte?**
Where's the purser's office?	**Où se trouve le bureau du commissaire?**
I feel sick, have you got anything for seasickness?	**J'ai mal au cœur, avez-vous quelque chose contre le mal de mer?**

115

■ **Please note:**

There are various routes from the UK and Ireland to the Continent, e.g.:

Dover–Calais:

by ferry	1 hour 30 minutes
by hovercraft (no lorries)	35 minutes

Dover–Boulogne:

by ferry	1 hour 40 minutes
by hovercraft (no lorries)	35 minutes
by catamaran (no lorries)	45 minutes

Ramsgate–Dunkerque:

by ferry	2 hours 30 minutes

Folkestone–Boulogne:

by ferry	1 hour 50 minutes

Newhaven–Dieppe:

by ferry	4 hours

Portsmouth–Le Havre:

by ferry	5 hours 45 minutes

Portsmouth–Caen:

by ferry	6 hours

Portsmouth–Cherbourg:

by ferry	4 hours 45 minutes

Poole–Cherbourg:

by ferry	4 hours 15 minutes

Portsmouth–St Malo:

by ferry	9 hours

Southampton–Cherbourg:

by ferry	6 hours

Plymouth–Roscoff:

by ferry	6 hours

Cork (Ireland)–Roscoff:

by ferry	6 hours 30 minutes

Harwich–Hoek van Holland:
by ferry   6 hours 30 minutes

Hull–Zeebrugge:
by ferry   20 hours

If you are only going on a short business trip, ask for reduced rates,
valid for 60 or 120 hours, when buying your ferry tickets.
Otherwise car tariffs depend on the season and time of the day
(tariffs A–E).

Useful telephone numbers for information and booking:

Brittany Ferries:
Reservations/Enquiries Plymouth   (01752) 221321
                            Portsmouth   (01705) 827701

Hoverspeed:
Reservations/Enquiries Dover   (01304) 240241
                            Calais   21 96 67 10
                            Boulogne   21 30 27 26

P & O:
Reservations/Enquiries London   0181-575 8555
                            Dover   (01304) 203388
                            Paris   (1) 42 66 40 17
                            Brussels   (2) 231 1937

Sally Line   London   0181-858 1127
                            Ramsgate   (01843) 595522

Sealink/Stena Line   Ashford   (01233) 646047

3.5 Cars

Which is the best road to . . .?   **Quelle est la meilleure route
                                   pour . . .?**

How many kilometres is it
to . . .?   **Il y a combien de kilomètres
                                   jusqu'à . . .?**

Have you got a road map?   **Avez-vous une carte routière?**

Where does this road go to?	**Où conduit cette route?**
Where's the nearest garage, please?	**Où se trouve la station-service la plus proche/le garage le plus proche?**
Fill it up, please	**Le plein, s.v.p.**
200 francs worth, please	**Pour deux cents francs**
Please check the oil/tyres/battery/water	**Vérifiez le niveau d'huile/la pression des pneus/la batterie/l'eau, s.v.p.**
Where can I park?	**Où est-ce que je peux me garer?**
Wash and wax, please	**Laver et nettoyer, s.v.p.**
I've had an accident	**J'ai eu un accident**
My car has broken down	**Je suis en panne**

See Part II, 7.5 for Accidents and Breakdowns.

You may hear or read the following words in French:

le camion	lorry/truck
le gas-oil/gazole	diesel
la limitation de vitesse	speed limit
la location de voitures	car hire service
le numéro d'assurance	insurance number
le parking	car park
le parking à étages	multi-storey car park
le parking souterrain	underground car park
le permis de conduire	driving licence
la plaque d'immatriculation	registration number
le raccourci	short cut
sans plomb	lead-free, unleaded
le self-service	self-service
la station-service	petrol station/garage
la voiture d'occasion	secondhand car

■ Please note:

Information on traffic regulations, motorways, etc. can be
obtained from the AA and RAC in England before beginning your
journey.

AA: Automobile Association
Tel: 0181-954 7373

RAC: Royal Automobile Club
Tel: 0181-686 2525

and the French Automobile Club:

Automobile Club de France
6 place de la Concorde
75008 Paris
Tel: (1) 42 65 34 70

Documents:

When travelling to France in your own or a hired car, you will need
your (national) driving licence, vehicle registration documents, the
green insurance card and your passport. You must have a warning
triangle, unless you have got emergency lights ('feux de détresse').

Traffic regulations:

In France you drive on the right and overtake on the left. Vehicles
coming from the right have the right of way ('priorité à droite'). At
roundabouts ('carrefours aménages') a vehicle already on the
roundabout has the right of way.

It is compulsory for all passengers to wear safety belts even for
short journeys in built-up areas.

British automobile associations will be able to give you further
advice.

1. Carrefour à sens giratoire
The vehicle already on the roundabout has right of way

2. Arrêt au poste de péage
Stop, toll station (e.g. at the entry or exit of a motorway)

3. Voie de détresse à droite
Escape lane on a steep hill

4. Parc National   National Park

5. Entrée d'une zone à stationnement de durée limitée
Parking zone with limited parking duration

6. Entrée d'une zone à stationnement unilatéral à alternance semi-mensuelle
Parking on one side of the road only, alternating every half-month

Emergencies:

In cases of emergency on a motorway ('autoroute') you can make a phone call from an emergency telephone – never further than 1 km away – the direction and distance of which are shown on a blue sign.

In case of an accident it is important to note down the details ('le constat'). The police will come only if someone has been injured.

See Part II, 7.5 for Accidents and Breakdowns.

Speed limits:

Speed limits are determined (among other things) by the weather conditions:

	Under normal traffic conditions	In adverse weather conditions
Built-up areas	50 km/h	50 km/h
Main roads	90 km/h	80 km/h
Dual carriageways	110 km/h	100 km/h
Motorways	130 km/h	110 km/h

Motorways:

There are two types of motorways in France: 'autoroutes à péage' (toll roads); and 'autoroutes de liaison', which are free of charge. Except for a few short stretches, tolls must be paid on the former kind of motorways at a toll house called a 'Poste de Péage'.

There are three different methods of payment both at the beginning and at the end of the motorway section you want to use:

1 Kiosks where you are handed a ticket at the beginning, or where you pay at the end; a green light then allows you to pass.

2 Kiosks where the exact amount in coins for the intended distance is thrown into a container, and then a green light allows you to pass.

3   Kiosks with automatic ticket machines. To obtain a ticket you
    press a button. When you take the ticket the light turns green
    and you can proceed.

Some 'autoroutes':

A1   Autoroute du Nord   Lille–Paris–Poitiers–Bordeaux–Biarritz
A4   Autoroute de l'Est   Paris–Reims–Metz
A6/7 Autoroute du Soleil   Paris–Lyon–Marseille

Open or closed kiosks are indicated by green or red crosses or
arrows respectively. If you drive through when the light is red or
the point is closed an extremely loud siren sounds.

Road signs:

Motorways in France are indicated by a blue sign (with the letter A
and a number) The speed limit is 130 km/h.

Green signs indicate the best routes connecting important towns.

Signs with a white background indicate all other routes.

Main roads ('routes nationales') are indicated by the letters RN or
N and the number.

You can obtain reports on traffic conditions and road congestion
by telephone from 'Inter Service Routes' or via Minitel:
(16–1) 3614 code ASFA, as well as 'Information Bisons Futés'.

The 'Les Routiers' restaurants are appreciated by lorry drivers for
their cuisine but also by the general travelling public.

Parking:

When parking your car you should watch out for the following
restrictions:

side of the street
There might be a sign indicating whether you can park on the
desired side of the street only on even/uneven dates, or during the
first or second half of the month.

parking meters
If you see the word 'Payant' marked on the road you will be near a

ticket machine where you will be able to get a parking ticket, or
where there will be parking meters.

On parking ticket machines you can read the following:

Payant, tous les jours de 9 h à 19 h sauf samedi, dimanche, jours fériés et mois d'août	Payable every day from 9.00 am to 7.00 pm except Saturdays, Sundays, public holidays and in August.
Durée limitée à 2 heures	Stay limited to two hours
Prenez un ticket au distributeur	Take a ticket out of the machine
Faites l'appoint, la machine ne peut pas rendre la monnaie	Please insert the exact amount of money as the machine cannot give change
En cas de panne, veuillez utiliser l'appareil le plus proche et la signaler au No de téléphone suivant . . .	In case of a breakdown please use the nearest machine and call the following number . . .
Monnaie	Small change
Ticket	Ticket
Annulation	Cancel

Petrol:

Gas-oil or gazole is diesel
(Essence) ordinaire is '2 star'
(Essence) super is '4 star'
Sans plomb is unleaded petrol

Petrol is sold in litres.

Litres and Gallons:

Gallons	1.1	2.2	4.4
Litres	5	10	20

Petrol stations are frequently closed between 12.00 noon and 2.00 pm but they are generally open during normal shopping hours. You can usually buy petrol more cheaply at supermarkets.

Maps for motorists:

Michelin series (1:200,000)
Very detailed street maps, with many tips

Grands Itinéraires de France (1:100,000)
Green arrows indicate the most favourable alternative routes ('itinéraires de dégagement') which avoid traffic build-ups. There is also a table showing the likely areas of congestion and another one giving the distances between the most important towns as well as driving times. Information is also given in English.

You should avoid motorways on the following dates:
Easter Monday, Whit Monday, the last weekend in June, weekends in July, August, September, 14 July, 15 August.

Distances are expressed in km
1 km is 0.622 mile
1 mile is 1.609 km

Table of distances

	BOR	CAL	DUN	GRE	LYO	MAR	NAN	PAR	STR	TOU
Bordeaux	—	872	871	661	543	648	325	579	920	244
Calais	872	—	41	859	755	1066	677	295	623	993
Dunkerque	871	41	—	858	754	1064	676	293	598	992
Grenoble	661	859	858	—	105	272	717	566	548	537
Lyon	543	755	754	105	—	313	613	462	490	537
Marseille	648	1066	1064	272	313	—	974	773	801	404
Nantes	325	677	676	717	613	974	—	384	867	569
Paris	579	295	293	566	462	773	384	—	490	700
Strasbourg	920	623	598	548	490	801	867	490	—	1025
Toulouse	244	993	992	537	537	404	569	700	1025	—

The French like to use their horns a lot and they drive rather fast.

3.6 Car hire

Is there a car hire service nearby?

Est-ce qu'il y a à proximité une location de voitures?

I'd like to hire a car	**Je voudrais louer une voiture**
I need a big/small car for one week	**J'ai besoin d'une grosse/petite voiture pour une semaine**
How much does it cost per week/per day/per weekend?	**Quel est le prix par semaine/par jour/pour le week-end?**
What do you charge per kilometre?	**Quel est le prix au kilomètre?**
What type of petrol does it run on?	**La voiture roule à quoi?**
Is the mileage unlimited?	**Est-ce que le nombre de kilomètres est illimité?**
How much is the insurance?	**Combien coûte l'assurance?**
Do I have to pay a deposit?	**Dois-je donner une caution?**
Here's my driving licence/my identity card	**Voilà mon permis de conduire/ma carte d'identité**
Do you accept credit cards?	**Accepter-vous les cartes de crédit?**
What documents do I need?	**De quels papiers ai-je besoin?**
Third-party insurance	**Assurances responsabilité-civile**
Passenger insurance	**Assurance passagers**
Collision damage waiver	**Rachat de franchise**

If you hire a car you may read or hear the following sentences in French:

Puis-je voir votre permis de conduire?	May I see your driving licence?
Pouvez-vous remplir cela, s.v.p.?	Fill in this form, please
Une assurance est obligatoire	Insurance is required
Avez-vous actuellement une assurance voiture?	Are you currently insured?

Souhaitez-vous une assurance supplémentaire?	Would you like the extra insurance?
Où voulez-vous rendre la voiture?	Where would you like to leave the car?
Voulez-vous la rapporter ici?	Would you like to return it here?
Veuillez lire les conditions au verso	Please read other side for conditions
Je déclare que les informations données ici sont exactes	I hereby declare that the above statements are true
Veuillez signer ici, s.v.p.	Please sign here
Procès de constat amiable	Accident report
par jour/semaine	per day/week

■ Please note:

When hiring a car in France you must produce a valid driving licence and a passport. You must be at least 21 years of age, in some cases 23. You must have had a full driving licence for at least one year. A deposit is not necessary if you have a credit card. Always inquire whether insurance is included in the price.

Compulsory insurance: Third-party insurance	**Assurance responsabilité-civile (incendie, bris de glace)**
Optional insurance: Collision damage waiver (CDW)	**Rachat de franchise**
Personal accident (PA)/and personal effects (PAPE)	**Garantie pour le conducteur et les personnes transportés et effets personnels**

There are several car-hire companies in France, e.g.:

Euro Rent	**Autorent**
(1) 45 67 82 17	**(1) 45 54 22 45**

Avis Train and Auto	**Budget Train and Auto**
(1) 46 09 92 12	**(1) 46 68 55 55**
Century	**Europcar**
(1) 42 61 68 68	**(1) 30 43 82 82**
Hertz	
(1) 47 88 51 51	

with chauffeur:

Michka	**Espaces Limousines**
(1) 47 07 99 22	**(1) 42 65 63 16**

You will also find offices at airports and major railway stations. Travel agencies and tourist information centres can also give you additional addresses.

Information on renting a car can also be obtained from French Railways (SNCF).

Usually, it is best to hire a car for France while you are still in the UK, e.g.

> **Avis Rent-a-Car:**
> **Hayes Gate House**
> **Uxbridge Road**
> **Hayes**
> **Middlesex UB4 0JN**
> **Tel: 0181-848 8733**

> **Hertz Rent-a-Car:**
> **Radnor House**
> **1272 London Road**
> **London SW16 4XW**
> **Tel: 0181-679 1799**

4

Hotels and Restaurants

4.1 Hotels

Have you got a room free?	**Avez-vous une chambre de libre?**
Can I have a quiet room, please?	**Puis-je avoir une chambre calme?**
. . . not facing the street	**. . . qui ne donne pas sur la rue**
. . . a single room	**. . . une chambre pour une personne**
. . . a double room	**. . . une chambre pour deux personnes**
. . . a double bed	**. . . un lit pour deux personnes**
. . . twin beds	**. . . deux lits jumeaux**
. . . with/without a bath/shower	**. . . avec/sans bain/douche**
. . . with breakfast	**. . . avec petit déjeuner**
. . . with half board	**. . . avec demi-pension**
. . . with full board	**. . . avec pension complète**
I made a reservation by phone	**J'avais réservé par téléphone**
Can I see the room please?	**Puis-je voir la chambre, s.v.p.?**
I'll take it	**Je la prends**
I'm sorry, it's too small/too noisy	**Je regrette, mais elle est trop petite/trop bruyante**
Can you show me another room, please?	**Pouvez-vous me montrer une autre chambre?**

Requests:

Can you wake me at 7 o'clock, please?	**Pouvez-vous me réveiller à sept heures, s.v.p.?**
Can you call a taxi, please?	**Pouvez-vous m'appeler un taxi, s.v.p.?**
Where can I leave my luggage?	**Où puis-je laisser mes bagages?**

128

Where can I deposit our valuables?	**Où puis-je déposer mes objets de valeur?**
Where can I post a letter?	**Où puis-je poster une lettre?**
Could you forward my post to . . ., please?	**Pouvez-vous faire suivre mon courrier à l'adresse . . ., s.v.p.?**
Could you bring me . . ., please?	**Pourriez-vous s.v.p. m'apporter . . .?**
. . . some coathangers	**. . . quelques cintres**
. . . a blanket	**. . . une couverture**
. . . a pillow	**. . . un oreiller**
. . . an ash-tray	**. . . un cendrier**
What's the voltage here? (In France: 220 volts, 50 Hz)	**Le voltage est de combien ici?**
The lights are not working	**La lumière ne marche pas**
Can you repair this?	**Pouvez-vous le/la réparer?**
The TV needs repairing	**Il faudrait réparer la télévision**
switch/socket/plug	**le bouton/la prise/la fiche**

British plugs cannot be used in most French hotels, so you should take a multiple adapter with you.

Can I have the bill, please?	**Pouvez-vous me donner la note, s.v.p.?**
Is service included?	**Est-ce que le service est compris?**
We're leaving tomorrow	**Nous partons demain**
Thank you for everything, we enjoyed ourselves very much	**Merci pour tout, nous nous sommes beaucoup plu**

Services:

I'd like to have my shoes cleaned, please	**J'aimerais faire nettoyer mes chaussures**
Can you wash these clothes, please?	**Pourriez-vous me faire laver ces vêtements, s.v.p.?**

129

Can you dry-clean and press my suit, please?	**Pouvez-vous nettoyer à sec et repasser mon costume?**
Can I have it back as soon as possible?	**Pourrais-je le récupérer le plus vite possible?**
Can you repair these shoes, please?	**Pouvez-vous réparer ces chaussures?**
How much do I owe you?	**Je vous dois combien?**
Is there a hairdresser's in the hotel?	**Est-ce qu'il y a un coiffeur dans l'hôtel?**
I'd like a haircut, please	**J'aimerais me faire couper les cheveux**

General questions:

Has anyone asked for me?	**Est-ce que quelqu'un m'a demandé?**
Are there any messages for me?	**Est-ce que quelqu'un a laissé un message pour moi?**
Can you post these letters for me, please?	**Pouvez-vous me poster ces lettres?**
Is there a good restaurant nearby?	**Est-ce qu'il y a un bon restaurant près d'ici?**
I need an interpreter who speaks English	**J'ai besoin d'un interprète qui parle anglais**

What you might read or hear in French at your hotel:

Puis-je vous aider?	Can I help you?
Vous avez réservé une chambre?	Have you booked a room?
. . . avec/sans salle de bain/ douche	. . . with/without a bath/shower
Combien de temps voulez-vous rester?	How long do you want to stay?
C'est pour une nuit seulement?	Just for one night?

C'est pour combien de nuits?	For how many nights, please?
C'est pour quand s.v.p.?	For what time, please?
Je suis désolé, mais nous sommes complets	I'm sorry, we're fully booked
Nous sommes malheureusement complets	Sorry, we're full
Vous désirez voir la chambre?	Would you like to see the room?
La chambre est à . . .	The room costs . . .
Avec/sans le petit déjeuner	Breakfast is/is not included
Le petit déjeuner est servi de . . . à . . .	Breakfast is served from . . . to . . .
Vous avez l'ascenseur là-bas en face de vous	There's a lift over there
Le garçon va porter vos bagages dans votre chambre	The porter will take your luggage up
Pouvez-vous remplir cette fiche, s.v.p.?	Could you sign the register, please?
Je peux voir votre passeport, s.v.p.?	May I see your passport, please?
Avez-vous des papiers?	Do you have some means of identification?
Pourriez-vous remplir cette fiche, s.v.p.?	Could you fill in this form, please?
Veuillez signer ici, s.v.p.?	Please sign here
Quelle est votre profession?	What's your occupation?
Vos initiales, s.v.p.?	Your initials, please?
Votre adresse d'origine, s.v.p.?	Your home address, please?
Vous désirez payer comment, en liquide ou avec une carte de crédit?	How would you like to pay: in cash or by credit card?

Réception	Reception
Prière de ne pas déranger	Please do not disturb
Standardiste	Switchboard Operator
Porteur	Porter
Femme de chambre	Chambermaid
Les clients sont priés de libérer leur chambre avant midi le jour de leur départ	Guests are requested to vacate their rooms before 12.00 noon on the day of departure

On the registration form you will find:

Prière de Remplir en Caractères d'Imprimerie:	Please Complete in Block Letters:
Nom de Famille	Surname
Prénoms	First Names
Nationalité	Nationality
Profession	Occupation
Date de Naissance	Date of Birth
Lieu de Naissance	Place of Birth
Adresse d'Origine	Home Address
Numéro de Passeport	Passport No.
Emis à:	Issued at:
Date d'Arrivée	Date of Arrival
Date de Départ	Date of Departure
Allant à	Next Destination
Signature	Signature

Breakfast:

During breakfast at your hotel you may read or hear the following:

Quel est votre numéro de chambre?	What's your room number, please?
Vous voulez commander?	Are you ready to order?
Qu'est-ce que vous prenez au petit déjeuner?	What would you like for breakfast?
du thé, du café	tea, coffee

au lait/avec du sucre/au citron	with milk/sugar/lemon
du chocolat chaud	hot chocolate
des petits pains	rolls
avec du beurre/de la confiture	with butter/jam

Breakfast at French hotels usually consists of croissants (pastry in the form of a crescent), baguettes (French stick), butter, jam and coffee, or tea, or hot chocolate.

If you want to order something else, you can say:

Est-ce qu'il serait possible d'avoir aussi . . .	Is it possible to order . . .
des œufs sur le plat	fried eggs
des œufs durs	hard-boiled eggs
un œuf à la coque	a soft-boiled egg
du jus d'orange	orange juice

■ Please note:

The following types of accommodation are available in France:

Hôtel	Hotels ranging from one to four star quality
Hôtel garni	offers only bed and breakfast
Château-Hôtel	luxury accommodation often in very beautiful buildings
Relais de Campagne	simple accommodation in the country
Logis de France	one to two star hotels of good quality, and reasonably priced.
Relais de Tourisme	country hotel, often offering good food
Relais Routiers	a kind of motel
Auberge	country inn, offering simple accommodation
Chambres d'hôte	with half or full board (not numerous in France)

Note than an 'Hôtel de Ville' is not a hotel but a town hall.

Hotel categories:

A blue and white octagonal sign indicates the category:

H Hôtel, simple	basic
1 star Hôtel, confort moyen	average
2 star Hôtel, bon confort	good
3 star Hôtel, grand confort	high standard
4 star Hôtel, très grand confort	excellent
4 star L Hôtel, Palace, hôtel hors classe	luxury

Information on hotels is available from:

> **Direction du Tourisme**
> **17 rue de l'Ingénieur Robert Keller**
> **75740 Paris Cedex 15**

Tea-making facilities are not provided in hotel rooms. If you can't live without a cup of tea, take an immersion heater with you, as well as an adapter. The voltage is the same (220/240 volts, 50 Hz).

The prices for overnight accommodation usually include VAT (Value Added Tax), known in France as TVA (Taxe de la Valeur Ajoutée), but breakfast is charged separately.

If you require facilities to organize conferences in France or want to open an office at short notice, contact:

> **ASPAC**
> **29 rue de Saint Pétersbourg**
> **75008 Paris**
> **Tel: (1) 44 69 99 99**
> **Fax: (1) 45 22 62 23**

ASPAC can help you rent offices. As well as telephone, fax and photocopying services, secretarial and translation services are also available. If required, you can even have a business address in France. ASPAC branches are widely distributed across France.

The French–British Chamber for Commerce and Industry in Paris
can also rent impressive rooms for business use.

> **French–British Chamber of Commerce
>   and Industry
> 7 rue Cimarosa
> 75116 Paris
> Tel: (1) 45 05 13 08
> Fax: (1) 45 53 02 87**

Hotel reservations:

You are strongly advised to book accommodation in advance. For
lists of hotels please write to:

> **French National Tourist Office
> 179 Piccadilly
> London W1V 0BA
> Tel: 0171 409 12224**

It is also a good idea to write to the French Tourist Office in Paris
for the following useful brochures:

Accueil de France Réservation d'Hôtels
Available from:

> **Office du Tourisme et des Congrès de Paris
> 127 avenue des Champs Élysées
> 75008 Paris
> Tel: (1) 49 52 53 54**

This brochure lists the addresses of 45 French tourist offices which
will help you to book hotel accommodation all over France (at the
latest, one week in advance; telephone reservations not
accepted).

Paris–Côte d'Azur: Hôtels–Restaurants–Tourisme
INI (Les Itinéraires Nationaux et Internationaux)
A list of hotels between Paris and Toulon
Available from:

> **Accueil de France
> 127 avenue des Champs Élysées
> 75008 Paris**

or:

**Maison de la France
8 avenue de l'Opéra
75001 Paris**

or:

**INI
35 avenue Edouard-Vaillant
921100 Boulogne**

Résidence de Tourisme
Listings of furnished flats and houses for rent on a weekly or
monthly basis. This brochure is obtainable from the French Tourist
Office.

Some useful telephone numbers of hotel booking services:

Resinter
**Tel: (1) 6077 2727/6087 4463
Fax: (1) 6991 0563
Télex: 600 644 601 320**

INITEL
**Hotels and Restaurants through Minitel
(1) 49 10 09 39**

Paris Séjour Réservation PSR
**Tel: (1) 42 56 30 00
Télex: 643 945
Fax: (1) 42 89 42 97**

Paris Neotel
(1) 40 44 81 81

Pullmann
**Tel: (1) 42 68 22 88
Télex: 215 059**

If you want to know whether a hotel has rooms suitable for conferences and business meetings, you can ask the question:

Est-ce que vous avez une salle de conférences?

See Part I, 4.

Book tips:

Le Bottin Gourmand
(Hotels and restaurants)
Éditions Bottin, Paris

Guide Gault Millau Paris
(Hotels, restaurants, bars, museums, shopping, services; 6500 addresses)
Médiazur, Paris

Michelin France
(Hotels and restaurants)
Michelin, Paris

Guides Régions
(Bretagne, Auvergne, Alsace-Lorraine, etc.)
Michelin, Paris

The Penguin Guide to France
(Hotels, restaurants, activities, shopping)
Penguin Books, Harmondsworth

Guide des Maisons d'Hôte de Charme en France
(Bed and Breakfast à la française; 288 addresses)
Rivages, Paris

Guide Bleu: France
(Travel, sightseeing, vocabulary, information, maps, street plans)
Hachette – Guides Bleus, Paris

4.2 Food and drink

Can you reserve a table for two, please, for 8 o'clock	**Pouvez-vous réserver une table pour deux personnes? Nous viendrons à huit heures.**
Could we have a table by the window, please?	**Pouvons-nous avoir une table près de la fenêtre?**
Is this seat taken?	**Cette place est occupée?**
Waiter/waitress	**Monsieur/Madame/ Mademoiselle**
We'd like something to drink, please	**Nous aimerions boire quelque chose**
May I have the menu, please?	**Je peux avoir la carte, s.v.p.?**
May I see the wine list, please?	**Donnez-moi la carte des vins, s.v.p.?**
What would you recommend?	**Qu'est-ce que vous me recommandez/conseillez?**
main course	**le plat principal**
cover charge	**le couvert**
the set meal	**la table d'hôte**
hors d'œuvres/starters	**les entrées/les hors-d'œuvre**
soup	**la soupe/le potage**
salad	**la salade**
meat	**la viande**
poultry	**la volaille**
fish/sea food	**le poisson/les fruits de mer**
vegetables	**les légumes**
potatoes/rice	**les pommes de terre/le riz**
cheese	**le fromage**
fruit	**les fruits**

dessert	**le dessert**
pie	**une tourte**
baked/grilled	**cuit au four/grillé**
boiled/steamed	**cuit à l'eau/cuit à la vapeur**
roasted	**cuit à la poêle/rôti**
What's today's special?	**Quel est le plat du jour?**
I'm hungry/thirsty	**J'ai faim/soif**
I only want a snack	**J'aimerais manger seulement un petit en-cas**
For starters I'll have . . .	**Comme hors-d'œuvre je voudrais . . .**
I'm in a hurry, can I have the bill, please?	**Je suis pressé, l'addition, s.v.p.?**
We'd like to pay separately	**Nous aimerions payer séparément**
Is everything included?	**Tout est compris?**
Is service included?	**Le service est compris?**
How much is it?	**Combien ça coûte?**
I'm afraid you have made a mistake	**Excusez-moi, je crois qu'il y a une erreur**
Do you accept traveller's cheques/credit cards?	**Vous acceptez les chèques/les cartes de crédit?**
Thank you, that's for you	**Merci, ça c'est pour vous**
Keep the change	**C'est juste/ça fait le compte**
Where are the toilets?	**Où sont les toilettes?**
It tastes very good/nice	**C'est très bon**
I've enjoyed the meal	**J'ai beaucoup aimé le repas**

I'm afraid that's not what I ordered	**Ce n'est pas ce que j'avais commandé**
It's too cold/tough/salty	**C'est trop froid/dur/salé**

What you may hear or read in French in a restaurant:

Par ici, s.v.p.	Come this way, please
Que désirez-vous boire?/Et comme boisson?	What would you like to drink?
Je peux vous recommander . . .	I can recommend . . .
Que prenez-vous comme hors-d'œuvre?	What would you like to start with?
Qu'est-ce que vous prenez? **. . . comme plat principal** **. . . comme dessert**	What would you like . . .? . . . as a main course . . . as a dessert?
Votre steak, vous le voulez comment?	How would you like your steak done?
bien cuit/à point/saignant	well-done/medium-rare/rare
Malheureusement nous n'avons pas de . . .	Sorry we don't have any . . .
Malheureusement nous sommes fermés le lundi	I'm sorry, we are closed on Mondays
Plat du jour	dish of the day
Spécialités de la maison	speciality of the house
'fait maison'	home-made
Le chef recommande	We recommend
Spécialité locale	local specialities
Une spécialité régionale	regional speciality
Table d'hôte	menu of the day
Menu à prix fixe	set meal
Supplément	additional charge

Sur commande	to be ordered in advance
la carte/le menu	menu

■ **Please note:**

When going out for a meal in France you can choose between the following:

Buffet:	Buffets are to be found at stations: the food served is often excellent.
Bar:	You can drink coffee, aperitifs, beer and eat light snacks, served at your table.
Bistro:	A bistro is mostly a simple type of pub, with small snacks and a limited choice of meals. In bistros you should ask for the dish of the day ('plat du jour').
Brasserie:	Usually larger than bistros, serving food and drink.
Cabaret:	A restaurant with a floor show.
Crêperie:	Delicious pancakes ('crêpes') are served here – with every imaginable flavour and filling.
Hostellerie:	Country inn with good cuisine, sometimes quite expensive.
Relais Routier	On motorways, for long-distance lorry drivers; often serve excellent cuisine.
Restaurant:	Restaurants cover all price ranges, and you can either try them out for yourself or rely on one of the numerous restaurant guides.
Restauroute:	Motorway service station including a restaurant.
Rôtisserie:	A restaurant specializing in grilled dishes.
Salon de Thé	Rather like a coffee shop, serving tea, coffee, cake and ice cream.

Good meals are also to be found in restaurants attached to museums, e.g. in the Pompidou Centre, Paris.

Tipping:

All restaurant bills now include a service charge of 15%. It is customary to leave some small change as well.

Meals in France:

Breakfast:	A typical breakfast consists of a croissant, a piece of baguette with butter and jam, white coffee ('café au lait') and sometimes a 'brioche', a kind of Danish pastry.
Lunch:	This is regarded as the most important meal of the day in France; it is eaten either at home or in a restaurant. Lunch-breaks normally last two hours.
Dinner:	The French usually have dinner at about 8 pm, at home with the family.

Before starting your meal in France you usually wish one another 'bon appétit' (enjoy your meal!).

Typical dishes:

If you want to try out typical dishes in France the following are highly recommended.

bœuf en daube	beef casserole
pot-au-feu	beef and vegetable hotpot
coq au vin	chicken in red wine
foie gras	goose/duck liver paté
choucroute d'Alsace	sauerkraut and sausage
entrecôte	rib(-eye) steak
crêpes	thin pancakes, various fillings and flavours
bœuf bourguignon	beef cooked in red wine
gratin dauphinois	potatoes cooked in butter and egg yolks
ratatouille	casserole of onions, courgettes, green peppers, aubergines

Menu

Entrées froides:
Cocktail d'avocat aux crevettes
Terrine spéciale
Saumon fumé norvégien avec toast
Salade frisée aux lardons et croûtons
Bloc de foie gras de canard

Entrées chaudes:
Moules d'Espagne farcie (les 12)
Escargots de Bourgogne (les 6)
Soupe à l'oignon gratinée

Poissons:
Sole meunière ou grillée
Saumon frais grillé béarnaise
Gambas grillées sur lit du mesclin

Viandes et Grillades:
Filet de bœuf grillé
Filet au poivre
Côte de bœuf grillée béarnaise
Escalope de veau
Côte d'agneau vert pré
Steak tartare garni de frites ou salade
Choucroûte au jarret de porc

Fromages:
Camembert
Emmental
Roquefort
Chèvre
Cantal

Desserts:
Mousse au chocolat
Crème renversée au caramel
Tarte du jour
Tarte normande flambée
Ananas frais
Profiteroles au chocolat
Crêpes Maison flambées au Grand
  Marnier

Glaces:
Coupe parisienne
Mystère ou Parfait café
Fraise ou Pêche Melba
Sorbet parfums divers

Drinks:

I'd like . . .	**Je voudrais . . .**
. . . a black coffee	**. . . un café noir**
with cream	**au lait/un café crème**
without sugar	**sans sucre**
. . . a tea	**. . . un thé**
with lemon/milk	**au citron/lait**
. . . a glass of milk	**. . . un verre de lait**
. . . a hot chocolate	**. . . un chocolat chaud**
. . . a glass of mineral water	**. . . un verre d'eau minérale**
. . . lemonade	**. . . de la limonade**
. . . orange juice	**. . . du jus d'orange**
. . . a beer/lager	**. . . une bière blonde/brune**
. . . a cognac/brandy	**. . . un cognac**
. . . a gin and tonic	**. . . un gin tonic**
. . . a red/white wine	**. . . du vin rouge/blanc**
. . . dry/medium-dry/sweet	**. . . sec/demi-sec/doux**
. . . champagne	**. . . du champagne**
. . . sherry	**. . . du sherry**
. . . dry/medium-dry/sweet	**. . . sec/demi-sec/doux**
. . . a whisky with/without ice	**. . . un whisky avec/sans glace**
. . . a glass of tap water	**. . . un verre d'eau du robinet**
waiter/waitress	**Monsieur/Madame**
The bill, please	**L'addition s.v.p.**
Is service included?	**Le service est compris?**

French wines:

Excellent wines are produced in the following wine-growing districts in France: Loire Valley, Burgundy, the Rhône, Savoie, Bergerac, Bordeaux, Languedoc, Provence, Cognac, Armagnac, Alsace and Champagne.

In Burgundy you can drink Chablis, a dry white wine, or Beaujolais, a light-bodied red wine.

In Bordeaux there are some very famous red wines, such as Médoc and Graves, as well as white wines like Sauternes, a sweet wine.

The Anjou district is well known for its sweet and rosé wines. In Alsace there are, among others, very good, light dry white wines like Riesling or Muscadet.

In the Rhône district a number of red wines are produced such as the well-known Châteauneuf du Pape, a full-bodied red wine.

What you might read on labels of French wine bottles:

AC	**Appellation d'origine controllée** (registered district of origin)
VDQS	**Vin délimité de qualité supérieure** (wine of superior quality produced in a certain area)
VDP	**Vin de pays** (local wine)
sec	dry
brut	very dry
doux	sweet
leger	light
corsé	full-bodied
blanc	white
rouge	red
rosé	rosé
mise en bouteille	bottled

If you do not know which wine to choose you could ask:
'Quel vin pouvez-vous nous recommander?'

For 'cheers', you say 'à votre santé' or 'à la vôtre'.

Book tips:

Larousse Les Vins
Larousse, Paris, 1990

Vins et Vignobles du Monde
Nathan, Paris, 1987

Le Vrai Livre du Vin
Éditions Princesse, 1987

Pocket Wine Book
Hugh Johnson
Mitchell Beazley, London, 1990

The World Atlas of Wine
Hugh Johnson
Mitchell Beazley, London, 1985

Guide Dussert-Gerber des Vins de France '92
Éditions Albin Michel, Paris, 1991

Le Guide des Gourmands 1992
Elisabeth de Meurville and Michel Creignon
Éditions 01/Gourmands Associés, Paris, 1991

4.3 Bars

There are no pubs in France. If the French want to socialize they
often invite each other for a meal at home. You will, however,
find bars on every corner. Here you can have a drink, a snack or a
light meal. You should wait to be served at your table.

What you might read or hear in a French bar:

Débit de boissons	Off-licence
Encore une bière	Another beer?
Une petite ou une grande?	Large or small?
La même chose?	The same again?
Que voulez-vous boire, c'est moi qui paie cette tournée?	What are you drinking, it's my round?
Que voulez-vous boire? ▶ **Je voudrais une bière pression, s.v.p.**	What will you have? ▶ I'll have a draught beer, please

▶ Quelque chose de non-alcoolisé, s.v.p.

▶ A soft drink, please/A non-alcoholic drink, please

Et avec ça?
▶ Non merci, ça va pour le moment

Anything else?
▶ No, thank you, not just at the moment

A votre santé!

Cheers! Your good health!

Je vous l'offre
▶ C'est très gentil de votre part, merci

Let me pay, please
▶ That's very nice of you, thank you

On a bar menu you could find the following:

Buffet froid
  Assiette de saucisson — sausage
  Assiette de rillette — pork potted meat
  Assiette de crudités — cucumbers, carrots, beetroot, hard-boiled egg
  Terrine de canard — duck pâté
  Assiette complète (jambon, pâté, saucisson, cantal) — ham, sausage, pâté, cantal cheese

Buffet chaud
  Croque Monsieur — sandwich of ham and cheese grilled and served hot
  Croque Madame — as above, with egg or pineapple
  au pain Poilane — with farmhouse bread
  Assiette de frites — chips
  Quiche Lorraine — cheese, bacon and egg flan

Desserts
  Tarte du jour — tart of the day
  Tarte aux pommes — apple tart
  Tarte aux poires — pear tart
  Crème caramel — caramel cream
  Mousse au chocolat — chocolate mousse
  Sorbet — sorbet
  Profiteroles — choux pastry filled with whipped cream and covered in a chocolate sauce

Apéritifs:		**Digestifs:**
Anis:	Porto	Rémy Martin
Ricard	Americano	Armagnac
Pernod	Ambassador	Irish Coffee
Pastis	Kir au Champagne	Vieux Calvados
Casanis	Kir au Riesling	Kirsch
	Coupe de Champagne	Whisky
	Martini blanc, rouge	
	Muscadet	
	Noilly	

5

In Town

5.1 Asking the way

Can you help me, please, I've lost my way	**(Madame, Monsieur) pouvez-vous m'aider, s.v.p.? Je me suis perdu**
How do I get to . . .?	**Pour aller à . . .?**
I'm looking for . . .	**Je cherche . . .**
I wonder if you can tell me the way to . . .?	**Monsieur, pourriez-vous me dire par hasard, où se trouve . . .?**
Where's the nearest bank?	**Mademoiselle, où se trouve la banque la plus proche, s.v.p.?**

- ▶ straight on at the traffic lights
- ▶ (to the) right
- ▶ (to the) left
- ▶ straight ahead
- ▶ first left
- ▶ second right
- ▶ at the roundabout
- ▶ you'll see it opposite
- ▶ you'll see it on your right

- ▶ **aux feux tout droit**
- ▶ **à droite**
- ▶ **à gauche**
- ▶ **tout droit**
- ▶ **la première à gauche**
- ▶ **la deuxième à droite**
- ▶ **au rond-point**
- ▶ **c'est en face**
- ▶ **c'est sur votre droite**

▶ I'm afraid you're going in the wrong direction
▶ I'm afraid I don't know
▶ I couldn't tell you, you'd better ask someone else

▶ J'ai bien peur que vous soyez dans la mauvaise direction
▶ Je suis désolé, je ne sais pas
▶ Je ne peux pas vous dire, demandez à quelqu'un d'autre

Is it far?/Is it near?
▶ it's five minutes' walk
▶ ten minutes by car
▶ take the bus/train/ Underground
▶ You can't miss it

C'est loin? C'est près d'ici?
▶ c'est à cinq minutes à pied
▶ c'est à dix minutes en voiture
▶ prenez le bus/le train/le Métro
▶ Vous ne pouvez pas le manquer

5.2 Public transport: buses, Underground, RER, taxis

Buses:

How often do the buses run?	Il y a des bus tous les combien?
Do you go near . . .?	Vous allez du côté de . . ./de quel côté?
Do you go to Grand Rue?	Est-ce que vous allez dans la Grand Rue?
Whereabouts in avenue Dumont?	A quelle hauteur de l'avenue Dumont?
How much is it to place de la Bastille?	Ça coûte combien jusqu'à la place de la Bastille?
Please let me know when we arrive at the station	Pouvez-vous me prévenir, quand nous arriverons à la gare?
Would you let me off, please?	Vous me laissez descendre, s.v.p.?
Are you getting off at the next stop?	Vous descendez au prochain arrêt?
Does this bus go to . . .?	Est-ce que le bus va à . . .?

■ Please note:

The French for 'bus' is 'car', or 'bus' (in town), or 'autocar' (for long-distance journeys).

Bus tickets are available from automatic ticket machines. You should always ask for a day ticket ('abonnement d'un jour') and a booklet of ten ('un carnet'). You can get information on bus connections at the local bus stations ('Gare routière').

Bus timetables can be obtained from the SNCF and, for Paris, from the RATP (Réseau Autonome de Transport Parisien), the public transport network in Paris.

You have to punch ('composter') your ticket on the bus although not the 'carte jaune' or other special tickets. For longer distances you need to validate several tickets, one for each section. There are large maps in the buses which show the various sections.

Press a button if you want to get off at the next stop.

Useful information, such as routes serving the stop, interchange between routes, timetables and number of tickets required, is displayed at each bus stop.

'Noctambus' is the name for 10 bus routes that operate from Châtelet to the outskirts of Paris throughout the night.

Information on international bus routes can be obtained from:

**Gare Internationale de la Villette
3 avenue Porte de la Villette
75019 Paris
Tel: (1) 40 38 93 93**

Underground/Metro/RER:

Where's the nearest Underground station, please?	**Où se trouve la station de Métro la plus proche?**
Where can I buy tickets?	**Où est-ce que je peux acheter des tickets?**
▶ at the counter	▶ **au guichet**
▶ at the automatic ticket machine	▶ **au distributeur automatique**

Do I have to change?	**Faut-il changer?**
Where do I change for place St Jean?	**Pour aller à la place Saint Jean, où est-ce qu'il faut changer?**
Is the next station Palais Royal?	**Est-ce que la prochaine station est le Palais-Royal?**
Where do I have to get off?	**Où est-ce que je dois descendre?**
Are you getting off at the next station?	**Vous descendez à la prochaine station?**
Could you tell me when we get there, please?	**Prévenez-moi, s.v.p., quand nous arriverons?**

In this connection you might hear or read the following:

Distributeur de tickets	Ticket machine
Montée à l'avant	Entry at the front
Montée à l'arrière	Entry at the rear
Préparez votre monaie	Exact fare, please
Sortie de secours	Emergency exit
Freins de secours	Emergency brake
Il faut prendre le vingt-cinq	You want the number 25 (bus)
Je vais vous dire quand nous y serons	I'll tell you when we get there
L'usager sans ticket	Fare-dodger
Accès aux quais	To the platforms
Préparez votre monnaie	Exact fare, please

■ Please note:

There are Métros in Paris, Lyon, Marseille and Lille. Information on the Métro can be obtained in Paris at the Métro stations, the Tourist Office ('Office du Tourisme') and alongside RATP information.

RATP information	**SNCF information**
Tel: (1) 43 46 14 14	**Tel: (1) 45 82 50 50**
Minitel 3615 code RATP	**Minitel 3615 code SNCF**

The Métro in Paris operates daily from 5.30 am to 1 am.

In addition to single tickets there are several special tickets: Le Carnet (booklet of ten single tickets), La Carte Paris Visite (valid for three or five days), Le Forfait Formule 1 (valid for one day), La Carte Orange (very cheap, but a passport photo is necessary). Some of them can be used for buses, the Métro and RER (Paris Visite, Carte Orange).

A single underground ticket is valid for only one journey, i.e. as long as you don't pass through the barrier. If you want to use a different means of transport, you need another ticket; on longer journeys you may need several tickets according to the number of sections.

Tourist tickets, Formule (valid for one day), Paris Visite (valid for three or five days), and Carte Orange (valid for one week, cheaper than Paris Visite, but requiring a passport photo) can be used for RER, Métro and buses combined.

These tickets are available from the Paris Tourist Office (127 Champs Élysées) and Underground stations, in RATP offices (place de la Madeleine and in some others), at SNCF stations and at the Orly and Roissy–Charles de Gaulle airports. When the amounts to be paid exceed 100 FF you can also use a credit card at the Métro cash desk.

When travelling by Underground note the final destination of the train as this is the direction in which it is travelling. This is important when changing trains; look for the sign 'correspondance'.

Maps of the Métro network in the train carriages and at the stations show connections and changing points. The RER, Métro and bus maps can be obtained at the RATP, RER and SNCF offices. Maps of the Métro and bus networks can also be found at all Métro station exits.

Large-scale maps of the immediate neighbourhood around the station for orientation can be found near the exits.

Smoking is not permitted on the Métro.

Do not throw your ticket away during the journey, but keep it until you have left the station at the end. You may have to show it to a ticket inspector or you may need it at the automatic exits (at some stations). Otherwise you will have to pay an on-the-spot fine ('indemnité forfaitaire'). Notices to this effect are displayed on carriage windows in the Métro as follows:

Conservez votre titre de transport jusqu'à la sortie. Votre titre de transport peut être contrôlé en voiture et en station

Keep your ticket until you leave the Métro. Your ticket might be checked in the carriage or in the station.

In the event of an emergency you can call the stationmaster via the alarm system at most Métro stations. Yellow signs with the word 'Alarme' show where and how the alarm system can be activated:

Pour appeler le chef de station appuyez et relâchez le bouton, Attendez.

To alert the station master press the button, release it and then please wait.

If you are carrying heavy suitcases, you should know that there are relatively few escalators on the Paris Underground.

People do not queue at bus stops in such an orderly fashion as they do in Britain.

RER (Réseau Express Régional) is the express rail network that operates between the centre and the outskirts of Paris. It also passes through the centre of Paris. Combined use of the Métro and RER can sometimes make your journey a lot easier.

Situ Information from Situ machines in Paris enables you to find out (within a few seconds) the best possible bus, Métro and RER connections and combinations for any destination in Paris and its surroundings. This service is free of charge, and is located at 60 points in Paris as well as under Minitel 3615 RATP and 3616 SITU.

Taxis:

Where can I find a taxi?

Où est-ce que je peux trouver un taxi?

Can you call me a taxi, please?

Appelez-moi un taxi, s.v.p.

Is there a taxi rank nearby?	**Est-ce qu'il y a une station de taxis à proximité?**
Is there any chance of hailing a taxi at this time of day?	**Est-ce qu'il y a des taxis qui passent ici à cette heure?**
To the . . . Hotel, please	**A l'hôtel . . ., s.v.p.**
Can you take me to . . .?	**Pouvez-vous me conduire à . . .?**
What's the fare to . . .?	**Combien coûte la course pour aller à . . .?**
I'm in a hurry, can you take the shortest route, please?	**Je suis pressé, prenez le chemin le plus court s.v.p.**
Can you stop on the corner, please?	**Arrêtez au coin, s.v.p.**
Can you wait, please?	**Pouvez-vous attendre, s.v.p.?**
Could you put my bags into the taxi, please	**Pouvez-vous mettre mes sacs dans le taxi, s.v.p.?**
Can you give me change, please?	**Pouvez-vous me faire la monnaie?**
Keep the change, please	**Gardez la monnaie/Ça va**

■ Please note:

Taxi ranks can be found at stations and in town centres, and can be recognized by the notice 'Taxis', or 'Tête de station'. A passing taxi that is free can also be hailed. The usual tip is between 10% and 15%.

'Libre' means 'for hire'; 'Tête de station' means please queue here. If you want to order a taxi by telephone you can either call a taxi rank near your hotel or one of the radio taxis, the numbers of which you can find in the telephone directory.

Some numbers of taxi companies in Paris:

G7 Radio	**47 39 47 39**
Les Taxis Bleus	**49 36 10 10**
Alpha Taxis	**45 85 85 85**

Artaxi	**42 41 50 50**
Taxi Radio 'Étoile'	**42 70 41 41**

You can smoke in taxis if there is no notice expressly forbidding you to.

5.3 Shopping

antique shop	**(l')antiquitaire/la brocante**
baker's	**(la) boulangerie**
bookshop	**(la) librairie**
boutique, clothes shop	**(la) boutique de mode**
chemist's	**(la) pharmacie/la droguerie**
china shop	**(le) magasin de vaisselle**
confectioner's	**(la) pâtisserie**
(currency) exchange	**(le) bureau de change**
dairy	**(la) crèmerie**
department store	**(le) grand magasin/grande surface**
dry cleaner's	**(la) teinturerie/le pressing**
electrical supplies shop	**(le) magasin d'électro-ménager**
flea market	**(le) marché aux puces**
florist's	**(le) magasin de fleurs**
furniture shop	**(le) magasin de meubles**
furrier's	**(le) magasin de fourrures**
greengrocer's	**(le) magasin de légumes**
grocer's	**(l')épicerie**
haberdasher's	**(la) mercerie**
hairdresser's	**(le) salon de coiffure**
health food shop	**(le) magasin de produits biologiques**
ironmonger's	**(la) quincaillerie**
jeweller's	**(la) bijouterie**
laundry/laundrette	**(la) laverie**
leather shop	**(la) maroquinerie**
market	**(le) marché**
music shop	**(le) magasin d'instruments de musique**
newsagent	**(le) magasin de journaux**
off-licence	**(le) magasin de spiritueux**

optician	(l')opticien
perfumery	(la) parfumerie
photographer's	(le) photographe
record shop	(le) magasin de disques
self-service	(le) self-service
shoe shop	(le) magasin de chaussures
souvenir shop	(le) magasin de souvenirs
sports shop	(le) magasin de sport
stationer's	(la) papeterie
sweet-shop	(la) confiserie
supermarket	(le) supermarché
tailor's/dressmaker's	(le) tailleur/la couturière
toyshop	(le) magasin de jouets
tourist information centre	(l')office de tourisme/(le) syndicat d'initiative
travel agency	(l')agence de voyages
watchmaker's	(l')horloger
wine merchant's	(le) magasin de vins

Where are the biggest department stores?	Où sont les plus grands magasins?
Can you tell me where I can find a good bookshop?	Où est-ce qu'il y a une bonne librairie?
Where can I buy . . ./get . . .?	Où est-ce que je peux acheter . . .?
Is it far/nearby?	C'est loin/près d'ici?
How do I get there?	Comment est-ce que je peux y aller?
Which floor is the gift department on, please?	Le rayon des cadeaux est à quel étage?
Can you help me, please?	Pouvez-vous m'aider, s.v.p.?
I'd like an electrical adapter, please	Je voudrais un adaptateur électrique
Can you show me . . ., please?	Pourriez-vous me montrer . . ., s.v.p.?

Can you show me some other . . . please?	**Pourriez-vous m'en montrer d'autres?**
Can I try it on?	**Est-ce que je peux l'essayer?**
How much is this?	**Ça coûte combien?**
Could you write it down for me, please?	**Pouvez-vous me l'écrire, s.v.p.?**
It's too expensive/small	**C'est trop cher/petit**
Have you got anything cheaper?	**Avez-vous quelque chose de moins cher?**
It's fine, I'll take it	**C'est bien, je le prends**
No, thank you, I don't like it	**Merci, mais ça ne me plaît pas**
I think I'll leave it, thank you	**Je crois que je ne vais pas le prendre, je vous remercie**
I'll come back later	**Je vais revenir**
I'd rather take . . .	**Je préfère prendre . . .**
I'm just looking	**Je regarde seulement**
I'm being served, thank you	**Merci, on me sert déjà**
Can I pay with traveller's cheques?	**Je peux payer avec des chèques de voyage?**
Do you accept credit cards?	**Vous acceptez les cartes de crédit?**
Has VAT been deducted?	**La TVA est déduite?**
Can I have a receipt, please?	**Je peux avoir un reçu?**
Can I have a carrier-bag, please?	**Je peux avoir un sac (en plastique)?**
Can you wrap it up for me, please?	**Pouvez-vous me faire un paquet?**
Would you send it to this address, please?	**Pourriez-vous l'envoyer à cette adresse, s.v.p.?**

Can I change this, please?	**Est-ce que je peux faire un échange?**

See Part II, 7.6 for phrases on the subject of returning goods.

When shopping you might hear the following:

Je peux vous aider?	Can I help you?
Vous désirez?	What would you like?
Quelle taille/quelle couleur cherchez-vous?	What size/colour would you like?
Quelle taille faites-vous?	What size are you/What size do you take?
C'est au rez-de-chaussée/au premier/au deuxième étage	It's on the ground/first/second floor
Je regrette, nous n'en avons plus	I'm afraid we are out of stock
Nous n'avons pas de . . .	We haven't any . . .
C'est malheureusement tout ce que nous avons	I'm sorry, that's all we have
La caisse est là-bas en face	The cash desk is over there
Comment payez-vous? En liquide/par chèque/avec une carte de crédit?	How are you paying? In cash/by cheque/with a credit card?
C'est votre reçu	This is your copy/receipt
Signez ici, s.v.p.	Sign here, please
Je suis désolé, mais nous n'acceptons pas les chèques de voyage	I'm sorry, we don't accept traveller's cheques
Je ne peux pas changer ce billet	I can't change that note
La TVA	VAT (Value Added Tax)
Je peux vous faire un avoir	I can give you a credit note
Et avec ça?	Anything else?

Fermeture du magasin	Closing time
Le vendeur/la vendeuse	Shop assistant

Quelle couleur voulez-vous?	Which colour would you like?
clair/foncé	light/dark
blanc/noir	white/black
rouge	red
bleu/bleu foncé	blue/navy blue
jaune/vert	yellow/green
brun/beige	brown/beige
mauve	lilac
violet	violet
pourpre	purple
rose	pink
gris	grey
doré/argent	gold/silver

Clothing sizes

Women's clothing:

UK	10	12	14	16	18	20	22
France	38	40	42	44	46	48	50

Menswear:

UK	36	38	40	42	44	46
France	46	48	50	52	54	56

Men's shirts:

UK	14	14½	15	15½	16	17
France	36	37	38	39	40	42

Shoes:

UK	5	6	7	8	9	10	11
France	38	39	41	42	43	44	45

French shops are usually open between 8.00 am – 9.00 am in the morning through to 6.00 pm or 7.00 pm in the evening. They usually close during lunch and on Mondays. Supermarkets and hypermarkets are open until 10.00 pm ('en nocturne') and on Mondays.

The names of some of the large chain stores are:

Les Galeries Lafayette
40 boulevard Haussmann
Tel: (1) 42 82 34 56
Métro: Chaussée d'Antin

Le Printemps
64 boulevard Haussmann
Tel: (1) 42 82 50 00
Métro: Havre-Caumartin

La Samaritaine
19 rue de la Monnaie
Tel: (1) 40 41 20 20
Métro: Pont-Neuf

Le Bon Marché
rue de Sèvres/rue du Bac
Tel: (1) 44 39 80 00
Métro: Sèvres – Babylone

There is a French 'invention' which is still not found anywhere else – 'hypermarché' – a huge supermarket with a very wide selection of goods, from food to spare parts for cars. There are chains called Casino, Mammouth, Carrefour, Hypermarché.

Tabacs:

You can buy cigarettes and tobacco in these shops, as well as stamps, telephone cards, and carnets for local public transport. Very often 'Tabacs' are linked with bars or newsagents. They can be identified by a red rhombus sign.

Book tips:

Gault Millau Paris
Lists a whole series of shops in Paris, e.g. for fashion, sports, food, books, gifts, furniture, antiques and department stores.

5.4 At the bank

Where's the nearest bank, please?
. . . a bureau de change

Où est la banque la plus proche?
. . . un bureau de change

I'd like to change £100

Je voudrais changer 100 livres

What's the exchange rate, please?	**Le change est à combien?**
Where can I buy French currency?	**Où est-ce que je peux acheter des francs?**
I'd like to cash traveller's cheques, please	**Je voudrais changer des chèques de voyage**
What commission do you charge?	**A combien s'élèvent les frais?**
I've got a credit card	**J'ai une carte de crédit**
I'd like fifty/two hundred franc notes, please	**Je voudrais des billets de cinquante/deux cents francs, s.v.p.**
One hundred francs in small notes, please	**Cent francs en petites coupures, s.v.p.**
Some small change, please	**Petite monnaie, s.v.p.**
Can foreigners open an account here?	**Est-ce que c'est possible pour les étrangers d'ouvrir un compte ici?**
I'd like to open a current/deposit/business account	**J'aimerais ouvrir un compte courant/un compte-épargne/un compte commercial**
I'd like to pay money into my account/to draw money from my account	**J'aimerais mettre de l'argent sur mon compte/retirer de l'argent de mon compte**

You might read or hear the following at a bank:

Je peux voir votre passeport, s.v.p.?	May I see your passport, please?
Signez ici, s.v.p.	Sign here, please
Allez à la caisse, s.v.p.	Go to the cash desk, please

Comment voulez-vous votre argent?	How would you like your money?
La monnaie étrangère	foreign currency
Le numéro de banque	bank sort code
Le chèque payable au comptant	cash cheque
Les frais (bancaires)	handling charge/bank charge
L'ordre de virement permanent	standing order
Le service des devises	foreign exchange department
Prélèvement automatique	direct debit
Le compte de virement	current account
La carte de crédit	credit card
Le service-information pour les clients	customer advisory service
Le compte-épargne	deposit account, savings account
Le virement	remittance, transfer
Le chèque barré	crossed cheque
Le bureau de change	foreign exchange office
Le mandat	money order
Prendre un crédit	to raise a loan/to borrow money from the bank

■ Please note:

You cannot change money at every bank branch. You need your passport to change money. You will also find 'bureaux de change' in larger towns. Compare the rates of exchange beforehand as they are generally less favourable in bureaux de change.

Opening times of banks:
9.00 am – 12.00 pm and 1.30/2 pm – 4.30/5.00 pm.

The bureaux de change at Orly and Roissy Airports, as well as those at Gare du Nord, Gare de Lyon and Gare d'Austerlitz stations, are open longer. The bureau de change at 115 Champs Élysées is open daily from 8.30 am to 8.00 pm, except Sundays.

The French franc is divided into 100 centimes
Coins: 1, 2, 5, 10 Francs
      5, 10, 20, 50 centimes
Notes: 20, 50, 100, 200, 500 Francs

'En grosses/petites coupures' means notes of higher or lower denomination.

Travellers' cheques and Eurocheques are accepted in hotels, restaurants and stores. You can also obtain money from a 'Cashpoint', by using a Visa card. Notices in the windows of stores, hotels and restaurants indicate which credit cards are accepted.

'Cours quotidien des principales devises' gives the daily rates of exchange of the most important currencies.
Tel: (1) 42 47 13 14 (24h)

Important banks in France:

Banque de France
39 rue Croix des Petits-Champs
75001 Paris
Tel: (1) 42 92 42 92
Télex: 220932

Crédit Lyonnais
Direction des Financements et
  Services aux Entreprises
1–3 rue des Italiens
75009 Paris
Tel: (1) 42 95 27 40

Banque Nationale de Paris
16 boulevard des Italiens
75009 Paris
Tel: (1) 42 44 45 46
Télex: 280605

Banque Française du
  Commerce Extérieur
21 boulevard Haussmann
75009 Paris
Tel: (1) 42 47 47 47
Télex: 660370

Société Générale
29 boulevard Haussmann
75009 Paris
Tel: (1) 42 98 20 00
Télex: 290842

Crédit Commercial de France
103 avenue des Champs
  Élysées
75008 Paris
Tel: (1) 40 70 70 40
Télex: 630300

Barclays Bank
33 rue du Quatre Septembre
75002 Paris
Tel: (1) 40 06 85 85
Télex: 210015

Midland Bank
6 rue Piccini
75761 Paris
Tel: (1) 45 02 80 80
Télex: 658022

Standard Chartered Bank
4 rue Ventadow
75001 Paris
Tel: (1) 42 61 82 20
Télex: 213097

Lloyds Bank France Ltd
43 boulevard des Capucines
75083 Paris
BP 7802

5.5 At the post office

Where's the nearest post office?	**Où se trouve le bureau de poste le plus proche?**
What time does it close?	**Il ferme à quelle heure?**
At which counter can I get stamps, please?	**A quel guichet est-ce que je peux avoir des timbres?**
A stamp for a postcard to England, please	**Un timbre, s.v.p., pour une carte postale pour l'Angleterre**
How much is a letter to . . .?	**Combien coûte une lettre pour . . .?**
Two two-franc stamps, please	**Deux timbres à deux francs, s.v.p.**
Do you have any special editions?	**Vous avez des timbres de collection?**
I'd like to send a telegram	**J'aimerais envoyer un télégramme**
How long will this letter take to get to England?	**Cette lettre pour l'Angleterre va mettre combien de temps?**
By airmail?	**Par avion?**
By surface mail?	**Par courrier normal?**

How much is the postage? **Combien coûte le port?**

You might see the following signs at post office counters:

Achat d'emballages	Packing material
Avis de réception	Receipt
Caisse d'épargne de la Poste	Post office savings bank
Cartes postales	Postcards
Change	Exchange
Chronoposte	Chronoposte
Colis postaux	Parcel post
Colissimo intra/extra-départemental	Coli-service within and outside departments
Encaissement des mandats	Money orders cashed
Envoi des mandats télégraphiques	Telegraphic remittances (money order)
Envoi des mandats	Transfer (money order)
Envoi des lettres et paquets et de collection	Despatch of letters and parcels and collection items
Imprimés	Printed matter
Journaux	Newspapers
Paquet ou lettre recommandé(e)	Registered post
Paiement des redevances	Payment of official fees
Petits paquets	Small parcels
Poste restante	Poste restante
Poste aérienne	Airmail
Postéclair	Express delivery
Postexpress	Express delivery
Redevances diverses	Various official fees
Réexpédition du courrier	Mail-forwarding service
Retrait des lettres/paquets	Collection of letters, parcels
Retraits à vue	Cash withdrawals
Taxe d'affranchissement	Delivery charges
Télégrammes	Telegrams
Timbres-poste en gros versement sur CCP	Stamps in large quantities and payment using post office giro account

■ Please note:

P et T stands for Postes et Télécommunications.

The opening hours of French post offices are:

    daily   8.00 am – 12 noon/2.00 pm – 5.30 pm (7.00 pm)
    Saturdays   8.00 am – 12.00 noon

In Paris post offices are open daily from 8.00 am to 7.00 pm and on Saturdays from 8.00 am to 12 noon.

The address of the main post office in Paris (open 24 hours a day) is

> **52 rue de Louvre**
> **75001 Paris**
> **Tel: (1) 45 33 71 60**

Postage stamps:

In France stamps can be bought from vending machines, at 'Tabac-Journaux' or 'Bar-Tabac' shops, or at your hotel. There are two types of mail: 'tarif normal' (first class) and 'tarif réduit' (second class).

Letterboxes:

Letterboxes are yellow. In Paris they have two slots marked respectively Paris and 'Autres Destinations' (other destinations). Sometimes there is another slot, 'Aérienne' (airmail).

You may read the following on French letterboxes:

heures des levées	collections
jours ouvrables	weekdays
dimanches et jours fériés	Sundays and public holidays
bureau le plus proche	nearest post office
carnets de timbres (poste)	books of stamps

Express delivery:

For urgent letters and parcels there is the 'EMS Chronopost'. Chronopost deliveries reach their destination anywhere in France before midday on the day after dispatch. Letters and parcels can be handed in at one of the 12,000 post offices, a Chronopost office, or, in large towns, collected by calling 05 05 24 00.

Between some towns there is a service where the delivery time is six hours or less. Information on this as well as on the international express service can be obtained by calling: 05 43 21 00 or Minitel 3614 code EMS.

Corresponding EMS services to France from abroad are faster than some of the private courier services.

Information on various express services is obtainable from:

> **Syndicat Français des Courriers**
> **Internationaux**
> **3 rue du Faubourg St-Honoré**
> **75008 Paris**

Telegrams:

They can be handed in at P et T offices and also phoned in under (1) 42 33 21 11 (from Paris to a foreign country) and under 3655 in all other cases.

Telex and fax services are available under: (1) 45 50 34 34

Information on postal services can be obtained from:

> **Centre des Renseignements Postaux**
> **61–63 rue de Donal**
> **75009 Paris**
> **Tel: (1) 42 80 67 89**

List of French Départements (Métropole/Europe)

Post code	Département	Post code	Département
59	Nord Pas de Calais	62	Pas de Calais
80	Somme	2	Aisne
8	Ardennes	76	Seine Maritime
60	Oise	55	Meuse
57	Moselle	27	Eure
51	Marne	54	Meurthe et Moselle
67	Bas-Rhin	88	Vosges
68	Haut-Rhin	52	Haute-Marne
10	Aube	77	Seine et Marne
95		93	

94		92	
75	Paris	91	
78		14	Calvados
50	Manche	61	Orne
28	Eure et Loire	29	Finisterre
22	Côtes du Nord	56	Morbihan
35	Ille et Vilaine	53	Mayenne
72	Sarthe	44	Loire-Atlantique
49	Maine et Loire	41	Loir-et-Cher
37	Indre et Loire	45	Loiret
18	Cher	36	Indre
89	Yonne	58	Nièvre
21	Côte d'or	71	Saône et Loire
70	Haute-Saône	90	Territoire de Belfort
25	Doubs	39	Jura
74	Haute-Savoie	1	Ain
69	Rhône	42	Loire
73	Savoie	38	Isère
26	Drôme	7	Ardèche
3	Allier	43	Haute-Loire
15	Cantal	19	Corrèze
23	Creuse	87	Haute-Vienne
86	Vienne	79	Deux-Sèvres
16	Charente	17	Charente-Maritime
85	Vendée	33	Gironde
24	Dordogne	47	Lot-et-Garonne
40	Landes	64	Pyrénées-Atlantiques
46	Lot	12	Aveyron
82	Tarn et Garonne	81	Tarn
32	Gers	31	Haute-Garonne
65	Hautes-Pyrénées	9	Ariège
48	Lozère	30	Gard
34	Hérault	11	Aude
66	Pyrénées-Orientales	84	Vaucluse
13	Bouches du Rhône	5	Hautes-Alpes
4	Alpes de Haute Provence	6	Alpes-Maritimes
83	Var	2A	Haute-Corse
2B	Corse du sud		

5.6 Telephones

Where can I find a public telephone (call) box?	**Où puis-je trouver une cabine téléphonique?**
I'd like to make an international phone call	**Je voudrais téléphoner à l'étranger**
What's the cost of the call?	**Combien coûte la communication?**
May I use your telephone, please?	**Je peux utiliser votre téléphone?**
Have you got a phone book?	**Avez-vous un annuaire téléphonique?**
Information, please	**Les renseignements, s.v.p.**
I'd like the number . . ., please	**Je voudrais avoir le numéro . . ., s.v.p.**
Can I dial direct?	**Je peux faire le numéro directement?**
Can you put me through to . .?	**Pouvez-vous me passer . .?**
I'd like extension 123, please	**J'aimerais avoir le poste 123, s.v.p.**
Can I call abroad from here?	**Est-ce que je peux d'ici téléphoner à l'étranger?**
I'd like to reverse the charges, please	**J'aimerais avoir une communication en PCV**
Dupont speaking	**Ici, Monsieur Dupont**
Can I speak to . ., please?	**Est-ce que je pourrais parler à . . .?**
▶ Speaking	**▶ A l'appareil**
▶ Sorry, he isn't in	**▶ Je suis désolé, il n'est pas là**
When will he be back?	**Quand est-ce qu'il sera là?**
Could you take a message, please?	**Pouvez-vous lui faire une commission?**
Please tell him I called	**Pouvez-vous lui dire s.v.p., que j'ai appelé**

Please ask him to call back	**Dites-lui s.v.p. de me rappeler**
I'll give you a ring	**Je vous appellerai**
I'm ringing about . . .	**Je vous téléphone à cause de . . .**
Could you give her a message, please?	**Pourriez-vous lui laisser un message?**

The following French words and sentences might be heard on the telephone:

Un coup de téléphone pour vous	There's a telephone call for you
Une communication urbaine/ interurbaine	A local/national call
Une communication internationale	An international call
Une communication en PCV	A reverse charges call
Qui est à l'appareil?	Who's calling, please?
Ici, Monsieur Dupont	Dupont speaking
Je regrette, elle n'est pas là en ce moment	Sorry, she's out at the moment/ she's not available
Il est en conférence	He's in a meeting
Est-ce qu'il peut vous rappeler?	Can he call you back?
Est-ce que je peux avoir votre numéro?	Can I take your number?
Que dois-je lui dire, qui a appelé?	Who shall I say called?
Désirez-vous laisser un message?	Would you like to leave a message?
Malheureusement personne ne répond	I'm sorry, there's no answer
Le poste est occupé, voulez-vous patienter?	The line's engaged, will you hold?

Ne quittez pas	Hold the line, please
Toutes les lignes sont occupées	All the lines are engaged
Je vous passe Mr . . .	I'll put you through
Ce n'est pas le bon numéro/je me suis trompé de numéro	Sorry, wrong number
Il n'y a pas d'abonné au numéro que vous avez demandé	Number unobtainable
Le numéro n'existe pas	There's no such number
La communication n'est pas très bonne malheureusement	Sorry, it's a bad line
Le téléphone est hors-service	The phone is out of order
Nous avons malheureusement été coupés	I'm afraid we were cut off

■ Please note:

You can make long-distance telephone calls from any telephone box. Should you need any help there is a special telephone service at post offices between 8.00 am and 7.00 pm. Local calls can still be made from 'bistros'.

You can make telephone calls by using coins (fewer and fewer public telephones), telephone cards, telephone credit cards and general credit cards (still not very common).

Coin-operated telephones:

To make a telephone call you can use 50 centimes (rarely), 1, 2 and 5 franc coins. Coin-operated telephones are becoming increasingly rare and you should definitely buy a telephone card.

Card-operated 'publiphones':

In Paris and throughout France there are 56,000 public payphones operating with telephone cards ('cartes téléphoniques') to the value of 50 or 120 units. These may be purchased from tobacconists ('Tabac') and ticket offices, as well as Telecom agencies. When using telephone cards you may read the following phrases in the telephone box:

pour téléphoner	in order to make a telephone call
décrocher	lift receiver
introduire la carte	insert the card (close flap)
numérotez	dial the number
retirez votre carte	withdraw your card
points de vente télécartes	places that sell telephone cards
Agence France Telecom	AFT
Bureau de Poste	Post Office
Bureau de Tabac	Tobacconists
Revendeurs agréés	Licensed selling points

You can also receive telephone calls in a telephone box:

Cette cabine peut être appelée à ce numéro . . .	This telephone box can be called by dialling the following number . . .

To phone the UK from France:

1 Dial 19
2 Wait for the tone
3 Dial 44 for UK
4 Wait for the second tone
5 Dial the area code without the 0
6 Dial the number you want

Dialling tones:

Dialling tone: continuous sound
Ringing tone: series of long sounds
Engaged: interrupted signal
Unobtainable: recorded message saying: 'Le numéro que vous avez demandé n'est plus en service actuellement.'

There are no dialling codes in France. These are already included in the given telephone number; only Paris (and its surroundings) has a code: 1.

If you dial another town from Paris you have to dial the 16 first, otherwise there are only eight digits.

Telephone numbers are given in pairs in French. You would therefore read the number of the Paris Chamber of Commerce and Industry (1) 42 89 75 75 as:
un – quarante-deux – quatre-vingt-neuf – soixante-quinze – deux fois.

Some useful numbers:

Directory Enquiries	12
Service Commercial Télex	14 (connects you with the various sections/services: telex, fax, etc.)
Telegrams	42 33 21 11/3655
Telemessages	05 23 21 11
	(You can send English telegrams by dialling this number) 05 33 44 11 for sending English telexes

Numbers free of charge (**numéros gratuits**):

Pompiers	Fire Brigade	18
Police	Police	17
Samu	Ambulance	15
Renseignement	Information	12
Renseignement	International Directory Enquiries	19/ 33/ 12/ country code
Appareil en panne	Out of order	13
Numéro vert	05 Service	
	Phone calls made under numbers beginning with 05 are free of charge. Information is given under 05 11 00 12	

If you phone directory enquiries you may hear the following phrases:

Cette communication vous sera facturée trois francs soixante-cinq.	You will be charged 3 F 65 for this call.
Nous vous invitons à rappeler ultérieurement ou si vous possédez un Minitel composez le 11.	Please call back later or if you have a Minitel dial 11.
Les premières minutes étant gratuites.	The first minutes are free.
Nous vous remercions de bien vouloir patienter quelques instants pour faire votre demande.	Please wait a moment before stating your question, many thanks.

International Telephone Alphabet

A	Amsterdam	J	Jerusalem	S	Santiago
B	Baltimore	K	Kilogram	T	Tripoli
C	Casablanca	L	Liverpool	U	Uppsala
D	Denmark	M	Madagascar	V	Valencia
E	Edison	N	New York	W	Washington
F	Florida	O	Oslo	X	Xantippe
G	Gallipoli	P	Paris	Y	Yokohama
H	Havana	Q	Quebec	Z	Zürich
I	Italy	R	Roma		

The French Telephone Alphabet

A	Anatole	J	Joseph	S	Suzanne
B	Berthe	K	Kléber	T	Thérèse
C	Célestin	L	Louis	U	Ursule
D	Désiré	M	Marcel	V	Victor
E	Eugène	N	Nicolas	W	William
F	François	O	Oscar	X	Xavier
G	Gaston	P	Pierre	Y	Yvonne
H	Henri	Q	Quintal	Z	Zoë
I	Irma	R	Raoul		

5.7 Telecommunications (telex, fax, Minitel, data transmissions)

Fax services and/or telex services are available by dialling 14 or via Minitel 3614 code Mictel. There are telex facilities in central post offices, and also in Paris, among other places, 7 place de la Bourse.

The regional 'agence commerciale' of Telecom can be contacted by dialling 05 11 00 12. They will gladly give you detailed information on the numerous services of Telecom. There are brochures in English on some of the services.

Minitel:

If you want to establish long-term business connections in France it is very important to know what Minitel is and what it offers. In 1990 Minitel offered 12,000 services and had 5 million subscribers.

Minitel is the equivalent of the British Prestel (about 150,000 users). If your Prestel is compatible with Minitel, you can use the French Teletel service, either via:

PSS Computer Service
Tel: 0171-920 0661
or
PSS Customer Service, Manchester
Tel: 0161-2366702
or
Infonet in London

or
Intelmatique SA
175 rue de Chevaleret
75013 Paris
Tel: (1) 40 77 68 40
Fax: (1) 45 82 21 16

Compatible machines are not readily available at the moment, but you can buy them from:

Alcatel Business Systems Ltd
PO Box 3
South Street
Romford
Essex RM1 2AR

Philips Business Systems Division
Elektra House
Bergholt Road
Colchester
Essex CO4 5BE

6

Leisure Time

6.1 Tourist information offices

Where's the tourist information centre, please?	**Où se trouve l'office de tourisme/le syndicat d'initiative, s.v.p.?**
When does it open/close?	**Ça ouvre/ferme à quelle heure?**
Are there any sightseeing tours?	**Est-ce que vous proposez des visites en bus organisées?**
Can you make a booking, please?	**Pouvez-vous réserver quelque chose?**
When's the sightseeing tour of the town/city?	**Quand est-ce qu'il y a une visite de la ville?**

What are the most interesting sights, please?	**Quelles sont les curiosités les plus intéressantes?**
▶ the old town	▶ **la vieille ville**
▶ the library	▶ **la bibliothèque**
▶ the botanical garden	▶ **le jardin botanique**
▶ the monuments	▶ **les monuments**
▶ the cathedral/churches	▶ **la cathédrale/les églises**
▶ the market	▶ **le marché**
▶ the museums	▶ **les musées**
▶ the castle	▶ **le château**
▶ the university	▶ **l'université**

Have you got a map of the town?	**Avez-vous un plan de la ville?**
a list of events	**un calendrier des manifestations**
a list of hotels	**une liste des hôtels**
a bus timetable	**un plan des bus**
in English, please	**en anglais, s.v.p.**

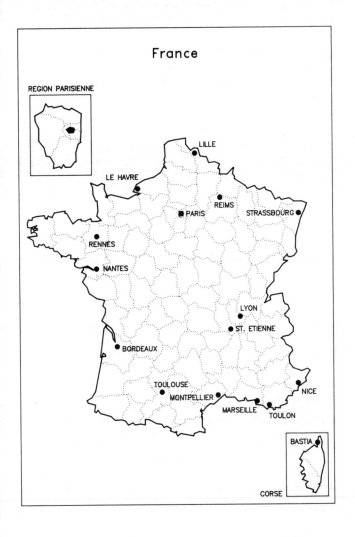

France

REGION PARISIENNE

LILLE

LE HAVRE

REIMS

PARIS

STRASSBOURG

RENNES

NANTES

LYON

ST. ETIENNE

BORDEAUX

TOULOUSE

MONTPELLIER

NICE

MARSEILLE

TOULON

BASTIA

CORSE

Do you have any information on . . ?	**Avez-vous de la documentation sur . . ?**
Do you have any brochures in English about . . ?	**Avez-vous des brochures en anglais sur . . ?**
Can you recommend a good restaurant, please?	**Pouvez-vous me recommander un bon restaurant?**
Thank you very much for your help	**Merci beaucoup pour votre aide**
Three tickets, please	**Trois billets, s.v.p.**
Two full price	**Deux plein tarif**
One half price	**Un demi-tarif**
Two adults, one child	**Deux adultes, un enfant**
Where can I book seats for . . ?	**Où est-ce que je peux réserver des billets pour . . ?**
When I do have to pick them up?	**Quand est-ce que je dois venir les chercher?**
How much do I owe you?	**Je vous dois combien?**
Where's the town hall?	**Où se trouve la mairie?**
▶ Straight on at the traffic lights	▶ **Au feu rouge tout droit**
▶ You can't miss it	▶ **Vous ne pouvez pas le manquer**

■ Please note:

Most towns and holiday resorts have tourist information centres or travel agencies where you can reserve a room, obtain information and booklets, street maps, entrance tickets, forthcoming events, programmes, etc., and book excursions. Tourist information centres are identified by the sign 'i'. Look out for the words 'Syndicat d'Initiative' or 'Office de Tourisme'.

Office du Tourisme et des Congrés de Paris
Bureau d'Accueil Central
127 Champs Elysées
75008 Paris
Tel: (1) 49 52 53 54
Télex: 611 984
Fax: (1) 47 23 56 91
(open daily from 9.00 am to 8.00 pm except
   on 25 December and 1 January)

French Government Tourist Office
178/179 Piccadilly
London W1V 0AL
Tel: 0171-493 6594/6694

Direction du Tourisme
(Centre for Tourism)
17 rue de l'Ingénieur Robert Keller
75740 Paris

Paris Sélection Loisirs
Tel: (1) 47 20 88 98
(Information in English)

For a list of French tourist information centres, see Part III, 11.

6.2 Entertainment

Have you got an entertainments guide?

Avez-vous un calendrier des manifestations?

What's on at the cinema/at the theatre?

Qu'est-ce qu'on joue au cinéma/au théâtre?

Can you recommend a show, please?

Pouvez-vous me recommender un spectacle?

When does the performance begin?

Quand commence la séance?

Are there any tickets for . .?	**Avez-vous des billets pour . .?**
. . . the concert	**. . . le concert**
. . . the exhibition	**. . . l'exposition**
. . . the dance/the ball	**. . . le ballet/le bal**
. . . the circus	**. . . le cirque**
. . . the play	**. . . la pièce de théâtre**
Can I book in advance?	**Est-ce que je peux réserver à l'avance?**
discos and nightclubs	**boîtes (de nuit), disco, discothèque**
with subtitles (films)	**sous-titré (films)**
original version	**version original/VO (films)**
café with entertainment	**café-théâtre**
café with music	**café-concert**
Are you doing anything tonight?	**Vous êtes occupé ce soir?**
What about a film?	**Si on allait au cinéma?**
▶ That would be nice	**▶ Ça serait bien**
▶ That's a good idea	**▶ C'est une bonne idée**
▶ I'm not sure, I'd prefer a concert	**▶ Je ne sais pas, je préférerais aller à un concert**
▶ I don't mind	**▶ Ça m'est égal**
Is there a good film on tonight?	**Il y a un bon film ce soir?**
Can you tell me when the performance finishes?	**A quelle heure finit la séance?**

What you might hear or read in French:

Vente des Billets	Booking Office
Location	Advance Booking
Vestiaire	Cloakroom
Orchestre	Stalls
La Première Rangée	Dress Circle
La Rangée du Fond	Upper Circle
C'est malheureusement complet	I'm sorry we're sold out

▶ **Please note:**

Programmes of events are available at tourist information offices and hotels. You can also find information on theatres, cinemas, cabarets and revues and exhibitions in newspapers, e.g. in *Le Monde* under the heading 'Spectacles' and 'Paris en Visite'.

You can buy programmes of events in Paris at newsagents:
Pariscope – une semaine de Paris
L'Officiel des Spectacles
Paris – Le journal d'information de la ville de Paris
Figaroscope
(These give information on cinema, theatre, exhibitions, music, museums, sports, conferences and nightlife).

A monthly calendar of interesting cultural events called *Paris Sélection* is published by the tourist office in Paris. In the same brochure you will also find useful tips for sightseeing tours, shopping, public transport, etc. This useful brochure is available not only at the main tourist office but also at the following branch offices:

Tour Eiffel	(Tel: 45 51 22 15)
Gare de Lyon	(Tel: 43 43 33 24)
Gare du Nord	(Tel: 45 26 94 82)
Gare de l'Est	(Tel: 46 07 17 73)
Gare d'Austerlitz	(Tel: 45 84 91 70)

Allo Paris is published in Paris every Wednesday; it is free and contains addresses of restaurants, theatre programmes, cabarets, cinemas, concerts and shopping tips.

You can obtain information on leisure activities in English by dialling the following number:

Informations Loisirs 24h/24h
Tel: (1) 49 52 53 56

It is important to know that usherettes in theatres and cinemas should be given a tip of one or two francs.

Museums:

Museums are closed on Tuesdays.
Information about arts:
Tel: (1) 42 77 12 33 Ext. 6081
Minitel 3615 code ARTS

Discos:

You often have to pay for admission, but in most cases this
includes the price of the first drink.

Festivals in France:

There are a number of interesting festivals, for example, theatre
festivals in Avignon, Nantes or Bourges. *France en Fête*, a brochure
available from French tourist information centres, gives you a
comprehensive listing.

Book tips:

The Paris Address Book
Berlitz Cityscope

6.3 Invitations

Are you free tonight?	**Vous êtes libre ce soir?**
Are you doing anything tonight?	**Vous avez déjà des projets pour ce soir?**
Could you come for dinner tomorrow?	**Vous pouvez venir dîner demain soir?**
▶ I'd like to come	▶ **Avec plaisir/volontiers**
▶ I'm sorry, I can't make it	▶ **Je regrette, mais je ne peux pas**
Can we meet tomorrow morning?	**On peut se voir demain matin?**
What about 10 o'clock	**A dix heures, ça va?**
Where shall we meet?	**On se retrouve où?**

I'll pick you up at the hotel	**J'irai vous chercher à votre hôtel**
Can I give you a lift?	**Je peux vous emmener en voiture?**
▸ Thank you, that's really not necessary	▸ **Merci, ce n'est vraiment pas la peine**
Thank you very much for a delightful evening	**Merci beaucoup pour cette agréable soirée**
I enjoyed it very much	**Cela m'a beaucoup plu**
Thank you very much for asking me out	**Je vous remercie d'être sorti avec moi**
▸ The pleasure was all mine	▸ **Mais j'ai été enchanté**
Thank you very much for your hospitality	**Je vous remercie beaucoup de votre hospitalité**
The meal was delicious	**Le repas était délicieux**
I'm afraid I must go/leave now	**Il faut que je parte malheureusement**
Nice to have met you	**J'ai été très content de vous voir**
It was very interesting	**C'était très intéressant**

You might hear the following in French:

Vendredi nous organisons une petite soirée	We're having a party on Friday
Voulez-vous être des nôtres?	Would you like to come?
▸ **Avec plaisir**	▸ I'd love to
▸ **Je regrette, j'ai déjà quelquechose vendredi**	▸ What a pity, I'm busy on Friday
Répondez s'il vous plaît	RSVP
Faites comme chez vous	Make yourself at home
Que voulez-vous boire?	What are you drinking?

Servez-vous, s.v.p.	Please help yourself
Pouvez-vous me passer le fromage, s.v.p.?	Could you pass me the cheese, please?
Voulez-vous encore un peu de vin?	Would you like some more wine?
▶ **Oui, s.v.p.**	▶ Yes, please
▶ **Non, merci**	▶ No thanks
Encore un peu?	Would you like some more?
Non, merci, ça va	I think I've had enough, thank you.
Quelle soirée réussie, vous ne trouvez pas?	Wonderful party, don't you think?
Cela nous a fait plaisir de vous avoir chez nous	It was nice of you to have come
Revenez nous voir bientôt	Come and see us again soon

■ Please note:

If you have received a private invitation, it is customary in France to take along a little gift, usually flowers, a plant, a bottle of wine or chocolates, for the hostess.

If you have been invited for dinner in the evening, remember that before beginning your meal you wish one another 'Bon appétit' (Enjoy your meal). The answer is 'Merci, vous aussi' (Thank you, the same to you).

If you want to send a thankyou letter for an invitation, you will find the model letters in the Appendix useful.

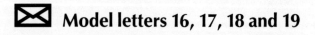 **Model letters 16, 17, 18 and 19**

7

Problems

7.1 At the doctor's

Please call a doctor	**Vous pouvez appeler un médecin, s.v.p.?**
Is there a doctor in the hotel?	**Est-ce qu'il y a un médecin à l'hôtel?**
When does the doctor hold his surgery?	**Quelles sont les heures de consultations?**
Please call an ambulance	**Pouvez-vous appeler une ambulance, s.v.p.?**
I feel sick	**J'ai mal au cœur**
It hurts here	**J'ai mal ici**
I have a pain in . . .	**J'ai mal à . . .**
Can you give me something for . . .	**Pouvez-vous me prescrire un remède contre . . .**
I suffer from . . .	**Je souffre de . . .**
attack/fit	**(la) crise**
asthma	**(l')asthme**
backache	**(le) mal de dos**
blood pressure (too high/too low)	**(la) tension (trop élevée/trop basse)**
bronchitis	**(la) bronchite**
cancer	**(le) cancer**
circulatory trouble	**(les) troubles circulatoires**
a cold	**(le) rhume**
concussion	**(la) commotion cérébrale**
cough	**(la) toux**
constipation	**(la) constipation**
diabetes	**(le) diabète**
diarrhoea	**(la) diarrhée**
dizziness	**(le) vertige**

fever/temperature	(la) fièvre
flu	(la) grippe
fracture	(la) fracture
hayfever	(le) rhume des foins
headache	(le) mal de tête
heart trouble	(les) troubles cardiaques
heartburn	(le)s aigreurs d'estomac
indigestion	(les) problèmes de digestion
an infected wound	une blessure infectée
infection	(l')infection
insomnia	(l')insomnie
migraine	(la) migraine
nausea	(la) nausée, le mal de cœur
nephritis	(la) néphrite
phlebitis	(la) phlébite
rheumatism	(le) rhumatisme
sciatica	(la) sciatique
skin disease	(la) maladie de peau
a sore throat	(le) mal de gorge
stomachache	(les) maux d'estomac
sunburn	(le) coup de soleil
toothache	(le) mal de dent
upset stomach	(l')indigestion
vomiting	(le) vomissement

At the doctor's you might hear the following:

Quels sont vos problèmes?	What's the trouble?
Où est-ce que vous avez mal?	Where does it hurt?
Qu'est-ce que je peux faire pour vous?	What can I do for you?
Veuillez vous déshabiller, s.v.p.	Get undressed, please
Allongez-vous ici, s.v.p.	Lie down here, please
Respirez fort	Breathe deeply, please
Ouvrez la bouche, s.v.p.	Open your mouth, please
Je vais prendre votre tension	I am going to take your blood pressure

186

Je vais vous faire une piqûre	I am going to you an injection
J'aimerais vous faire faire une radio	I'd like you to have an X-ray
Ce n'est rien de grave	It's nothing serious
Je vais vous prescrire quelque chose	I'll prescribe something for you
Prenez un cachet après le repas trois fois par jour	Take one pill three times a day after meals
C'est un antibiotique	This is an antibiotic
Il faut que vous restiez trois jours au lit	You must stay in bed for three days
Revenez dans trois jours	Come back in three days
Service des urgences	Emergency ward

■ Please note:

Before travelling to France you should make enquiries at travel agents about what formalities should be observed for medical treatment in France. In any case, if your trip lasts for more than a few days, you should take an E111 form (obtainable from post offices) with you. You can, of course, take out additional medical insurance for the trip with your travel agent.

When you go to a doctor in France you will receive a receipt with the price of the consultation ('la visite') and any prescriptions. The chemist will add the cost ('la vignette') of the prescribed medicine and return the receipt. You will need the receipt to obtain a refund on your return to the UK.

You have to pay a French doctor directly after receiving treatment. You also have to pay for the medicine. Dental treatment also has to be paid for in cash, but dentists are very expensive, so if it's not an emergency, go to your own dentist in the UK.

There is a 24 hour emergency dental service, the telephone numbers of which are printed in the local paper.

Samu is the emergency medical service, and this must also be paid for. You will find the number in the telephone book under SOS Médecin; emergency number in Paris: 47 07 77 77 or 43 37 77 77.

7.2 At the chemist's

Where is the nearest chemist please?	Où se trouve la pharmacie la plus proche?
Which chemist is open at night?	Quelle est la pharmacie de service?
I'd like some pills for . . .	Je voudrais des comprimés pour . . .
Do I need a prescription?	Est-ce qu'il faut une ordonnance?
adhesive plaster	du sparadrap
after/before each meal	après/avant chaque repas
analgesics, headache pills	des cachets contre le mal de tête
aspirin	de l'aspirine
burn ointment	de la pommade pour les brûlures
charcoal (indigestion) tablets	des comprimés de charbon
cotton wool	du coton
cough medicine	un médicament contre la toux
eye drops	des gouttes pour les yeux
for external use	usage externe
first-aid kit	une boîte de premier secours
indigestion tablets	des cachets contre le mal d'estomac
for internal use	à avaler
laxative	un laxatif
pain-killers	un calmant, un analgésique
pills/tablets	les cachets/les comprimés
sleeping pills	le somnifère
valerian (herbal antispasmodic)	la valériane

■ **Please note:**

The sign for a Pharmacy is a green cross. In larger towns there usually is a night and Sunday service ('la pharmacie de garde'), the rotas for which are displayed on the pharmacy windows, and also published in the local papers.

SOS Pharmacie – emergency number in Paris:
(1) 45 62 02 41 (84 Champs Elysées)
(1) 43 43 19 03 (6 place Félix-Eboué)

7.3 Lost property

Where's the lost property office, please?	Où se trouve le bureau des objets trouvés?
I've lost my . . .	J'ai perdu . . .
. . . wallet	. . . (mon) portefeuille
. . . handbag	. . . (mon) sac à main
. . . identity card	. . . (ma) carte d'identité
. . . passport	. . . (mon) passeport
. . . purse	. . . (mon) portemonnaie
. . . cheque card/banker's card	. . . (ma) carte bancaire
. . . watch	. . . (ma) montre

■ **Please note:**

If you have lost something you should go to the local police station or the local lost property office.

The lost property office in Paris is:

> **Objets trouvés**
> **36 rue des Morillons**
> **Tel: (1) 45 31 14 80**
> **Métro: Convention**
> **Open: Mondays to Fridays, 8.30 am to 5.00 pm**

7.4 The police

Please call the police	**Allez chercher la police, s.v.p.**
I've been robbed	**On m'a volé**

I'd like to report a theft/a crime	**Je voudrais déclarer un vol/un délit**
My car has been broken into	**On a forcé la porte de ma voiture**
My briefcase is missing	**Ma serviette a disparu**
Thank you very much for your help	**Merci beaucoup pour votre aide**
You've been very helpful	**Vous m'avez beaucoup aidé**
You've been very kind	**C'était vraiment très gentil de votre part**
You are very kind	**Vous êtes bien aimable**
Thank you very much	**Merci beaucoup**
▶ Don't mention it/Not at all	▶ **De rien, je vous en prie**

Calls for help:

Au Secours	Help
Arrêtez	Stop
Vite	Quick
Aux Voleurs	Stop, thief
Au Feu	Fire
Attention	Watch Out/Careful
Poison	Poison
Danger	Danger
Pompiers	Fire Brigade
Ambulance	Ambulance
Police	Police

At a police station you may hear the following:

Vous pouvez me le décrire?	Could you describe it for me?/What was it like?
Quand l'avez-vous perdu exactement?	When exactly did you lose it?
Est-ce que je peux voir vos papiers, s.v.p.?	Can I see your papers, please?

Donnez-moi s.v.p. votre nom et adresse	May I have your name and address, please?
Can anyone here speak English?	**Est-ce qu'il y a quelqu'un qui parle anglais ici?**
I need an interpreter	**J'ai besoin d'un interprète**
I need a lawyer	**J'ai besoin d'un avocat**
I'd like to speak to the British consulate please	**J'aimerais parler avec le consulat d'Angleterre**
Where's the British embassy?	**Où se trouve l'ambassade britannique?**

Useful telephone numbers:
Police   17
Fire Brigade   18

You will also find emergency numbers in telephone boxes. If you are in serious difficulties, for example, if you have lost your passport, or you have had an accident, please contact your embassy or consulate:

Ambassade du Royaume-Uni
35 rue du Faubourg Saint-Honoré
75383 Paris Cedex 08
Tel: (1) 42 66 91 41
Télex: 650264
Fax: (1) 42 66 98 96

Consulat Britannique de Paris
9 avenue Hoche
75383 Paris Cedex 8
Tel: (1) 42 66 38 10

There are also British consulates in Marseille, Bordeaux, Lille, Lyon, Biarritz, Toulouse, Boulogne, Calais, Cherbourg, Dunkerque, Nantes, Le Havre, St Malo, Nice.

In the event of minor general problems contact the police (civilian) or gendarmerie (military).

7.5 Accidents and breakdowns

I've had an accident	**J'ai eu un accident**
My car has broken down	**Je suis en panne**
Could you take me to the nearest garage, please?	**Pouvez-vous m'emmener, s.v.p. jusqu'au prochain garage?**
Could you send someone to repair my car, please?	**Pouvez-vous envoyer quelqu'un pour réparer ma voiture?**
Can you tow the car into town?	**Pouvez-vous remorquer ma voiture jusqu'en ville?**
Can you send a mechanic at once, please?	**Pouvez-vous s.v.p. envoyer tout de suite un mécanicien?**
How long will it take?	**Combien de temps ça va prendre?**
How much do I owe you?	**Je vous dois combien?**
This is my insurance certificate	**Voilà mes papiers d'assurance**

See also Part II, 3.5.

I think there's something wrong with the engine	**Je crois qu'il y a quelque chose dans le moteur qui ne va pas**
accelerator	**la pédale d'accélérateur**
battery	**la batterie**
brake	**les freins**
bumper	**le pare-chocs**
clutch	**l'embrayage**
engine	**le moteur**
exhaust	**le pot d'échappement**
headlight	**le phare**
horn	**le klaxon**
ignition	**l'allumage**
spark plug	**la bougie**
starter	**le démarreur**
steering wheel	**le volant**
windscreen wiper	**l'essuie-glace**
wing mirror	**le rétroviseur de côté**

Have you got . .?	**Vous avez . .?**
. . . a rope	**. . . une corde**
. . . a monkey wrench	**. . . une clé anglaise**
. . . a spanner	**. . . une clé à écrous**
. . . a screwdriver	**. . . un tournevis**
. . . spare parts	**. . . les pièces de rechange**
The engine is overheating	**Le moteur chauffe**
The keys are locked inside the car	**Les clés sont enfermées dans la voiture**

In case of an emergency on a motorway (autoroute) you can make a phone call from an emergency telephone, which is never further than 1 km away, the direction and distance of which are shown on a blue sign. Just press the button and you will be directly connected to the police or gendarmerie. Make your report as follows:

1 Give your identity
2 Give your position
3 The direction in which you are travelling
4 The number of your emergency telephone
5 The distance of your vehicle from the telephone
6 Type of car
7 Its make
8 Its colour
9 The registration number
10 Reason for the breakdown, as far as you can tell

The police/gendarmerie will then inform the authorized breakdown service immediately.

If you have an accident it is important to note down the details on a special form (le constant amiable). This is a standardized notification of claim used on French territory. The police will help you with it. When travelling do not forget to carry proof of your insurance cover, insurance certificate (seal to be affixed to the windscreen) and green card.

7.6 Problems when returning goods

Can you change this, please?	**Est-ce que je peux échanger ça?**

Can I return this?	**Est-ce que je peux rendre ça?**
I bought it yesterday	**Je l'ai acheté hier**
Here is the receipt	**Voilà le ticket de caisse**
This is dirty/torn/damaged	**C'est sale/déchiré/abîmé**
Can I have the money back	**Est-ce qu'on peut me rembourser?**
Can I see the manager, please?	**Est-ce que je peux parler au responsable?**

7.7 Problems with the tone of voice

If you hear the following expressions or sentences you are probably being insulted, or at least not being treated very politely.

C'est vraiment ennuyeux	This is a damn nuisance
Ça m'énerve beaucoup	It really gets on my nerves
J'en ai assez (de . . .)	I'm fed up (with . . .)
Ça suffit	I've just about had enough
Quelle bêtise	It's rubbish
C'est vraiment comique	Don't make me laugh
C'est tout simplement du vol	It's a rip-off
Et alors?	So what?
Ça m'est égal	I couldn't care less
Vraiment!	Really!
Malheur à vous!	Don't you dare!
Sales étrangers	Stupid foreigners
Fichez le camp	Get lost
Fermez-la	Shut up
Fichez-moi la paix	Leave me alone
Mais qu'est-ce que vous vous imaginez?	What on earth do you think you're doing?
Ça va pas la tête?	What on earth are you thinking of?

8

What You Say If You Want To . . .

8.1 . . . make a request

Pourriez-vous s.v.p. . .?
Est-ce qu'il serait possible de . .?
Auriez-vous l'obligeance de . .?
Est-ce que cela vous ennuierait/dérangerait de . .?

. . . respond to a request

Volontiers
Si vous voulez
Mais bien sûr
Avec plaisir

Malheureusement non
Je regrette, mais ce n'est pas possible
Il m'est vraiment impossible de . . .

8.2 . . . say thank you

Merci
Merci beaucoup
Merci mille fois
Je vous remercie beaucoup
Je vous suis très reconnaissant(e)
Je vous remercie de votre aide

. . . respond to thanks

De rien
Je vous en prie
C'est tout naturel
Je suis très content(e) d'avoir pu vous aider

8.3 . . . ask for permission

Est-ce que je peux/pourrais . . . ?
Est-ce que vous me permettez de . .?
Est-ce qu'il est permis de . .?
Est-ce que cela vous dérangerait si . .?

. . . grant or refuse permission

Oui
Volontiers
Oui, bien sûr

Oui, je vous en prie
Naturellement
Si tu veux
Si vous voulez
D'accord
En ce qui me concerne, je ne vois pas de problèmes
En ce qui me concerne, je n'y vois pas d'inconvénients

Non
J'ai bien peur que non
Je regrette, mais ce n'est pas possible
Il ne vaudrait mieux pas . . .
A vrai dire non

8.4 . . . have something repeated

Pardon?
Comment?
Qu'est-ce que vous avez dit?
Excusez-moi, mais je n'ai pas tout à fait compris la dernière phrase
Vous pouvez répéter, s.v.p.?

. . . show that you are listening

Ah bon
C'est tout à fait ça

C'est vrai
Vraiment?

. . . sum up

En résumé . . .
Ça veut dire que . . .
Ça signifie donc que . . .
Si je résume . . .
En tout et pour tout on peut dire que . . .

8.5 . . . ask for advice or suggestions

Qu'est-ce que vous en dites?
Quelle est votre opinion?
Vous avez une proposition à faire?
Qu'est-ce que vous me conseillez?
Qu'est-ce que vous diriez/feriez à ma place?

. . . offer advice/make a suggestion

Pourquoi ne feriez-vous pas . .?
Moi, à votre place, je ferais . . .
Je trouve que vous devriez . . .
Ça serait bien si vous . . .
Avez-vous déja pensé à . .?
Je vous conseillerais de . . .

. . . respond to some advice

Entendu
C'est une bonne idée
Votre suggestion me plaît

Non, je ne trouve pas votre proposition très bonne
Je pense que ce ne serait pas très bien/malin/astucieux/ingénieux

8.6 . . . ask for someone's opinion

Qu'est-ce que vous pensez de . .?
Quel est votre avis sur . .?
Je vous serais très reconnaissant de bien vouloir donner votre avis

. . . give your opinion

Je suis d'avis que . . .
Je pense/crois que . . .
D'après moi/à mon avis/en ce qui me concerne . . .
Je pars du principe que . . .
Je suis tout à fait sûr(e)/convaincu(e)/persuadé(e) que . . .
Il n'y a aucun doute que . . .
Il est évident que . . .

Peut-être que . . .
Il est possible que . . .
Cela dépend de . . .
Eventuellement/Je reconnais que . . ./ça ce peut que . . .

Certainement pas
Je ne crois pas que . . .
Je ne suis du tout sûr(e) que . . .
C'est (tout à fait) impossible . . .

J'ai bien peur que cela ne soit pas possible

8.7 . . . express delight

Merveilleux!
Sensationnel!
Extraordinaire!
Je suis très content(e) que . . .
Je suis très heureux (heureuse) d'apprendre que . . .

. . . show that you are angry

Ah non!
Pas comme ça!
Ah vraiment!
C'est vraiment très ennuyeux!

Ça ne peut pas continuer comme ça!
C'est intolérable!
Vous n'êtes pas sérieux!

8.8 . . . make a complaint

Veuillez m'excuser, mais . . .
Est-ce que cela vous dérangerait beaucoup de ne pas . . .
Je dois malheureusement vous dire que . . .
Je regrette de devoir me plaindre
Je suis très mécontent(e) de . . .

. . . admit that you were wrong

Je suis désolé(e)
C'est ma faute
Je crois que vous avez raison
C'est moi qui ai mal compris
Ça doit être un malentendu

. . . apologize

Pardon
Excusez-moi/Pardonnez-moi
Veuillez m'excuser (de + Infinitive)
C'est de ma faute
Je suis absolument désolé(e) que . . .
Pouvez-vous me pardonner encore une fois?
Je suis vraiment impardonnable

. . . respond to an apology

Ça ne fait rien
Je vous en prie
Ça peut arriver
Ne vous en faites pas
Ce n'est pas la peine de vous excuser
Ça peut arriver à tout le monde

8.9 . . . invite someone

Si on allait à . . .
Si on faisait . . .
Je serais très content(e) si . . .
Je vous invite à (+ Infinitive) . . .
J'aimerais vous inviter à . . .

. . . accept or decline an invitation

Volontiers
D'accord
Avec plaisir
Merci beaucoup pour votre invitation
Je vous remercie, c'est vraiment très gentil à vous

Je suis vraiment désolé(e), mais . . .
J'aurais été vraiment très content(e), mais . . .
Malheureusement, je ne peux pas, j'ai déja quelque chose.

8.10 What you say if you don't know what to say . . .

. . . hein . . .
. . . euh . . .
. . . oui, euh . . .
. . . bon, enfin . . .
. . . bon . . . ben . . .
. . . et bien . . .
. . . et ben . . .
. . . tiens . . .
. . . disons . . .
. . . à part ça . . .
. . . alors . . .
. . . bof . . .
. . . et oui . . .
. . . ma foi . . .
. . . comment dirais-je . . .
. . . je veux dire . . .
. . . voilà, (et) voilà . . .

PART III

1

Abbreviations

abs	aux bons soins	care of
ACF	Automobile Club de France	French Automobile Club
ANCE	Agence Nationale pour la création d'entreprises	National Agency for New Business Development
AFNOR	Association Française de Normalisation	French standards association
agce	agence	agency
angl	anglais	English
ANPE	Agence Nationale pour l'emploi	National employment agency
appt	appartement	flat
apr.J.-C.	après Jésus Christ	A.D.
av.J.-C.	avant Jésus Christ	B.C.
AR	accusé de reception	acknowledgement of receipt
av	avenue	avenue
à vdre	à vendre	for sale
bacc	baccalauréat	French equivalent of A levels
Banq, Bque	banque	bank
bd/bld	boulevard	boulevard
BP	Boîte postale	post office box
°C	degrés Celsius	degrees Celsius/ centigrade
CA	chiffre d'affaires	turnover
c-à-d	c'est-à-dire	that is
CAF	coût, assurance, fret	cost, insurance, freight
c/c	compte courant	current account
CCI	Chambre de Commerce et d'Industrie	Chambre of Commerce and Industry
CCP	Compte Chèques Postaux	postal account

202

CEE	**Communauté Économique Européenne**	European Economic Community
cert	**certificat**	certificate
C&F	**coût et fret**	cost and freight
cf	**reportez-vous à**	see
CFE	**Centre de Formalités des Entreprises**	Company Registration Office
CV/ch	**cheval vapeur**	horse power
CIE/Co.	**compagnie**	company
CNPF	**Confédération du Patronat Français**	Equivalent of CBI in the UK
connt	**connaissement**	Bill of Lading
cpte	**compte**	account
CV	**curriculum vitae**	curriculum vitae
dép/dept	**département**	department
Dr	**Docteur (en médicine)**	doctor
EOOE	**Erreur Ou Omission Exceptée**	Errors and Omissions Excepted
E-U	**États-Unis**	United States
EUR	**Europe**	Europe
ex	**par exemple**	for example
exp.	**expéditeur**	sender
FAB	**franco à bord**	free on board
Fco	**franco**	free of charge
FF/frs/fcs	**francs**	francs
fig	**figure**	illustration
gal	**général**	general
GB	**Grande-Bretagne**	Great Britain
gvt	**gouvernement**	government
h	**heure**	hour
HS	**hors service**	out of order
HT	**hors taxes**	no duties included
INC	**Institut National de la Consommation**	Consumers' Association
INPI	**Institut National de la Propriété Industrielle**	National Institute for Industrial Property

IRPP	**impôt sur le revenu des personnes physiques**	income tax
jr	**jour**	day
KF	**kilofrancs**	1,000 francs
LC	**lettre de crédit**	letter of credit
livr	**livraison**	delivery
loc	**location**	hire
LR	**lettre recommandée**	registred letter
M/MM	**Monsieur/Messieurs**	Mr/Messrs.
Mme	**Madame**	Mrs
Mlle	**Mademoiselle**	Miss
mar	**maritime**	marine
M^e	**Maître**	lawyer, solicitor
mens	**mensuel**	monthly
NB	**Nota Bene**	please note
nbrx	**nombreux**	many
n/c	**notre compte/ commande**	our account/order
NF	**norme française**	French standard
No	**numéro**	number
No tél	**numéro de téléphone**	telephone number
p	**page**	page
PCV	**percevable à l'arrivée**	reverse charge call
PDG	**Président-Directeur Général**	Managing Director/ Chairman
P et T	**Postes et Télécommunications**	Post Office and telecommunications
PIB	**produit intérieur brut**	Gross Domestic Product
PNB	**produit national brut**	Gross National Product
PJ	**pièce(s) jointe(s)**	enclosure(s)
pp	**pages**	pages
p.p.	**port payé**	postage paid
PR	**poste restante**	poste restante/to be called for
pr ts rens	**pour tous renseignements**	for further information

PS	post scriptum	postscript
PV	procès verbal	minutes
RC	registre du commerce	business register
RdV	rendez-vous	appointment
RN	route nationale	national/major road
RP	relations publiques	public relations
RSVP	répondez s'il vous plaît	please reply
rte	route	road
s	sur	on
SA	Société Anonyme	Public Limited Company
SARL	Société à Responsabilité Limitée	Limited Liability Company
s/c	sous couvert de	care of
se & p	sauf erreur et omission	errors and omissions excepted
SF	sans frais	free of charge
SI	Syndicat d'Initiative	Tourist Information
SIREN	Système informatique pour Répertoire des Entreprises	Databank
SMIC	Salaire minimum de croissance	basic minimum wage
SNC	Société en Nom Collectif	General Partnership Company
SNCF	Société Nationale des Chemins de Fer Français	French railways
SS	Sécurité sociale	French social security
SVP	s'il vous plaît	please
TSVP	tournez, s'il vous plaît	please turn over
TTC	toutes taxes comprises	all duties included
TU	temps universel	Greenwich Mean Time
TVA	taxe sur la valeur ajoutée	Value Added Tax
urgt	urgent	urgent
virt	virement	transfer

VRP	voyageur, représentant, placier	travelling salesman

2

Signs

A l'Étage Supérieur	On the Top Floor
A Louer	To Rent/To Let
A Vendre	For Sale
Adultes	Adults
Agence de Voyages	Travel Agency
Aller à Gauche/à Droite	Keep Left/Keep Right
Allumez vos Phares	Lights On
Ambulances	Ambulance
L'Appareil Rend la Monnaie	Returned Coins
Appuyer, Pousser	Push
Arrivée	Arrivals
Ascenseur	Lift
Attention	Attention
Attention au Chien	Beware of the Dog
Attention à la Marche	Mind the Step
Attention aux Trains	Beware of the Train
Attention Fragile	Handle with Care
Baignade Interdite	No Swimming
Bas	Downstairs
Boîte aux Lettres	Letterbox
Bureau des Informations	Information Office
Cabine d'Essayage	Changing Room
Caisse	Cash Desk
Caissier/Caissière	Cashier
Carrefour Aménage	Roundabout
Chambres Libres	Vacancies (rooms)
Chaud, Brûlant	Hot
Complet	No Vacancies

Consigne	Left Luggage
Croisement/Carrefour	Crossroads
Danger	Danger
Danger de Mort	Danger of Death
Départ	Departures
Détritus, Ordures	Litter
Déviation	Diversion
Douane	Customs
Eau Non Potable	Not Drinking Water
Eau Potable	Drinking Water
Entrée	Entrance/Entry
Entrée/Sortie	Way In/Way Out
Entrée Interdite	No Entry
Entrée Interdite aux Personnes Étrangers	No Admission for Unauthorized persons
Entrée Libre	Admission Free
Entrez Sans Frapper	Walk Straight In (without knocking)
Épuisé	Sold Out
Escalator, Escalier Roulant	Escalator
Fermé	Closed
Feu	Fire
Feux	Traffic Lights
Frappez	Knock (door)
Freins de Secours	Emergency Brake
Froid	Cold
Guide	Guide
Haut	Upstairs
Heures d'Ouverture	Office Hours/Opening Hours
Hôpital	Hospital
Hors d'Usage/Hors Service	Out of Order
Impasse	Dead End
Indicatif	Dialling Code
Interdiction de Déposer des Ordures	No Tipping

Interdiction d'Entrer	No Trespassing
Interdiction de Fumer	No Smoking
Interdiction de se Garer	No Parking
Interdiction de Tourner à Droite	No Right Turn
Interdit	Prohibited
Jour de Repos	Closed All Day
Levée	Collection
Libre	Vacant
Libre pour les Riverains	Access to Residents
Limitation de Vitesse	Speed Limit
Liquidation Totale	Clearance Sale
Métro	Underground (railway)
Mettre des Pièces de Monnaie	Insert Coins
Mode d'Emploi	Instructions for Use
Monter à l'Avant	Enter at the Front
Ne Pas Déranger S.V.P.	Do Not Disturb
Ne Pas Marcher sur la Pelouse	Keep off the Grass
Ne Pas Ouvrir	Do Not Open
Ne Pas Se Pencher au Dehors	Do Not Lean Out
Ne Pas Toucher	Do Not Touch
Objets Trouvés	Lost Property
Occupé	Engaged
Offre Spéciale	Special Offer
Ouvert de . . . à . . .	Open from . . . to . . .
Parking	Multi-storey Car Park, Car Park
Parking Gardé	Supervised Car Park
Passage Interdit	No Through Road
Peinture Fraîche	Wet Paint
Pension	Bed and Breakfast
Piétons	Pedestrians
Police	Police
Porteur	Porter
Premier Étage	First Floor
Premiers Secours	First Aid

Presse	Press
Propriété Privée	Private Grounds
Prudence/Attention	Caution
Quai	Platform
Réception	Reception
Réservé	Reserved
Rez-de-Chaussée	Ground Floor
Salle d'Attente	Waiting Room
Salle de Restaurant	Dining Room
Self-Service	Self-Service
Sens Giratoire	Clockwise
Service Après-Vente	Customer Service
Soldes	Sale
Sonnez, S.V.P.	Ring (the bell)
Sortie	Exit
Sortie de Voitures	Keep Entrance Clear
Sortie de Secours	Emergency Exit
Sous-Sol	Basement
Standard Téléphonique	Operator
Stop	Stop
(Taxi) Libre	For Hire
Téléphone Publique	Public Telephone
Tirer	Pull
Toilettes – Dames	Women's/Ladies' Toilets
Toilettes – Messieurs	Men's Toilets
Toilettes Publiques	Public Conveniences
Tout Droit	Straight On
Train-Couchettes	Couchette
Transit/Toutes Directions	Through Traffic
Travaux de Voierie	Roadworks
TVA (Taxe sur la Valeur Ajoutée)	VAT (Value-Added Tax)
Vente de Billets	Ticket Office/Box Office
Vers les Quais	To the Trains
Vestiaire	Cloakroom
Vitesse Maximum	Maximum Speed

Voie à Sens Unique	One Way Street
Voie Privée	Private Road
Vol Régulier	Scheduled Flight
Volt	Voltage
Wagon-Lit	Sleeper
Wagon-Restaurant	Dining Car
WC	Toilets

3

Numbers

0	zéro	21	vingt et un
1	un	22	vingt-deux
2	deux	23	vingt-trois
3	trois	30	trente
4	quatre	40	quarante
5	cinq	50	cinquante
6	six	60	soixante
7	sept	70	soixante-dix
8	huit	71	soixante et onze
9	neuf	72	soixante-douze
10	dix	80	quatre-vingts
11	onze	81	quatre-vingt-un
12	douze	90	quatre-vingt-dix
13	treize	91	quatre-vingt-onze
14	quatorze		
15	quinze	100	cent
16	seize	1,000	mille
17	dix-sept	10,000	dix mille
18	dix-huit	100,000	cent mille
19	dix-neuf	1,000,000	un million
20	vingt		

Please note:

137   **cent trente-sept**
9465 **neuf mille quatre cent soixante-cinq**

Decimal fractions:

A comma is used rather than a point as in Britain. In French, 2.5 becomes 2,5 ('deux virgule cinq').

Fractions:

a half	**un demi**
a third	**un tiers**
a quarter	**un quart**
three-quarters	**trois quarts**
two tenths	**deux dixièmes**

Ordinal numbers:

1st	**le premier/la première**	1er (1ère)
2nd	**le/la deuxième/second(e)**	2ème
3rd	**troisième**	3ème
4th	**quatrième**	4ème
5th	**cinquième**	5ème
6th	**sixième**	6ème
7th	**septième**	7ème
8th	**huitième**	8ème
9th	**neuvième**	9ème
10th	**dixième**	10ème
11th	**onzième**	11ème
12th	**douzième**	12ème
13th	**treizième**	13ème
20th	**vingtième**	20ème
21st	**vingt et unième**	21ème
22nd	**vingt-deuxième**	22ème
30th	**trentième**	30ème
31st	**trente et unième**	31ème

4

Weights and Measures

Mesures de longueur:		Lengths:
1 kilomètre	km	0.6214 miles
1 mètre	m	1.0936 yards
		3.2808 feet
		39.3701 inches
1 centimètre	cm	0.3937 inches
1 millimètre	mm	0.0394 inches

Mesures du superficie:		Areas:
1 kilomètre carré	km^2	0.3861 square miles
1 hectare	ha	0.0039 square miles
1 mètre carré	m^2	1.1960 square yards
		10.7639 square feet
1 centimètre carré	cm^2	0.1550 square inches

Mesures de volume:		Volumes:
1 mètre cube	m^3	1.3079 cubic yards
		35.3148 cubic feet
		219.9736 gallons (imperial)
1 litre	l	0.2200 gallons (imperial)
		1.7596 pint

Mesures de poids:		Weights:
1 tonne (1000 k)	t	0.9843 ton
1 kilogramme	kg	2.2046 pound
1 livre (0.5 kg)		1.1023 pound
1 gramme	g	0.0353 ounces
1 hundredweight		**50.8 kg**
1 pound		**453.59 g**
1 ounce		**28.25 g**

Celsius and Fahrenheit:

Temperatures are given in degrees Celsius (centigrade) in France.

Celsius	-10	-5	0	10	21
Fahrenheit	14	23	32	50	70

To convert Fahrenheit into Celsius subtract 32, then multiply by five and divide by nine. To convert Celsius to Fahrenheit, multiply by nine and divide by five, than add 32.

5

The Calendar

Days of the Week:

Sunday	**dimanche**
Monday	**lundi**
Tuesday	**mardi**
Wednesday	**mercredi**
Thursday	**jeudi**
Friday	**vendredi**
Saturday	**samedi**

Months:

January	**janvier**
February	**février**
March	**mars**
April	**avril**
May	**mai**
June	**juin**
July	**juillet**
August	**août**
September	**septembre**

October	**octobre**
November	**novembre**
December	**décembre**

Seasons:

spring	**le printemps**
summer	**l'été**
autumn	**l'automne**
winter	**l'hiver**
high season	**haute saison**
low season	**basse saison**

Bank Holidays:

1er janvier	**Jour de l'An**	New Year's Day
1er mai	**Fête du Travail**	Labour Day
8 mai	**Fête de la Libération**	Victory Day
14 juillet	**Fête Nationale**	National Holiday
1er novembre	**Toussaint**	All Saints' Day
11 novembre	**Armistice**	Armistice
25 décembre	**Noël**	Christmas Day

Movable Bank Holidays:

Vendredi Saint	Good Friday
Pâques	Easter
Ascension	Ascension
Pentecôte	Whitsun
Assomption	Assumption

If a holiday falls on a Thursday or a Tuesday, the French usually take an additional day off ('faire le pont'). You should bear this in mind when making appointments. Remember, too, that between the middle of July and the end of August half of France is on holiday, and it will be difficult to contact anybody. At this time many stores and restaurants in France close down completely for their annual holiday.

6

Job Titles

acheteur/acheteuse	buyer, purchaser
acteur/actrice	actor/actress
agent de change, courtier en valeur	stockbroker
agent de police/policier	policeman (-woman)
agent de voyages	travel agent
agent foncier	property/estate agent
analyste	computer systems analyst
archéologue	archaeologist
architecte	architect
archiviste	archivist
arpenteur, métreur	surveyor
arpenteur	survey technician
assistant(e) de recherches	research assistant
assistant(e) social(e)	welfare and social worker
assureur/agent d'assurances	insurance broker
avocat/avocate	solicitor, barrister, lawyer
bibliothécaire	librarian
biochimiste	biochemist
biologue	biologist
botaniste	botanist
boucher/bouchère	slaughterman (-woman)
brasseur	brewer
cadre supérieur en service exportation	export executive
chauffeur de taxi	taxi driver
chef des achats	purchasing manager
chef de publicité	advertising media executive
chef du secrétariat	office manager
chef de vente	sales manager
cheminot	railwayman (-woman)
chimiste	chemist (chemical scientist)
chimiste, préparateur/préparatrice	laboratory technician

coiffeur/coiffeuse	hairdresser
commissaire-priseur	auctioneer
comptable	bookkeeper, accountant
concierge, gardien/gardienne	caretaker, janitor
conseiller/conseillère	careers officer
conseiller/conseillère de distribution	marketing consultant
constructeur	construction engineer (design technician)
constructeur d'échafaudage	scaffolder
contractuel/contractuelle	traffic warden
contrôleur/contrôleuse de qualité	quality controller
coutourier/couturière	dressmaker
couvreur	roofer, thatcher
décorateur/décoratrice	window dresser
dentiste	dental surgeon
designer	designer
dessinateur/dessinatrice industriel(le)	draughtsman
directeur/directrice d'une caisse d'épargne-construction	building society manager(ess)
directeur/directrice chef	director/general manager(ess)
directeur/directrice d'hôtel	hotel/catering manager
directeur de publicité	public relations manager
économiste	economist
éditeur/éditrice	editor
électricien	electrician
emballeur/emballeuse	packer
employé(e)	clerk
employé(e) de banque	bank clerk
entraîneur/entraîneuse	sports coach
étalagiste	display assistant
expert-comptable	chartered accountant
fleuriste	florist
forgeron	blacksmith
géologue	geologist

géomètre	surveyor
gestionnaire, diplômé en gestion des entreprises	administrator, business economist
horloger/horlogère	watch and clock repairer
infirmière	nurse
infirmière diplômée	registered nurse
ingénieur de génie civil	civil engineer
ingénieur des mines	mining engineer
ingénieur-chimiste	chemical engineer
ingénieur en informatique	computer service engineer
ingénieur-électricien	electrical engineer
ingénieur-électronique	electronic engineer
ingénieur de fabrication	production engineer
ingénieur en aéronautique	aircraft engineer
ingénieur en construction mécanique	mechanical engineer
installateur	fitter
instituteur/institutrice	teacher (primary school)
instructeur, moniteur/monitrice	training manager
interprète	interpreter
jardinier/jardinière	gardener
journaliste	journalist
laveur de vitres	window cleaner
maçon	bricklayer
magasinier, manutentionnaire entrepositaire	warehouseman, warehousewoman
mathématicien/ mathématicienne	mathematician
mécanicien automobile	mechanic, mechanical engineer
mécanicien d'entretien	maintenance/service engineer
médecin	doctor
métallurgiste	metallurgist
météorologue	meteorologist
meunier	miller
moniteur/monitrice d'auto-école	driving instructor

monteur	assembler, fitter
opticien/opticienne	optician
outilleur	toolmaker
paveur	plasterer
peintre en bâtiment, artisan-peintre	decorator
pharmacien/ne	pharmacist, chemist
photographe	photographer
physicien/physicienne	physicist
pilote	(airline) pilot
plombier	plumber
porteur	porter
professeur	teacher (secondary school)
professeur d'éducation physique	PE teacher
projeteur	design technician
prothèsiste	dental technician
rédacteur/rédactrice	editor, sub-editor
rémouleur	grinder
représentant(e)	sales representative
restaurateur/restauratrice	restaurant owner
sapisseur	upholsterer
secrétaire à la réception	receptionist
serveuse/garçon de café	waiter/waitress
sidérurgiste, aciériste	steelworker
soudeur	welder
statisticien/statisticienne	statistician
tailleur	tailor
technicien/technicienne	engineer
technicien en télécommunications	telecommunications technician
technicien textile	textile worker
traducteur/traductrice	translator
urbaniste	town planner

verrier	glazier
vétérinaire	veterinary surgeon
zoologue	zoologist

7

Information on the Single European Market

Population and GNP of EU States

Country	Population in millions	GNP in billion ECU
Austria	7.9	143.2
Belgium	10.0	169.1
Denmark	5.2	110.1
Finland	5.0	81.9
France	57.2	1020.2
Germany	80.3	1498.5
Greece	10.3	60.1
Ireland	3.5	38.7
Italy	56.8	944.8
Luxembourg	0.4	8.2
The Netherlands	15.1	247.6
Portugal	9.8	74.3
Spain	39.1	444.1
Sweden	8.6	190.7
UK	57.7	805.6
	366.9	5837.1
Comparison with USA:	255.0	4586.2

Source: Eurostat 1994
1 ECU = 1.250 US$

Trade between the UK and other EU-States

	Imports in billion ECU	Exports in billion ECU
Austria	— *	— *
Belgium and Luxembourg	7.5	7.3
Denmark	3.2	2.2
Finland	— *	— *
France	16.4	15.7
Germany	25.4	20.9
Greece	0.5	1.0
Ireland	6.8	8.0
Italy	9.2	8.3
The Netherlands	12.4	9.0
Portugal	1.6	1.6
Spain	3.9	5.3
Sweden	— *	— *
Total Europe 12	86.9	79.3
World Total	171.4	144.5
Comparison with USA:	16.5	15.5

Source: Eurostat 1994
* States joined with effect of 1.1.95

The Ten Most Important Customers and Suppliers of the UK

Customers	Amounts in million pounds	Suppliers	Amounts in million pounds
1 Germany	15.052	1 Germany	19.038
2 USA	12.238	2 USA	13.713
3 France	11.490	3 France	12.221
4 The Netherlands	8.452	4 The Netherlands	9.910
5 Italy	6.153	5 Japan	7.453
6 Irish Republic	5.740	6 Italy	6.773
7 Belgium and Luxembourg	5.720	7 Belgium and Luxembourg	5.744

8	Spain	4.409	8	Irish Republic	5.067
9	Sweden	2.431	9	Switzerland	3.919
10	Japan	2.233	10	Norway	3.835
	Total World	106.775			120.546

Source: DTI 1994

EU-Countries/Languages/Currencies/Exchange Rates

Country	Language	Currency	Parity 1 ECU corresponds to:	
Austria	German	Austrian Schilling	13.315	ASch
Belgium	Flemish French German	Belgian Franc, Luxembourg Franc	39.018	FB
Denmark	Danish	Danish Crown	7.466	DKR
Finland	Finnish	Finnish Mark	6.308	FM
France	French	French Franc	6.545	FF
Germany	German	German Mark	1.893	DM
Greece	Greek	Greek Drachma	294.532	Drch
Ireland	English Gaelic	Irish Punt	0.792	IeP
Italy	Italian	Italian Lira	1995.579	Lit
Luxembourg	Letzeburg German French	Belgian Franc, Luxembourg Franc	39.018	FB
The Netherlands	Dutch	Dutch Gilder	2.120	Hfl
Portugal	Portuguese	Escudo	195.650	Esc
Spain	Spanish Katalan, Bask	Peseta	164.435	Pst
Sweden	Swedish	Swedish Crown	9.324	SKr
UK	English	Pound Sterling	0.783	£

Source: Eurostat 1995
Comparison USA: 1 ECU = 1.247 US$

Rates of exchange: January 28, 1995

		One French Franc is equivalent to:
Allemagne	DM	0.289
Autriche	Sch	2.035
Belgique	Bfr	5.962
Danemark	DKr	1.141
Espagne	Pta	25.126
Etats Unis	$	0.191
Europe	ECU	0.153
France	FF	1.000
Grece	DRA	45.045
Pays Bas	NFl	0.324
Irelande	IeP	0.121
Italie	LIT	304.925
Norvège	NKr	1.266
Portugal	Esc	29.895
Suède	Skr	1.425
Suisse	Sfr	0.243
Japon	Yen	124.118
Canada	Can$	1.763

Source: Banque de France

If you have any questions on the European Single Market you can contact various institutions, e.g. the Chambers of Commerce and Industry and:

Association of British Chambers of
   Commerce
9 Tufton Street
London SW1 3QB
Tel: 0171-222 1555

Euro-Chambers
B-1000 Brussels
Tel: (2) 230 0038

as well as:

> **Department of Trade and Industry**
> 1 Victoria Street
> London SW1H 0ET
> Tel: 0171-210 3000
>
> **DTI Hotline**
> Tel: 0171-200 1992

Further addresses:

> **SME Task Force**
> 200 rue de la Loi
> B-1049 Brussels
> Tel: 010 322 236 1676
> Fax: 322-236 1241
> Télex: 61 655 BURAP B

The SME Task Force was set up by the European Commission to help smaller and medium-sized businesses.

> **CBI (The Confederation of British Industry)**
> **Centre Point**
> **103 New Oxford Street**
> **London WC1A 1DU**
> Tel: 0171-379 7400
> Telex: 21322
>
> **Commission of the European Communities**
> **Brussels Office**
> **200 rue de la Loi**
> **B-1049 Brussels**
> Tel: 010 322 235 1111
> Télex: 21877
>
> **Bureau pour la France de la Commission**
>   **des Communautés Européennes**
> **(Press and Information Office of the EC in**
>   **France)**
> **61 rue des Belles-Feuilles**
> **75782 Paris Cedex 16**
> Tel: (1) 45 01 58 85
> Fax: (1) 47 27 26 07

European Investment Bank
Head Office
100 boulevard Konrad Adenauer
2950 Luxembourg
Tel: 352 43791
Télex: 3530

Department of Official Publications of the
    European Community
2 rue Mercier
2985 Luxembourg
Tel: 352 499281
Télex: 1324 pubog lu

Ministère des Affaires Européennes
(Ministry for European Affaires)
36 avenue Raymond Poincaré
75016 Paris
Tel: (1) 47 55 54 00

Euro-Info-Centres in Great Britain:

Euro-Info-Centre
Birmingham Chamber of Industry and
    Commerce
75 Harbone Road
PO Box 360
Birmingham B15 3DH
Tel: 0121-454 6171

Euro-Info-Centre
Scottish Development Agency
Atrium House
50 Waterloo Street
Glasgow G2 6HO
Tel: 0141-221 0999

Euro-Info-Centre
Department of Employment
Small Firms Services
Ebury Bridge House
2–18 Ebury Bridge Road
London SW1W 8QD
Tel: 0171-730 8451

Ireland:

European Business Information Centre
Irish Export Board/Coras Trachtala
Merrion Hall
PO Box 203
Strand Road
Sandymount
Dublin 4
Tel: (1) 6169 5011

Euro-Info-Centres are still being established. Please write to the following address for corrections and additions:

Jean-Pierre Haber
Commission of the European Community
GD XIII
200 rue de la Loi
B-1049 Brussels
Tel: (2) 235 0538

Euro-Info-Centres in France (Euroguichets):

Bordeaux Euroguichet
Comité d'Expansion Aquitaine
2 place de la Bourse
33076 Bordeaux Cedex
Tel: 56 52 65 47/56 52 98 94
Fax: 56 44 32 69

Lyon Euroguichet
Chambre de Commerce et d'Industrie de
   Lyon
16 rue de la République
69289 Lyon Cedex 02
Tel: 78 38 10 10
Fax: 78 37 94 00

Metz Euroguichet
Région de Lorraine
place Gabriel Hocquard, BP 1004
57036 Metz Cedex 1
Tel: 87 33 60 00
Fax: 87 32 89 33

225

Nantes Euroguichet
Chambre de Commerce et d'Industrie de
    Nantes
Centre des Salorges BP 718
16 quai Ernest Renaud
44027 Nantes Cedex 04
Tel: 40 44 60 60
Fax: 40 44 60 90

Strasbourg Euroguichet
Chambre de Commerce et d'Industrie de
    Strasbourg et du Bas-Rhin
10 place Gutenberg
67081 Strasbourg Cedex
Tel: 88 32 12 55
Fax: 88 22 31 20

Book Tips on the Single European Market:

Promotion of Research and Technology by the EC – A manual for applicants
(Commission of the European Community)

Publications of Statistics from various fields, e.g. foreign trade and industry, obtainable from:

Office of Statistics of the European
    Communities
Bâtiment Jean Monnet
rue Alcide de Gasperi
L-2920 Luxembourg

The Times Guide to 1992 – Britain in a Europe without Frontiers
Richard Owen and Michael Dynes
Times Books, London, 1989

1992 – The Facts and Challenges
Alison Press and Catherine Taylor
Industrial Society Press, London

*Completing the Internal Market of the European Community:
1992 Handbook*
Mark Brealey and Conor Quigley
Graham & Trotman

226

1992: Strategies for the Single Market
James W. Dudley
Kogan Page, London

Objectif 92: Le guide pratique du marché unique
Bruno Vever
ETP Paris

Europe en Chiffres
(*Europe in Figures*)
Office of Official Publications of the Commission of the European
Communities, Luxembourg

The Europe Review 1990
World of Information, Saffron Walden, Essex

Guide des Bonnes Manières et du Protocole en Europe
Fixot, 1989

Europages – The European Business Directory
(140,000 companies from 10 countries)
Available from:

> Eurédit
> 9 avenue de Friedland
> 75003 Paris
> Tel: (1) 42 89 34 66
> Télex: 650035 F
> Fax: (1) 42 89 34 73

Panorama de l'Industrie Communautaire 1990
(*Survey of the Industry of the Community 1990*)
(More than 165 industrial sectors)
Commission of the European Communities,
Luxembourg, 1989

L'Europe à votre Porte
(*Europe on your Doorstep*)
Collection d'Exportateur
Centre Français du Commerce Extérieur (CFCE)

Free EC publications

You can obtain EC publications free of charge from the press and information offices of the EC Commission:

Great Britain:

Jean Monnet House
8 Storey's Gate
London SW1P 3AT
Tel: 0171-222 8122

Windsor House
9/15 Bedford Street
Belfast BT2 7EG
Tel: (01232) 240 708

4 Cathedral Road
Cardiff CF1 9SG
Tel: (01222) 371 631

7 Alva Street
Edinburgh EH2 4PH
Tel: 0131-226 4015

Ireland:

39 Molesworth Street
Dublin 2
Tel: (1) 712 244

France:

61 rue des Belles-Feuilles
75782 Paris Cedex 16
Tel: (1) 45 01 58 85
Fax: (1) 47 27 26 07

CMCI Bureau 320
2 rue Henri-Barbusse
13241 Marseille Cedex 01
Tel: 91 91 46 00
Fax: 91 90 98 07

EC databanks:

Access to EC databanks (banques de données) can be made through:

> ECHO Customer Service
> European Commission Host Organisation
> BP 2373
> 177 Route d'Esch
> L-1023 Luxembourg
> Tel: 352 48804 1
> Télex: 2181 euro lu.
> Fax: 352 48804 0

Access to one of the most interesting databanks is possible through ECHO:

> TED (Tenders Electronics Daily)
> (Databank Supplement of the Official
> Gazette of the EC)
> (Survey of Public Contracts, Invitations to
> Tender and Supplemental Contracts)

Further databanks:

Details of large numbers of national and international databanks can be found in:

Les Banques de Données pour le Marketing et les Études
(*Databanks for Marketing and Market Research*)
International Year Book
Published by:

> ADETEM
> 221 rue La Fayette
> 75010 Paris
> Tel: (1) 40 38 97 10

Répertoire des Banques de Données TELETEL pour l'Entreprise
(*Teletel Databanks for Enterprises*)
Published by:

> FLA Consultants
> 27 rue de la Vistule
> 75013 Paris
> Tel: (1) 45 82 75 75

Delphes
Delphes is a databank run by the French CCI, access through:

> EDD (Européenne de Données)
> 164 ter, rue d'Aguesseau
> 92100 Boulogne Blancourt
> Tel: (1) 46 05 29 29
> Minitel 3615 1992

or in the UK:

> Data-Star
> Plaza Suite
> 144 Jermyn street
> London SW1Y 6HJ
> Tel: 0171-930 5503

in the USA:

> DIALOG

8

Reference Libraries and Bookshops

> Chambre de Commerce et d'Industrie de
>   Paris
> Le Centre de Documentation Economique
> 27 avenue de Friedland
> 75008 Paris
> Tel: (1) 42 89 70 77
> Télex: 650100

> Centre de Documentation Economique et
>   Financière
> 12 place Bataillon du Pacifique
> 750128 Paris
> Tel: (1) 40 24 99 30

> Centre Français du Commerce Extérieur
> Comité Français des Manifestations
>   Économiques à l'Étranger (CFCE/CFME)

(French Centre of Foreign Trade)
(French Committee on Economic Activities
   Abroad)
10 avenue d'Iéna
75783 Paris Cedex 16
Tel: (1) 40 73 30 30

Bibliothèque de l'INSEE
18 boulevard A. Pinard
75014 Paris
Tel: (1) 45 40 01 12/12 12

La Documentation Française
29 quai Voltaire
75007 Paris
Tel: (1) 14 50 70 70

Bookshops specializing in business books:

Librairie du Commerce International
10 avenue d'Iéna
75116 Paris
Tel: (1) 40 73 34 60
Télex: 206 811

World Trade Centre CNIT
92053 Paris – La Défense
Tel: (1) 46 92 26 03
Postal order:
BP 438, 75233 Paris Cedex 05
Fax: (1) 43 36 47 98
Télex: 206 811 F LICOMIN

FNAC
Métro: Les Halles

Forum des Halles
1 rue Pierre Lescaut
75001 Paris
Tel: (1) 40 41 40 00

9

Business Newspapers and Magazines

The following French newspapers and magazines contain useful
information for business people.

*La 30, 6
Tribune de l'Économie
Le Figaro
Le Monde
Le Nouvel Économiste
L'Expansion
Les Échos*

*Le Moci
EuroBusiness
L'Exportation
La Revue Économique
Valeurs Actuelles
Fortune
La Vie Française*

10

Useful UK Addresses for Part I

→1

**Market Research Society
175 Oxford Street
London W1R 1TA**

**European Marketing and Statistics
Euromonitor Publications
87–88 Turnmill Street
London EC1M 5QU**

→2

**Advertising Association
Abford House
15 Wilton Road
London SW1V 1NJ**

**Institute of Practitioners in Advertising
44 Belgrave Square
London SW1X 8QS**

232

→3   **British Telecom**
          Bureaufax International Centre
          BTI Communication Centre
          9 St Botolph Street
          London EC3A 7DT

The centre provides an extensive translation service in French/
English and English/French. Interpreters are available when
required.

→4   **British Exporters Association**
          16 Dartmouth Street
          London SW1H 9BL

          SITPRO
          (Simplification of International Trade
            Procedures)
          Almack House
          26–28 King Street
          London SW1Y 6QW

          Department of Trade and Industry Export
            Initiative
          1 Victoria Street
          London SW1H 0ET

→5   **Institute of Freight Forwarders Ltd**
          Redfern House
          Browells Lane
          Feltham
          Middlesex TW13 7ET

          Freight Transport Association
          Hermes House
          St John's Road
          Tunbridge Wells
          Kent TN4 9UZ

→6   **Lloyds of London**
          51 Lime Street
          London EC3N 7DQ

→7
British Institute of International and
    Comparative Law
Charles Clore House
17 Russell Square
London WC1B 5DR

The Law Society
113 Chancery Lane
London WC2A 1PL

→8
French Trade Delegation
12 Church Road
Edgbaston
Birmingham B15 3SR
Tel: 0121-454 0554

French Commercial Office
Sunley Tower
Piccadilly Plaza
Manchester M1 4BW
Tel: 0161-236 7949

Commercial Consultants
21–24 Grosvenor Place
London SW1X 7HU
Tel: 0171-235 7080

French Chamber of Commerce and
    Industry in the UK
Knightsbridge House
197 Knightsbridge
London SW7 1RB
Tel: 0171-2255 250
Telex: 269 132 FRACOM
Fax: 0171-225 5557

11

Chambers of Commerce and Industry and Tourist Information Offices

Unlike those in English-speaking countries, the CCI in France are public institutions ('établissements publics'), which represent the interests of trade and industry when dealing with government departments.

All firms within a given area ('circonscription') which appear in the register of companies are by law members ('résortissants') of the relevant CCI (151 local CCIs, 21 regional CRCI and eight overseas territories, 'les territoires d'outre-mer').

With 22,000 permanent employees, the CCI are important information and service centres for registered companies in France and provide the following:

– information and help for further development to companies in their district
– occupational training courses on all levels
– they act as management consultants and/or provide appropriate contacts
– they actively support the establishment of new firms in their areas.

CCIs and Tourist Information Centres in France

Town/Tourist Information Office	Chamber of Commerce and Industry
Paris	
Office du Tourisme et des Congrès de Paris 127 Champs Élysées 75008 Paris Tel: (1) 49 52 53 54 Fax: (1) 47 23 56 91 Télex: 611 984	CCI Paris 27 avenue de Friedland 75382 Paris Cedex 08 Tel: (1) 42 89 70 00 Télex: 650 100

Avignon
Office du Tourisme/
   Syndicat d'Initiative
41 cours Jean-Jaurès
84000 Avignon
Tel: 90 82 65 11
Télex: 432 877

CCI Avignon
46 avenue Jean-Jaurès
BP 158
84008 Avignon
Tel: 90 82 40 00
Télex: 431 919

Bordeaux
Office du Tourisme/
   Syndicat d'Initiative
12 cours du 30 juillet
33080 Bordeaux Cedex
Tel: 56 44 28 41
Télex: 570 362

CCI Bordeaux
12 place de la Bourse
33076 Bordeaux Cedex
Tel: 56 79 50 00
Télex: 541 048

Calais
Office du Tourisme/
   Syndicat d'Initiative
12 boulevard Clemenceau
62100 Calais
Tel: 21 96 62 40
Télex: 130 886

CI Calais
24 boulevard des Alliés
BP 199
62104 Calais
Tel: 21 97 99 70
Télex: 810 052

Dijon
Office de Tourisme
34 rue des Forges
21022 Dijon Cedex
Tel: 80 30 35 39
Télex: 350 912

CCI Dijon
1 place du Théâtre
21010 Dijon
Tel: 80 65 91 00
Télex: 350 038

Dunkerque
Office de Tourisme
Le Beffroi
4 place C. Valentin
Tel: 28 26 27 89
Télex: 132 011

CCI Dunkerque
1 quai Freycinet
BP 1.501
58383 Dunkerque Cedex
Tel: 28 22 70 00
Télex: 820 970

Grenoble
Office du Tourisme
14 rue de la République
BP 227
38019 Grenoble
Tel: 76 54 34 36
Télex: 980 718

CCI Grenoble
1 place André Malraux
BP 297
38016 Grenoble Cedex
Tel: 76 47 20 36
Télex: 320 824

Le Havre
Office de Tourisme/
    Syndicat d'Initiative
Forum de l'Hôtel de Ville
76059 Le Havre Cedex
Tel: 35 21 22 88
Télex: 190 369

CCI Le Havre
place Jules-Fery
BP 1.410
76067 Le Havre
Tel: 35 55 26 00
Télex: 190 091

Lille
Office de Tourisme/
    Syndicat d'Initiative
Palais/place Rihour
59002 Lille Cedex
Tel: 20 30 81 00
Télex: 110 213

CCI Lille–Roubaix–Tourcoing
place du Théâtre
59000 Lille
Tel: 20 63 77 77
Télex: 160 650

Limoges
Office de Tourisme/
    Syndicat d'Initiative
boulevard de Fleurus
87000 Limoges
Tel: 55 34 46 87
Télex: 580 705

CCI Limoges
6 place Jourdan
BP 403
87011 Limoges
Tel: 55 34 70 11
Télex: 580 915

Lyon
Office de Tourisme/
    Bureau des Congrès
place Bellecour
BP 2254
69214 Lyon Cedex 02
Tel: 78 42 25 75
Télex: 330 032

CCI Lyon
21 rue de la République
69289 Lyon Cedex 02
Tel: 72 40 58 58
Télex: 310 828

Marseille
Office de Tourisme
4 La Canebière
13001 Marseille
Tel: 91 54 91 91
Télex: 430 402

CCI Marseille
Palais de la Bourse
BP 1856
13222 Marseille
Tel: 91 91 91 51
Télex: 170 091

Metz
Office de Tourisme de
    Metz Cathédrale
Place d'Armes
57007 Metz
Tel: 87 75 65 21
Télex: 860 411

CCI Metz
10–12 avenue Foch
57016 Metz Cedex 1
Tel: 87 52 31 00
Télex: 860 362

Nancy
Office de Tourisme/
    Syndicat d'Initiative
14 place Stanislaus
54000 Nancy
Tel: 83 35 22 41
Télex: 960 414

CCI Nancy
40 rue Henri Poincaré
54042 Nancy Cedex
Tel: 83 36 46 43
Télex: 960 070

Nantes
Office du Tourisme
Maison du Tourisme
place du Commerce
44000 Nantes
Tel: 40 47 04 51
Télex: 710 905

CCI Nantes
16 quai Ernest Renaud
BP 718
44040 Nantes
Tel: 40 44 60 60
Télex: 700 693

Nice
Office de Tourisme/
    Syndicat d'Initiative
avenue Thiers-Gare SNCF
06000 Nice
Tel: 93 87 07 07
Télex: 460 042 Accueil Nice

CCI Nice
20 boulevard Carabacel
BP 259
06007 Nice
Tel: 93 55 91 55
Télex: 460 041

Nîmes
Office de Tourisme
6 rue Auguste
30000 Nîmes
Tel: 66 67 29 11
Télex: 490 926

CCI Nîmes
12 rue de la République
30032 Nîmes
Tel: 66 67 65 31
Télex: 490 981

Rennes
Office du Tourisme/Syndicat
  d'Initiative
8 place du Maréchal Juin
35025 Rennes Cedex
Tel: (1) 99 30 38 01
Télex: 741 218 Otsiren

CCI Rennes
2 avenue de la Préfecture
35042 Rennes
Tel: 99 33 66 66
Télex: 730 091

Strasbourg
Office de Tourisme/
  Syndicat d'Initiative
Palais des Congrès
67082 Strasbourg
Tel: 88 37 67 68
Télex: 870 860

CCI Strasbourg
10 place Gutenberg
67000 Strasbourg Cedex
Tel: 88 75 25 25
Télex: 870 068

Toulon
Office du Tourisme/
  Syndicat d'Initiative
8 avenue Colbert
83000 Toulon
Tel: 94 22 08 22
Télex: 400 479 Tournif

CCI Toulon
boulevard du Général Leclerc
BP 1.408
83056 Toulon
Tel: 94 89 90 00
Télex: 430 065

Toulouse
Office du Tourisme/
  Syndicat d'Initiative
Donjon du Capitole
31000 Toulouse
Tel: 61 23 32 00
Télex: 531 508

CCI Toulouse
Palais Consulaire
2 rue d'Alsace-Lorraine
31002 Toulouse
Tel: 61 33 65 00
Télex: 531 877

239

12

Reference Books

All French reference books are listed in the following publications:

Le Répertoire National des Annuaires Français
(*National Survey of French Year Books*)
La Bibliothèque Nationale

Le Répertoire d'Annuaires Français
(*Survey of French Year Books*)
édité par le Centre de Documentation Économique de la Chambre de Commerce et d'Industrie de Paris
Published by the Centre for Documentation of the Paris Chamber of Commerce and Industry

Le Bottin Administratif: 60.000 noms de représentants de la fonction publique
(*60,000 names of representatives of the Civil Service*)

Le Bottin Informatique: Les 10.000 entreprises qui comptent – les produits et services qu'elles proposent
(*The 10,000 leading companies: the products and services they offer*)

Francexport: 26.000 clients, entreprises exportatrices françaises
(*26,000 customers, French export companies*)
Obtainable from:

> Librairie du Commerce International
> 10 avenue d'Iéna
> 75116 Paris
> Tel: (1) 40 73 34 60
> Listing and mailing: (1) 40 73 39 78

How to start a business in France
(*Practical advice*)
Published by the Chambre de Commerce et d'Industrie de Paris

Annuaire des Chambres de Commerce et d'Industrie (CCI)
Assemblée Permanente des CCI
(Year Book of the Chamber of Commerce and Industry; describes
function and responsibility of the French Chambers of Commerce)

French Company Handbook 1990
> 3 rue des Batignolles
> 75017 Paris
> Tel: (1) 43 87 29 29
> Fax: (1) 45 22 49 13

Kompass National
(*Survey of products and services: vols 1 and 2*)
(Geographical order of companies: vols 3 and 4)
vols 1 and 2: Répertoire par produits et services
vols 3 and 4: Répertoire géographique des entreprises
Obtainable from:
> Kompass France SA
> 22 avenue F.D. Roosevelt
> 75008 Paris
> Tel: (1) 43 59 37 59
> Télex: 644911 F

Annuaire National des Transporteurs 1991
(*National Year Book of Carriers*)
Edition Louis Johanet, Paris

Annuaire du Marketing
(*Marketing Year Book*)
Published by:
> ADETEM
> Association Nationale pour la Recherche
>   sur le Développement des Marchés
> 221 rue La Fayette
> 75001 Paris
> Tel: (1) 40 38 97 10
> Fax: (1) 40 38 05 08

Annuaire ESOMAR
(*ESOMAR Year Book*)

ESOMAR
(Association Européenne pour les Études
d'Opinion et de Marketing)
(European Association of Opinion Research
and Marketing)
J.J. Viottastraat 29
1071 JP Amsterdam
The Netherlands
Tel: (20) 664 2141
Fax: (20) 664 2922

International Directory of Market Research Organisations
Published by:

The Market Research Society
175 Oxford Street
London W1R 1TA
Tel: 0171 439 2585

Les Grands de l'Assurance Européenne
(*The Largest European Insurance Companies*)
L'Argus, Paris

Qui représente qui en France: Répertoire Général de l'Importation
(*Who Represents Whom in France; general survey of import trade*)
34th edition
SNEJ, 1990

Market Book France: Boissons, bricollage, épicerie
(*About different sectors, e.g. drinks, Do It Yourself, spices, etc.*)
Les Éditions Concurrence

L'Annuaire de la Franchise (1990)
(*Franchising Year Book*)
Obtainable from:

Centre d'Étude de la Commercialisation et
de la Distribution
19 rue de Calais
75009 Paris

Annuaire Statistique de la France
(*Statistical Year Book of France*)
Obtainable from:

> Institut National de la Statistique et des
> Études Économiques (INSEE)
> 18 boulevard Adolphe-Pinard
> 75675 Paris Cedex 14
> Tel: (1) 45 40 12 12

Les Chiffres Clés du Commerce Extérieur
(*Key Statistics of Foreign Trade*)
Ministère de l'Industrie et de l'Aménagement du Territoire,
Ministère du Commerce Extérieur

Répertoire Français Commerce Extérieur
(*Survey of French Foreign Trade*)
(Alphabetical list of companies specializing in international trade
according to type of industry)
Published by UFAP Annuaires Professionnels

Annuaire Officiel '90
(*Official Year Book of Employers*)
Available from:

> Conseil National du Patronat Français
> ETP
> 31 avenue Pierre 1er de Serbie
> 75784 Paris Cedex 16

France 30.000
(*More than 30,000 enterprises*)
Available from:

> Dun & Bradstreet International
> 17 avenue de Choisy
> 75643 Paris Cedex 13
> Tel: (1) 40 77 07 07

Les 1000 Premières Entreprises Françaises
(1000 leading French companies)
Special edition published by L'Expansion/Dun & Bradstreet

Foires et Salons à Paris Calendrier
(Calendar of Trade Fairs and Exhibitions in Paris)
Available from Chambre de Commerce et d'Industrie, Paris

France Congrès: Guide de villes de congrès
(*Congresses in France: Guide to Congress Towns*)
Obtainable from:

> France-Congrès
> 24 avenue de l'Opéra
> 75001 Paris
> Tel: (1) 42 96 03 61
> Télex: 210311
> Fax: Code 328

Expo News Magazine: Salons – Foires – Congrès Tourisme d'affaires
(*Exhibitions, Trade Fairs, Congresses, Business Tourism*)
Supplement to *Expo News lettres*; weekly
Available from:

> Fédération des Foires et Salons de France
> 16 place Havre
> 75009 Paris
> Tel: (1) 45 26 17 69
> Fax: (1) 42 80 58 44

International Trade Exhibitions in France
Published by the Fédération Française des Salons Spécialisés et Promosalons
Representative in the UK:

> The Colonnades
> 82 Bishop's Bridge Road
> London W2 6BB
> Tel: 0171-221 3660
> Fax: 0171-792 3525

Annual Directory of the top 1200 companies
Supplement to the magazine *L'Expansion*

Les 100.000
(*The 100,000 Leading French Companies*)
Published by:

Bottin S.A.
31 cours des Juillottes
94706 Maisons Alfort
Tel: (1) 49 81 56 56
Fax: (1) 49 77 85 28

Qui produit
(*Who Produces What*)
(sur les 100.000 entreprises: l'entreprise, ses produits, ses services)
(*businesses, their products and services*)
Bottin, Paris

Qui décide: Savoir qui décide dans les 100.000 entreprises
(*Who decides: Who are the decision-makers in 100,000 leading French companies*)
Bottin, Paris

Annuaire Relais France Télécom:
(PAP)

Annuaire des entreprises/Secteurs d'activités
(*Annual Telecom Directory: Year Book of Companies and Activities*)

Télexport: Les exportateurs et importateurs français
(*French Exporters and Importers*)
Available from:

Chambre Français de Commerce et
d'Industrie
Association Télexport
2 rue de Viarmes
75001 Paris
Tel: (1) 45 08 36 43

Que Choisir
(*What to Choose*)
Published by:

> Union Fédérale des Consommateurs
> (Consumers' Federation)
> 11 rue Guénot
> 75555 Paris Cedex 11
> Tel: (1) 43 48 55 48

Publications of the French Chamber of Commerce in the UK:
INFO Magazine
Franco-British Trade Directory
Franco-British Transport Magazine

APPENDIX

1

Model Letters

 ## Model Letter 1

	Maison Beaumont	inside address
	12 rue du Palais	
	38002 Grenoble	
n/ref.:		reference
v/ref.:		
Objet:		subject line
	Grenoble, le 20 mars 1991	place, date
(1) Mesdames, Messieurs,	(2) Monsieur	salutation
	(3) Madame	
		body of the letter

(1) Nous vous prions (Je vous prie)
     d'agréer <. . . .> l'assurance de
     nos (mes) sentiments distingués. — *complimentary close three various forms <. . . .> please repeat the complete salutation*

(2/3) Veuillez accepter <. . . .>
     l'expression
     de nos (mes) sentiments distingués
     (dévoués).

Le Directeur Commercial — *status (e.g.)*

— *signature*

Gérard Leroy — *name*

Model Letter 2

Foire de Lyon 1992

Mesdames, Messieurs,

Nous sommes un groupe d'entreprises qui s'occupent
d'industrie mécanique et nous avons l'intention de présenter
la gamme de nos produits à la foire de Lyon.

Nous vous serions très reconnaissants de bien vouloir nous
faire part des conditions de participation requises.

En vous remerciant d'avance nous vous prions d'agréer,
Mesdames, Messieurs, l'expression de nos sentiments
distingués.

 # Model Letter 3

Mesdames, Messieurs,

Nous nous référons à votre annonce du . . . parue dans le
journal . . . du . . . Comme nous sommes vivement intéressés
par l'importation de vos produits, nous vous prions de nous
envoyer votre catalogue et votre liste de prix.

Dans l'attente d'une réponse rapide nous vous remercions
d'avance et vous prions d'agréer, Mesdames, Messieurs, nos
salutations distinguées.

Model Letter 4

Mesdames, Messieurs,

Nous vous remercions de votre lettre du . . . et de l'intérêt que vous portez à nos produits.

Nous sommes très contents de vous faire l'offre suivante:

(quantity, name of merchandise, quality, price)

Nous joignons à notre lettre nos conditions de livraison et de paiement.

Nous espérons être favorisés de votre ordre et vous assurons que nous l'exécuterons avec le plus grand soin.

Veuillez agréer, Mesdames, Messieurs, l'expression de nos sentiments les meilleurs.

Pièce jointe:
1 catalogue

 # Model Letter 5

Madame,

Nous vous remercions de votre offre du 27 janvier 1992 et vous prions de nous envoyer immédiatement franco domicile:

....

Prix: FF 200.000/pièce

Conditions de paiement: à 10 jours 2% d'escompte ou
                                          à 30 jours prix net

Pour la bonne règle, veuillez nous accuser réception de cette commande.
Veuillez agréer, Madame, l'expression de nos sentiments respectueux.

Model Letter 6

Objet: Notre commande No . . . du 03-01-1992

Mesdames, Messieurs,

Nous avons le regret de devoir vous informer que nous ne sommes pas satisfaits de l'exécution de notre commande citée ci-dessus.

La marchandise que vous nous avez livrée ne correspond pas à la qualité que nous avons commandée. Pour que vous puissiez vous en persuader vous-mêmes, nous vous en retournons un échantillon et vous prions de bien vouloir nous échanger cette marchandise.

Veuillez agréer, Mesdames, Messieurs, l'expression de nos sincères salutations.

Annexe

 Model Letter 7

Objet: Votre lettre du . . .

Mesdames, Messieurs,

Nous vous remercions de votre envoi d'échantillon. Malheureusement, suite à une erreur de notre service d'expédition, nous vous avons fait parvenir un article de moindre qualité. C'est pourquoi nous avons procédé aujourd'hui à un nouvel envoi à votre adresse franco domicile.

Veuillez nous réexpédier à nos frais la marchandise que nous vous avons envoyée par erreur.

Nous vous prions de bien vouloir nous pardonner cette erreur et espérons que notre collaboration continuera d'être des meilleures.

Recevez, Mesdames, Messieurs, l'assurance de nos meilleurs sentiments.

Model Letter 8

Mesdames, Messieurs,

Nous vous accusons réception de votre lettre du . . .

C'est avec beaucoup de soin que nous avons vérifié la qualité de l'échantillon que vous nous avez envoyé. Nous avons constaté qu'il s'agissait bien de la qualité référence No . . .

Comme vous pouvez le voir à la copie de votre commande, que nous vous joignons, la qualité livrée correspond à celle que vous nous avez commandée. Nous sommes cependant tout à fait prêts à vous reprendre la marchandise et à vous en livrer une autre de qualité supérieure.

Dans l'attente de connaître vos intentions, nous vous prions d'agréer, Mesdames, Messieurs, l'expression de nos sentiments distingués.

 # Model Letter 9

Mesdames, Messieurs,

En règlement de votre facture No . . . du . . ., nous vous adressons, ci-joint, un chèque barré d'un montant de

FF/£ . . .

Veuillez agréer, Mesdames, Messieurs, l'expression de nos sentiments distingués.

Pièce(s) jointe(s)
1 chèque

Model Letter 10

Objet: Votre facture No . . . du . . .

Nous avons chargé aujourd'hui la banque XY de virer la somme de

FF/£ . . .

à votre compte No. . . . à la banque XYZ.

Veuillez agréer, Mesdames, Messieurs, l'expression de nos sentiments distingués.

 # Model Letter 11

Premier Rappel

Sans doute avez-vous omis par erreur de nous régler la facture dont nous vous joignons une photocopie. Jusqu'au 31-12-91 votre compte reste débiteur du montant de cette facture.

Nous vous prions de bien vouloir virer immédiatement le montant de notre facture à notre compte No . . . à la banque XY.

Dans l'attente de votre règlement, nous vous prions de croire à l'expression de nos sentiments distingués.

Pièce jointe

Model Letter 12

Deuxième Rappel

Mesdames, Messieurs,

Nous nous référons à notre facture No . . . du . . , et à notre premier rappel du . . .

Malheureusement nous n'avons toujours pas reçu cette somme.

C'est pourquoi nous vous prions de régler notre facture d'un montant de

FF/£ . . . jusqu'au . . .

Veuillez agréer, Mesdames, Messieurs, nos salutations distinguées.

 # Model Letter 13

Lettre recommandée

Troisième Rappel

Objet: Facture No . . .

Mesdames, Messieurs,

En balançant nos écritures nous avons malheureusement eu le regret de devoir constater que malgré nos lettres du . . . et du . . . vous n'avez pas encore réglé la facture mentionnée ci-dessus.

Dans le cas où la somme de

FF/£ . . .

ne nous serait pas parvenue jusqu'au . ., nous nous verrions dans l'obligation de poursuivre le recouvrement de notre créance par les voies de droit.

Recevez, Mesdames, Messieurs, l'expression de nos sentiments distingués.

Model Letter 14

<u>**Strictement confidentiel**</u>

Mesdames, Messieurs,

Jusqu'à présent nous n'avons pas encore été en relations d'affaires avec l'entreprise dont vous trouverez le nom sur la feuille ci-jointe. C'est pourquoi nous vous serions très reconnaissants de bien vouloir nous faire part de votre jugement personnel et de nous communiquer quelques renseignements sur la solvabilité de cette entreprise.

Il va de soi que vous pouvez compter sur notre entière discrétion. Nous vous prions d'agréer, Mesdames, Messieurs, l'expression de nos sentiments distingués.

Annexe:

Model Letter 15

Curriculum Vitae

Nom de famille

Prénoms

Adresse

No de tél.

Date de naissance

Lieu de naissance

Nationalité

Situation familiale

Diplômes scolaires

Etudes/Formation professionnelle

Qualifications supplémentaires

Références

Model Letter 16

Cher Monsieur Johnson,

Nous avons le plaisir de vous inviter vous et votre épouse à notre réception donnée à l'occasion de l'anniversaire de notre entreprise, qui aura lieu

le 20 août 1992, à partir de 11 heures.

Nous vous prions de nous donner une réponse.

Croyez, cher Monsieur, à l'expression de mes meilleurs sentiments.

 # Model Letter 17

Cher Monsieur Dupont,

Nous vous remercions de votre aimable invitation à la réception du . . ., à laquelle mon épouse et moi aurons le plaisir de nous rendre.

Veuillez agréer, cher Monsieur, l'expression de mes meilleurs sentiments.

 # Model Letter 18

Cher Monsieur Dupont,

Ma femme et moi, nous vous remercions de votre aimable invitation, à laquelle nous avons le regret de ne pas pouvoir nous rendre, étant retenus par ailleurs.

Je vous prie d'agréer, cher Monsieur, l'expression de mes meilleurs sentiments.

Model Letter 19

Cher Monsieur Amiel,

Mon voyage d'affaires à travers la France étant maintenant terminé, je tiens par cette lettre à vous remercier de votre hospitalité et de votre coopération.

Ma visite chez vous m'a beaucoup apporté et c'est avec plaisir que je me rappelle les conversations animées que nous avons eues dans votre entreprise. Ma femme également a beaucoup apprécié les courses faites en compagnie de Madame, votre épouse.

Je vous adresse tous mes remerciements et je serais très heureux à mon tour de vous rendre votre hospitalité à Ramsgate.

Recevez, cher Monsieur Amiel, l'expression de mes meilleurs sentiments.

John S. Miller

2

Presentation of the Balance Sheet

Assets

Unpaid capital, called up
Expenses incurred in connection with the start-up or expansion of the business

A   Fixed assets
I   *Intangible assets*
    1   Licences, trade marks and patents, etc., as well as licences to such rights and assets
    2   Goodwill
    3   Advances paid on intangible assets

II   *Tangible assets*
    1   Land, rights similar to land, and buildings, including buildings on property owned by others
    2   Technical equipment and machinery
    3   Other equipment, office furniture and equipment
    4   Advances paid on fixed assets, and assets under construction

III   *Financial assets*
    1   Shares in group companies
    2   Loans to group companies
    3   Participating interests of 25% or more
    4   Loans to entities with which the enterprise is linked by virtue of participating interests of 25% or more
    5   Other investments – long term
    6   Other loans.

B   Current assets
I   *Inventories*
    1   Raw materials and supplies
    2   Work in progress; uncompleted projects
    3   Finished goods and goods for resale
    4   Advance payments on stocks

II   *Receivables and other current assets*
    1   Trade receivables
    2   Amounts due from group companies
    3   Receivables from entities with which the enterprise is linked by virtue of participating interests of 25% or more
    4   Other current assets

III   *Securities*
    1   Shares in group companies
    2   Treasury stock
    3   Other securities

IV   *Cheques, cash, deposits with Federal Bank and with Bank of Federal Postal System, Deposits with Commercial Banks*

C   Pre-paid expenses
    Excess of liabilities over assets to the extent not covered by shareholders' equity

Structure du Bilan

Actif

Capital souscrit non versé
Frais d'établissement et d'extension

A Immobilisations
I Immobilisations Incorporelles
1 Concessions, brevets, licences, marques et droits et valeurs similaires
2 Fonds de commerce
3 Acomptes versés sur immobilisations incorporelles

II Immobilisations corporelles
1 Terrains et droits similaires, constructions, y compris les bâtiments sis sur des terrains appartenant à des tiers
2 Installations techniques et machines
3 Autres installations, outillage et mobilier
4 Acomptes versés et immobilisations corporelles en cours

III Immobilisations financières
1 Parts sociales dans des entreprises liées
2 Créances sur entreprises liées
3 Participations (25% et plus)
4 Créances sur des entreprises avec lesquelles il existe un lien de participation de 25% et plus
5 Autres titres ayant le caractère d'immobilisations
6 Autre prêts

B Actif circulant
I Stocks
1 Matières premières et consommables
2 Produits en cours de fabrication
3 Produits finis et merchandises
4 Acomptes versés

II Créances et autres actifs circulants*
1 Créances résultant de ventes et prestations de services
2 Créances sur des entreprises liées
3 Créance sur des entreprises avec lesquelles il existe un lien de participation de 25% et plus
4 Autres actifs circulants

III Valeurs mobilières
1 Parts dans des entreprises liées
2 Actions propres ou parts propres
3 Autres valeurs mobilières

IV Avoirs en banques, avoirs en compte de chèques postaux et en caisse

C Compte de régularisation
Excédent des passifs par rapport aux actifs non couverts par les capitaux propres

* Indiquer les montants avec une durée à courir de plus d'un an

Liabilities and Shareholders' Equity

A **Shareholders' equity**
I *Share capital*
II *Capital reserve*
III *Earnings reserve*
1   Legal reserve
2   Reserve for treasury stock
3   Statutory reserves
4   Other earnings reserves

IV *Retained earnings/Accumulated deficit brought forward from previous year*

V *Net Income/Loss for the year*
Special reserves, to be taxed in subsequent years

B **Accruals**
1   Accruals for pensions and benefits
2   Accrued taxes
3   Other accruals

C **Liabilities**
1   Debenture loans (convertible)
2   Amounts due to banks
3   Advance payments received
4   Trade payables
5   Notes payable
6   Amounts due to group companies
7   Amounts owed to entities with which the enterprise is linked by virtue of participating interests of 25% or more
8   Other liabilities
taxes
in respect of social security

D **Deferred Income**

Contingencies and Commitments
Discounted notes, guarantees, guarantees given on notes and loans, other warranties, pledges on company assets to secure another party's liabilities, other contingencies and commitments

Passif

A Capitaux propres
I *Capital souscrit*
II *Prime d'émission et réserve de réévaluation*
III *Réserves*
    1 Réserve légale
    2 Réserve pour actions propres ou parts propres
    3 Réserves statutaires
    4 Autres réserves

IV *Résultats reportés (bénéfices ou pertes) en début d'exercice*

V *Résultat de l'exercice (bénéfice ou perte)*

B Provision pour risques et charges
    1 Provisions pour pensions et obligations similaires
    2 Provisions pour impôts
    3 Autres provisions

C Dettes*
    1 Emprunts obligataires avec mention séparée des emprunts convertibles
    2 Dettes envers des établissements de crédit
    3 Acomptes reçus sur commandes
    4 Dettes sur achats et prestations de services
    5 Dettes représentées par des effets de commerce
    6 Dettes envers des entreprises liées
    7 Dettees envers des entreprises avec lesquelles la société a un lien des participation de 25% et plus
    8 Autres dettes
      dont dettes fiscales
      dont dettes au titre de la sécurité sociale

D Compte de régularisation

Engagements et Impondérables
Effets escomptés, garanties, débiteurs pour engagements sur effets et prêts, garanties réelles constituées sur avoirs propres et autres engagements et impondérables.

* Indiquer les montants avec une durée à courir de plus d'un an

3

Presentation of the Statement of Earnings (Profit and Loss Account)

1 Sales
2 Increase or decrease in finished goods and work in progress
3 Other capitalized labour, overheads and materials
4 Other operating income
5 Materials
  (a) raw materials, supplies and purchased goods
  (b) purchased services (e.g. utilities, suncontracting costs, etc.)
6 Personnel costs
  (a) wages and salaries
  (b) Social security and pension costs, benefits
7 Depreciation, amortization and special provisions
  (a) on intangible and tangible assets, and on capitalized business start-up or expansion costs
  (b) on current assets to the extent that usual provisions made by corporations are exceeded
8 Other operating expenses
9 Income from participating interests of 25% or more, income from group companies
10 Income from group companies, other securities and long-term financial investments
11 Other interest and similar income from group companies
12 Write down of financial assets and of securities included in current assets
13 Interest and similar expenses incurred by companies
14 Results of ordinary operations
15 Extraordinary income
16 Extraordinary expenses
17 Extraordinary net
18 Taxes on income
19 Other taxes
20 Net income/loss for the year

Income and expenses arising from profit and loss pooling arrangements and similar contracts are to be presented as separate line items.

Structure du Compte de Pertes et Profits

1 **Chiffre d'affaires**
2 Variation du stock de produits finis et en cours de fabrication
3 Travaux effectués par l'entreprise pour elle-même et portés à l'actif
4 Autres produits d'exploitation
5 Matières premières et autres
   (a) matières premières consommables et achats de marchandises
   (b) charges externes (par exemple, électricité, gaz et eau, contractants
   . . .)
6 Frais de personnel
   (a) salaires et appointements
   (b) charges sociales, avec mention séparée de celles couvrant les
   pensions
7 Amortissements
   (a) sur immobilisations incorporelles et corporelles, ainsi que sur les
   frais d'établissement et d'extension de l'exploitation
   (b) sur les actifs circulants
8 Autres charges d'exploitation
9 Produits provenant des entreprises avec lesquelles il existe un lien de
  participation de 25% et plus avec mention séparée de ceux provenant
  d'entreprises liées
10 Produits provenant d'autres valeurs mobilières, avec mention séparée
  de ceux provenant d'entreprises liées
11 Autres intérêts et produits assimilés, avec mention séparée de ceux
  provenant d'entreprises liées
12 Amortissements sur immobilisations financières et sur valeurs
  mobilières faisant partie de l'actif circulant
13 Intérêts et charges assimilées, avec mention séparée de deux
  concernant des entreprises liées
14 **Résultats provenant des activités ordinaires**
15 Produits exceptionnels
16 Charges exceptionnelles
17 **Résultat exceptionnel (brut)**
18 Impôts sur le résultat
19 Autres impôts
20 **Résultat de l'exercice (bénéfice ou perte)**

Le produit et charges résultant d'une mise en commun de pertes et de
bénéfices ou d'opérations similaires doivent être présentés séparément.

4

English–French Index of Technical Vocabulary with Phonetic Transcriptions

f feminine
m masculine
pl plural

to accept an offer	**accepter une offre** *f*	aksepte yn ɔfʀ(ə)
accepted in the trade	**d'usage** *m* **dans le commerce** *m*, **d'usage** *m* **courant**	d'yzaʒ dɑ̃ lə kɔmɛʀs d'yzaʒ kuʀɑ̃
accordance	**accord** *m*	akɔʀ
account	**compte** *m*	kɔ̃t
accountant, bookkeeper	**comptable** *m*	kɔ̃tabl(ə)
accounting, bookkeeping	**comptabilité** *f*	kɔ̃tabilite
accruals	**charges** *f pl* **à payer**	ʃaʀʒ(ə) a peje
acknowledgement of order	**accusé** *m* **de réception de la commande**	akyze də resepsjɔ̃ də la kɔmɑ̃d
to acquire a licence	**acquérir une licence** *f*	akeʀiʀ yn(ə) lisɑ̃s
acquisition	**acquisition** *f*, **achat** *m*	akizisjɔ̃, aʃa
additional period of time	**délai** *m* **supplémentaire** *m*	dele syplemɑ̃tɛʀ
address	**adresse** *f*	adʀɛs
to adjust prices	**ajuster les prix** *m pl*	aʒyste le pʀi
adjustment	**règlement** *m* **des réclamations**	ʀɛɡləmɑ̃t de ʀeklamasjɔ̃
administration expenses	**frais** *m pl* **d'administration**	fʀɛ d'administʀasjɔ̃
advance order	**commande** *f* **d'avance**	kɔmɑ̃d d'avɑ̃s
advance payment	**paiement** *m* **d'avance**	pɛmɑ̃ d'avɑ̃s
advance, in . . .	**à l'avance**	al'avɑ̃s
advertisement (printed)	**annonce** *f* **publicitaire (insérée dans un journal)**	anɔ̃s pyblisitɛʀ
advertising	**publicité** *f*	pyblisite
advertising consultant	**conseiller** *m* **publicitaire**	kɔ̃seje pyblisitɛʀ
advertising gimmick	**cadeau** *m* **publicitaire**	kado pyblisitɛʀ
to advise	**informer, recommander**	ɛ̃fɔʀme, ʀəkɔmɑ̃de

affidavit	**déclaration** f **sur l'honneur, affidavit** m	deklɑʀasjɔ̃ syr l'ɔnœr, afidavit
after-sales service	**service** m **après-vente**	sɛʀvis apʀɛ vɑ̃t
after-tax profit	**bénéfices** m pl **après impôts**	benefis apʀɛ ɛ̃po
agenda	**ordre** m **du jour**	ɔʀdʀ(ə) dy ʒuʀ
agent, representative	**représentant/e** m/f	ʀəpʀezɑ̃tɑ̃/tə
agreement	**accord** m, **convention** f	akɔʀ, kɔ̃vɑ̃sjɔ̃
air cargo, airfreight	**fret** m **aérien**	fʀɛ aeʀjɛ̃
air transport	**transport** m **aérien**	tʀɑ̃spɔʀ aeʀjɛ̃
air waybill	**lettre** f **de transport aérien**	lɛtʀ(ə) də tʀɑ̃spɔʀ aeʀjɛ̃
all-in costs	**coût** m **total**	ku tɔtal
all-in price	**prix** m **tout compris**	pʀi tu kɔ̃mpʀi
to allow a claim	**accepter une réclamation** f	aksepte yn ʀeklamasjɔ̃
to amend a contract	**modifier un contrat** m	mɔdifje ɛ̃ kɔ̃tʀa
amortization instalment	**la tranche** f **d'amortissement** m	tʀɑ̃ʃ d'amɔʀtismɑ̃
amount overdue	**arriéré** m	aʀjeʀe
annual financial statement	**bilan** m **annuel**	bilɑ̃ anyɛl
annual general meeting of the shareholders	**assemblée** f **annuelle/ assemblée** f **générale ordinaire**	asɑ̃ble anyɛl asɑ̃ble ʒeneʀal ɔʀdineʀ
annual report	**rapport** m **annuel**	ʀapɔʀ anyɛl
application	**candidature** f, **inscription** f	kɑ̃didatyʀ, ɛ̃skʀipsjɔ̃
application software	**logiciel** m **d'application**	lɔʒisjɛl d'aplikasjɔ̃
to apply for	**se présenter à, solliciter un emploi** m	sə pʀezɑ̃te a, sɔlisite ɛ̃ ɑ̃plwa
to apply for space (at a fair)	**s'inscrire à (une foire)**	s' ɛ̃skʀiʀ a yn fwaʀ
to apply for the patent	**déposer un brevet** m	depoʒe ɛ̃ bʀɛvɛ
to appreciate	**savoir apprécier**	savwaʀ apʀesje
apprentice	**apprenti(e)** m/f	apʀɑ̃ti
arrears	**arriérés** m pl	aʀjeʀe
as per contract	**d'après le contrat** m	d'apʀɛ lə kɔ̃tʀa
as per invoice	**d'après la facture** f	d'apʀɛ la faktyʀ
as per your order, in accordance with your order	**d'après votre commande** f	d'apʀɛ vɔtʀ(ə) kɔmɑ̃d
assembly	**montage** m	mɔ̃taʒ
assembly instructions	**notice** f **de montage**	nɔtis də mɔ̃taʒ
assembly line	**chaîne** f	ʃɛn
assets	**actif** m	aktif

assignment of a debt	cession f d'une créance	sɛsjõ d'yn(ə) kʀeɑ̃s
at cost	au prix m coûtant, au prix m de revient	o pʀi kutɑ̃, o pʀi də ʀəvjɛ̃
at half price	à moitié prix m	a mwatje pʀi
at your/our expense	à vos/nos frais m pl	a vo/no fʀɛ
attached	ci-joint	siʒwɛ̃
attachment (seizure of goods)	saisie f	sezi
to attend a conference	prendre part à une conférence f	pʀɑ̃dʀ(ə) paʀ a yn kõfeʀɑ̃s
to attend an evening course	suivre des cours m pl du soir	suivʀ(ə) de kuʀ dy swaʀ
auditing	contrôle m	kõtʀol
back-up saving	sauvegarde f	sovgaʀd
bad debt	créance f irrécouvrable	kʀeɑ̃s iʀekuvʀabl(ə)
bag, sack	sac m	sak
balance	solde m	sɔld(ə)
to balance an account	solder, équilibrer un compte m	sɔlde, ekilibʀe œ̃ kõt
balance sheet	bilan m	bilɑ̃
bankruptcy, liquidation	faillite f	fajit
to bargain	marchander	maʀʃɑ̃de
barrel	tonneau m	tɔno
beneficiary	bénéficiaire m	benefisjɛʀ
to bill, to invoice	compter	kõte
Bill of Exchange (B/E)	traite, lettre f de change	tʀɛt, lɛtʀə də ʃɑ̃ʒ
Bill of Lading (B/L)	connaissement m	kɔnɛsmɑ̃
bill overdue	traite f non honorée, effet m en souffrance	tʀɛt nõ ɔnɔʀe, efɛ ɑ̃ sufʀɑ̃s
blank, space	blanc m	blɑ̃
blend (tea, coffee)	mélange m	melɑ̃ʒ
to book, to enter an order	enregistrer une commande f	ɑ̃ʀeʒistʀe yn kɔmɑ̃d
to book exhibition space	louer une surface f d'exposition	lwe yn syʀfas d'ɛkspozisjõ
book value	valeur f comptable	valœʀ kõtabl(ə)
bookings	rentrée f des commandes	ʀɑ̃tʀe de kɔmɑ̃d
bookkeeper, accountant	comptable m	kõtabl(ə)
bookkeeping, accounting	comptabilité f	kõtabilite
booth	stand m de la foire	stɑ̃d də la fwaʀ
bootstrap (computer term)	amorce f	amɔʀs(ə)

266

borrowed capital	capital *m* extérieur	kapital d'ɛksterjœr
boss	patron *m*, chef *m*	patrɔ̃, ʃɛf
to bounce (cheque)	être sans provision	ɛtr(ə) sã prɔviziʒɔ̃
branch	succursale *f*	sykyrsal
brand	marque *f*	mark(ə)
to bring an action against someone	porter plainte contre . . .	pɔrte plɛ̃tə kɔ̃tr(ə)
to bring forward a motion	présenter une demande *f*, une requête *f*	prezãte yn dəmãd, yn rəkɛt
brochure, leaflet	brochure *f*	brɔʃyr
brought forward (b/f)	report *m*	rəpɔr
budgetary accounting	planning *m* budgétaire	planiŋ bydʒetɛr
buffer	tampon *m*	tãpɔ̃
bulk goods	marchandises *f pl* en vrac	marʃãdiz vark
bulk haulage	transport *m* en vrac	trãspɔr ã vrak
business, company, firm	entreprise *f*	ãtrəpriz
business, to do . . .	faire des affaires *f pl*	fɛr dezafɛr
business letter	lettre *f* commerciale	lɛtr(ə) kɔmɛrsjal
business licence tax	taxe *f* professionnelle	taks prɔfesjɔnɛl
business partnerships	participations *f pl*	partisipasjɔ̃
business reply card	réponse *f* à une publicité, carte-réponse *f*	repɔ̃s a yn pyblisite, kart(ə) repɔ̃s
business reputation	renommée *f* commerciale, notoriété *f*	r(ə)nɔme kɔmɛrsjal, nɔtɔrjete
to buy, to purchase	acheter	aʃte
buyer	acheteur *m*	aʃtœr
buying conditions	conditions *f pl* d'achat	kɔ̃disjɔ̃ d'aʃa
c/o (care of)	aux bons soins *m pl* de (abs)	o bɔ̃ swɛ̃ də
cable connection	branchement *m*	brãʃmã
to calculate	calculer	kalkyle
calculation (of cost price)	calcul *m* (du prix de revient)	kalkyl
calculator (pocket)	machine *f* à calculer (de poche)	maʃin a kalkyle
call-money	argent *m* au jour le jour	arʒã o ʒur lə ʒur
can, metal container	bidon *m*	bidɔ̃
to cancel	annuler	anyle
to cancel a contract	annuler un contrat *m*	anyle œ̃ kɔ̃tra

capital gains	**plus-values** *f pl* **en capital**	plyvaly ɑ̃ kapital
capital goods	**biens** *m pl* **d'investissement**	bjɛ̃ d' ɛ̃vɛstismɑ̃
capital structure	**structure** *f* **des capitaux**	stryktyʀ de kapito
cardboard box, carton	**boîte** *f*	bwat
cargo, carriage, freight	**fret** *m*	fʀɛ
carriage	**transport** *m*	tʀɑ̃spɔʀ
carrier, forwarder	**transporteur** *m*	tʀɑ̃spɔʀtœʀ
to carry a motion	**adopter une résolution** *f*	adɔpte yn ʀezɔlysjɔn
carry forward (the balance)	**reporter**	ʀəpɔʀte
carry-over	**report** *m*	ʀəpɔʀ
case	**caisse** *f*	kɛs
cash against documents (CAD), documents against payment (D/P)	**comptant** *m* **contre documents** *m pl*, **documents** *m pl* **contre paiement**	kɔ̃tɑ̃ kɔ̃tʀ(ə) dɔkymɑ̃, dɔkymɑ̃ kɔ̃tʀ(ə) pɛmɑ̃
cash discount	**escompte** *m* **au comptant**	ɛskɔ̃t o kɔ̃tɑ̃
cash flow	**cash flow** *m*	kaʃ floʊ
cash on delivery (COD)	**paiement** *m* **à la livraison**	pɛmɑ̃ a la livʀɛzɔ̃
cash with order (CWO)	**payable à la commande** *f*	pɛjabl(ə) a la kɔmɑ̃d
catalogue	**catalogue** *m*	katalɔg
catalogue, latest . . .	**tout dernier catalogue** *m*	tu dɛʀnje katalɔg
central processing unit (CPU)	**unité** *f* **centrale**	ynite sɑ̃tʀal
to certify	**certifier, attester**	sɛʀtifje, atɛste
to certify the contract	**certifier un contrat** *m*	sɛʀtifje œ̃ kɔ̃tʀa
chairman	**directeur** *m* **général**	diʀɛktœʀ ʒeneʀal
chairperson	**président** *m*, **directeur** *m* **général**	pʀezidɑ̃, diʀɛktœʀ ʒeneʀal
channels of transmission	**voies** *f pl* **de transmission**	vwa de tʀɑ̃smisjɔ̃
charge, fee	**taxe** *f*	taks(ə)
to charge	**compter, débiter**	kɔ̃te, debite
chartered accountant	**expert** *m* **comptable**	ɛkspɛʀ kɔ̃tabl(ə)
circular	**circulaire** *f*	siʀkylɛʀ
circumstances beyond our control	**conditions** *f pl* **imprévisibles**	kɔ̃disjɔ̃ ɛ̃pʀevizibl(ə)

claim, debt	demande f d'indemnisation, réclamation f, déclaration f de sinistre	dəmãd d'ɛ̃dɛmnizasjɔ̃, ʀeklamasjɔ̃, deklaʀasjɔ̃ de sinistʀ(ə)
to clarify a position	exposer clairement son point m de vue	ɛkspoze klɛʀmã sɔ̃ pwɛ̃ də vy
classifications	classifications f pl	klasifikasjɔ̃
clerk	employé(e) m/f de commerce	ãplwaje də kɔmɛʀs(ə)
to close an account	arrêter, fermer un compte m	aʀete, fɛʀme ɛ̃ kɔ̃t
to close the meeting	clore une réunion f	klɔʀ yn ʀeynjɔ̃
collection agency	agence f d'encaissement	aʒãs d'ãkɛsmã
commercial	film m, spot m publicitaire	spɔt pyblisitɛʀ
commercial invoice	facture f commerciale	faktyʀ kɔmɛʀsjal
commercial quality	qualité f d'usage	kalite d'yzaʒ
commercial settlement of a dispute	règlement m d'un litige	ʀɛgləmã d'ɛ̃ litiʒ
commission	commission f	kɔmisjɔ̃
commission agent	commissionnaire m, courtier m	kɔmisjɔnɛʀ, kuʀtje
commodity, goods, merchandise	marchandise f, produit m	maʀʃãdiz, pʀɔdɥi
common market	marché m commun	maʀʃe kɔmɛ̃
communication line	passerelle f	pasʀɛl
Community Transport Procedure (CTP)	système m d'expédition en commun	sistɛm d'ɛkspozisjɔ̃ ã kɔmɛ̃
company, firm, business	entreprise f	ãtʀəpʀiz
to compel	obliger	ɔbliʒe
to compensate	dédommager	dedɔmaʒe
compensation	dédommagement m	dedɔmaʒmã
to compete	être en concurrence	ɛtʀ(ə) ã kɔ̃kyʀãs
competition	concurrence f	kɔ̃kyʀãs
competitive price	prix m concurrentiel	pʀi kɔ̃kyʀãsjɛl
competitor	concurrent m	kɔ̃kyʀã
to complain about	se plaindre de	sə plɛ̃dʀ(ə) də
complaint	réclamation f	ʀeklamasjɔ̃
composition	concordat m	kɔ̃kɔʀda
compound interest	intérêts m pl composés	ɛ̃teʀɛ kɔ̃poze
compromise	compromis m	kɔ̃pʀɔmi
compulsory sale	vente f forcée	vãt fɔʀse
concern, group	groupe m	gʀup
concerning	en ce qui concerne, au sujet de	ã sə ki kɔ̃sɛʀn, o syʒe də

269

conditions, terms	conditions *f pl*	kɔ̃disjɔ̃
conditions of participation	conditions *f pl* de participation	kɔ̃disjɔ̃ də partisipasjɔ̃
conference	conférence *f*	kɔ̃ferɑ̃s
consignee	destinataire *m/f*	destinatɛr
consignment, shipment	envoi *m* de marchandise	ɑ̃vwa də marʃɑ̃diz
consignment note, waybill	feuille *f* de route, lettre de voiture	fœj də rut, lɛtr(ə) də vwatyr
consignor, shipper	expéditeur *m*	ɛkspeditœr
consortium	consortium *m*	kɔ̃sɔrtiym
to constitute a quorum	atteindre le quorum *m*	atɛ̃dr(ə) lə kɔrɔm
consular invoice	facture *f* consulaire	faktyr kɔ̃sylɛr
consumer goods	biens *m pl* de consommation	bjɛ̃ də kɔ̃sɔmasjɔ̃
consumer price	prix *m* à la consommation	pri a la kɔ̃sɔmasjɔ̃
container	container *m*	kɔ̃tenɛr
contract (of employment)	contrat *m* de travail	kɔ̃tra də travaj
contract (of sale)	contrat *m* de vente	kɔ̃tra də vɑ̃t
to contract, to enter into a contract	conclure un contrat *m*	kɔ̃klyr œ̃ kɔ̃tra
contract clause	clause *f* du contrat	kloz dy kɔ̃tra
the contract expires	contrat *m* expire	kɔ̃tra ɛkspir
the contract is null and void	contrat *m* est nul et avenu	kɔ̃tra ɛ nyl e avny
contracting parties	parties *f pl* contractantes	parti kɔ̃traktɑ̃t
contractors, suppliers	fournisseur *m*	furnisœr
to control, check	contrôler, surveiller	kɔ̃trole, syrveje
convenience, at your earliest	aussitôt que possible	osito kə pɔsiblə
co-operation	collaboration *f*	kɔlabɔrasjɔ̃
corporation tax	impôt *m* sur les sociétés	ɛ̃po syr le sɔsjete
cost price	prix *m* de revient	pri də rəvjɛ̃
cost-covering	couvrant les frais *m pl*	kuvrɑ̃ le frɛ
cost-free, free of charge	gratuit, sans frais	gratɥi, sɑ̃ frɛ
costs	frais *m pl*, coûts *m pl*	frɛ, ku
country of destination	pays *m* de destination	pei də destinasjɔ̃
courtesy	obligeance *f*, complaisance *f*	ɔbliʒɑ̃s, kɔ̃plɛzɑ̃s
cover (insurance)	couverture *f*	kuvɛrtyr
to cover a risk	couvrir un risque *m*	kuvrir œ̃ risk(ə)
crate	cageot *m*, caisse *f*	kaʒo, kɛs
credit, short-/medium-/long-term	crédit *m* à court/moyen/long terme	kredi a kur/mwajɛ̃ lɔ̃ tɛrm(ə)

to credit	**créditer**	kʀedite
credit inquiry	**demande** f **de renseignements commerciaux**	dəmɑ̃d də ʀɑ̃sε ɲmɑ̃ kɔmεʀsjo
credit insurance	**assurance-crédit** f	asyʀɑ̃s kʀedi
credit note	**avis** m **de crédit**	avi də kʀedi
creditor	**créancier** m	kʀeɑ̃sje
current account	**compte** m	kɔ̃t
current assets	**actif** m **réalisable/de roulement**	aktif ʀealizabl(ə)/ də ʀulmɑ̃
curriculum vitae	**curriculum** m **vitae**	kyʀikylɔmvite
customer	**client** m	klijɑ̃
daisy wheel printer	**imprimante** f **à marguerite**	ɛ̃pʀimɑ̃t ɑ maʀgəʀit
damage	**dommage** m	dɔmaʒ
data acquisition	**saisie** f **de données**	sεzi də dɔne
data transfer	**traitement** m **de l'informatique**	tʀεtmɑ̃ də l'ɛ̃fɔʀmatik
databank	**banque** f **de données**	bɑ̃k də dɔne
database	**base** f **de données**	baz də dɔne
date of invoice	**date** f **de la facture**	da də la faktyʀ
date of shipment	**date** f **d'expédition**	da d'εkspedisjɔ̃
deadline	**délai** m **de livraison**	dele də livʀεzɔ̃
deadlines	**dates** f pl **limites, délais** m pl	dat limit, dele
debit note	**bordereau** m **de débit**	bɔʀdəʀo də debi
debt, claim	**créance** f	kʀeɑ̃s
debtor	**débiteur** m	debitœʀ
to decide on a motion	**décider d'une requête** f	deside dyn ʀəkεt
defect	**défaut** m	defo
defective goods	**marchandise** f **défectueuse**	maʀʃɑ̃diz defεktɥøz
delay	**retard** m	ʀətaʀ
to deliver	**livrer**	livʀe
to deliver within the specified time	**livrer dans les délais de livraison**	livʀe dɑ̃ le dele də livʀεzɔ̃
delivery	**livraison** f	livʀεzɔ̃
delivery note	**bulletin** m **de livraison**	byltɛ̃
demand	**demande** f	dəmɑ̃d
to demand compensation	**exiger des dommages et intérêts** m pl	εgziʒe de dɔmaʒ e ɛ̃teʀε
to demand payment	**exiger le paiement** m	εgziʒe lə pεmɑ̃
demonstration	**démonstration** f	demɔ̃stʀasjɔ̃
density	**densité** f	dɑ̃site
deposit, savings account	**compte** m **d'épargne**	kɔ̃t depaʀɲ(ə)
depreciations	**amortissements** m pl	amɔʀtismɑ̃

detailed information about . . .	**informations** f pl **détaillées sur . . .**	ɛ̃fɔʀmasjɔ̃ detaje syʀ
development (of a product)	**activité** f **de développement (d'un produit)**	aktivite də devlɔpmɑ̃ (d'œ̃ pʀɔdɥi)
development (of business), growth	**développement** m **des affaires**	devlɔpmɑ̃ dezafeʀ
digital	**numérique**	nymeʀik
direct labour	**salaires** m pl **directs**	saleʀ diʀekt
direct materials	**matériel** m **de fabrication**	mateʀiel də fabʀikasjɔ̃
direct memory access	**accès** m **direct**	akse diʀekt
discount	**escompte** m, **remise** f, **ristourne** f	ɛskɔ̃t, ʀəmiz, ʀistuʀn(ə)
discount rate	**taux** m **d'escompte**	to d'ɛskɔ̃t
disk	**disque** m, **disquette** f	disk(ə), disket
disk operating system (DOS)	**système** m **d'exploitation disque**	sistem d'ɛksplwatasjɔ̃
disk storage	**mémoire** m **à disque magnétique**	memwaʀ a disk(ə) maɲetik
to dismantle a stand	**démonter un stand**	demɔ̃te œ̃ stɑ̃d
dismissal	**licenciement** m	lisɑ̃simɑ̃
to dispatch, to send off, to ship, to forward	**envoyer, expédier**	ɑ̃vwaje, ɛkspedje
dispatch department	**service** m **d'expédition**	seʀvis d'ɛkspedisjɔ̃
dispatch note	**avis** m **d'expédition**	avi d'ɛkspedisjɔ̃
display, screen	**écran** m	ekʀɑ̃
display material	**matériel** m **d'exposition**	mateʀjel d'ɛksposisjɔ̃
dispute	**litige** m, **différend** m, **conflit** m	litiʒ, difeʀɑ̃, kɔ̃fli
distribution network	**réseau** m **de distribution**	ʀezo də distʀibysjɔ̃
dividend	**dividende** m	dividɑ̃d
to do business	**faire des affaires**	feʀ dezafeʀ
documents against acceptance (D/A)	**documents** m pl **contre acceptation**	dɔkymɑ̃ kɔ̃tʀ(ə) akseptasjɔ̃
domestic market	**marché** m **intérieur**	maʀʃe ɛ̃teʀjœʀ
dot-matrix printer	**imprimante** f **matricielle**	ɛ̃pʀimɑ̃t matʀisjel
doubtful debt	**créance** f **douteuse**	kʀeɑ̃s dutøz
down-payment	**acompte** m, **arrhes** f pl	akɔ̃t(ə), aʀ
draft	**traite** f	tʀet
to draw a cheque	**tirer un chèque** m	tiʀe œ̃ ʃek
to draw money from an account	**prélever, retirer**	pʀelve, ʀətiʀe
drive (disk)	**lecteur** m	lektœʀ
due date	**échéance** f, **date** f **d'échéance**	eʃeɑ̃s, dat d'eʃeɑ̃s

dunning letter, reminder letter	**lettre** f **de rappel/de sommation**	lɛtʀ(ə) də ʀapɛl/ də sɔmasjɔ̃
duplicate consignment note	**duplicata** m, **double** m **du bulletin de livraison/de la feuille de route**	dyplikata, dubl(ə) dy byltɛ̃ də livʀɛzɔ̃/də la fœj də ʀut
E & OE (errors and omissions excepted)	**sauf erreur**	sof ɛʀœʀ
economic position	**situation** f **économique**	sitɥasjɔ̃ ekɔnɔmik
education, training	**éducation** f, **formation** f	edykasjɔ̃, fɔʀmasjɔ̃
to effect delivery	**effectuer une livraison** f	efɛktɥe yn livʀɛzɔ̃
to effect payment, to pay,	**payer**	peje
electronic data processing	**traitement** m **électronique de l'information, informatique** f	tʀɛtmã elɛktʀɔnik də lɛ̃fɔʀmasjɔ̃, ɛ̃fɔʀmatik
electronic mail/E-mail	**mailing** m	mɛliŋ
electronic mailbox	**boîte** f **aux lettres électronique**	bwat o lɛtʀ(ə)zel ɛktʀɔnik
to employ, to engage, to take on	**embaucher**	ãboʃe
employee	**employé/e** m/f, **salarié/e** m/f	ãplwaje, salaʀje
employer	**employeur** m	ãplwajœʀ
enclosure	**pièce** f **jointe**	pjɛs ʒwɛ̃t
to engage, to employ, to take on	**embaucher**	ãboʃe
engineering	**conception** f **technique**	kɔ̃sɛpsjɔ̃ tɛknik
to enter, to book an order	**prendre note d'une commande** f	pʀãdʀ(ə) nɔt dyn kɔmãd
to enter into a contract, to contract	**passer un contrat** m	pase œ̃ kɔ̃tʀa
to entrust a firm with the agency	**accorder la représentation, se faire représenter par une entreprise**	akɔʀde la ʀəpʀezãtasjɔ̃, sə fɛʀ ʀəpʀezãte paʀ yn ãtʀəpʀiz
entry	**entrée** f	ãtʀe
equity capital	**capital** m **propre**	kapital pʀɔpʀ(ə)
to erase	**effacer**	efase
error, oversight	**erreur** f	ɛʀœʀ
to establish, to found	**fonder**	fɔ̃de
estimate	**devis** m	dəvi
estimated annual turnover	**chiffre** m **d'affaires estimé**	ʃifʀ(ə) d'afɛʀ ɛstime

to exchange the goods	échanger une marchandise f	eʃɑ̃ʒe yn maʁʃɑ̃diz
to execute an order	exécuter un ordre m	ɛgzekyte yn ɔʁdʁ(ə)
executive	cadre m supérieur	kɑdʁ(ə) sypeʁjœʁ
exhibit	pièce f d'exposition	pjɛs dɛkspozisjɔ̃
to exhibit, to show	exposer	ɛkspoze
exhibition	exposition f	ɛkspozisjɔ̃
exhibition centre	parc m des expositions	paʁk dezɛkspozisjɔ̃
exhibition regulations	règlement m de la foire	ʁɛglɑ̃mɑ̃ də la fwaʁ
exhibitor	exposant m	ɛkspozɑ̃
expected growth	développement m prévu	devlɔpmɑ̃ pʁevy
expenditure, expenses	dépenses f pl	depɑ̃s
expert	expert m	ɛkspɛʁ
to exploit a patent	exploiter un brevet m	ɛksplwate œ̃ bʁəvɛ
to export	exporter m	ɛkspɔʁte,
export packing	emballage f d'export	ɑ̃balaʒ d'ɛkspɔʁ
exporter	exportateur m	ɛkspɔʁtatœʁ
to extend a contract	prolonger un contrat m	pʁɔlɔ̃ʒe œ̃ kɔ̃tʁa
extension	prolongation f d'un crédit	pʁɔlɔ̃gasjɔ̃ d'œ̃ kʁedi
extras	frais m pl supplémentaires, faux frais m pl	fʁɛ syplemɑ̃tɛʁ, fo fʁɛ
factoring	affacturage m	afaktyʁaʒ
factory gate price	prix m à la production	pʁi a la pʁɔdyksjɔ̃
fair	foire f, exposition f	fwaʁ, ɛkspozisjɔ̃
fair average quality (f.a.q.)	qualité f moyenne	kalite mwajɛn
fair management	direction f de la foire	diʁɛksjɔ̃ də la fwaʁ
fair pass	carte f de la foire	kaʁt(ə) də la fwaʁ
fair price	prix m raisonnable	pʁi ʁɛzɔnabl(ə)
to fall due	tomber à échéance f	tɔ̃be a eʃeɑ̃s
fault	défaut m	defo
faulty material	matériau m défectueux	mateʁjo defɛktɥø
favourable price	prix m avantageux	pʁi avɑ̃taʒø
fax	télécopie f	telekɔpi
fee	taxe f	taks
file	fichier m	fiʃje
to file for bankruptcy	déclarer faillite f	deklaʁe fajit
file protection, write-lock	protection f du fichier	pʁɔtɛksjɔ̃ dy fiʃje
financial controller	chef m du service financier	ʃɛf dy sɛʁvis finɑ̃sje

English	French	Phonetic
financial standing	**situation** *f* **financière**	sitɥasjɔ̃ finɑ̃sjɛʀ
finished goods	**produits** *m pl* **finis**	pʀɔdɥi fini
firm, business, company	**entreprise** *f*	ɑ̃tʀəpʀiz
first-class quality	**qualité** *f* **de première classe**	kɑlite də pʀəmjɛʀ klɑs
fixed assets	**actif** *m* **immobilisé**	ɑktif imɔbilize
fixed costs	**frais** *m pl*/**charges** *f pl* **fixes**	fʀɛ/ʃɑʀʒ(ə) fiks
fixed price	**prix** *m* **fixe**	pʀi fiks
flat rate	**taux** *m* **uniforme**	to ynifɔʀm(ə)
flexible working hours, flexitime	**horaire** *m* **aménagé, travail** *m* **à la carte**	ɔʀɛʀ amenaʒe, tʀavaj a la kaʀt
floor plan	**plan** *m* **d'ensemble (de la foire)**	plɑ̃ d'ɑ̃sɑ̃bl(ə) (də la fwaʀ)
floor space	**surface** *f* **d'exposition**	syʀfɑs d'ɛkspɔsisjɔ̃
floppy disk	**disque** *m* **souple, disquette** *f*	disk(ə) supl, diskɛt
flowchart	**organigramme** *m*	ɔʀganigʀam
follow-up letter	**lettre** *f* **publicitaire de relance**	lɛtʀ(ə) pyblisitɛʀ də ʀəlɑ̃s
for the attention of (att . . .)	**à l'attention** *f* **de . . .**	a l'atɑ̃sjɔ̃ də
foreign currency	**monnaie** *f* **étrangère**	mɔnɛ etʀɑ̃ʒɛʀ
foreign exchange department	**service** *m* **des devises**	sɛʀvis de dəviz
foreign language secretary	**secrétaire** *f* **bilingue/ trilingue/multilingue**	səkʀetɛʀ bilɛ̃g/ tʀilɛ̃g/myltilɛ̃g
foreman	**contre-maître** *m*, **agent** *m* **de maîtrise**	kɔ̃tʀəmɛtʀ(ə), aʒɑ̃ də mɛtʀiz
to forward, to send off, to ship, to dispatch	**envoyer, expédier**	ɑ̃vwaje, ɛkspedje
forwarder, carrier	**transporteur** *m*	tʀɑ̃spɔʀtœʀ
forwarding/freight charges	**frais** *m pl* **de transport**	fʀɛ də tʀɑ̃spɔʀ
to found, to establish	**fonder**	fɔ̃de
franchise	**franchise** *f*, **concession** *f*	fʀɑ̃ʃiz, kɔ̃sesjɔ̃
franchised dealer	**commerçant** *m* **en franchise, concessionnaire** *m*	kɔmɛʀsɑ̃ ɑ̃ fʀɑ̃ʃiz kɔ̃sesjɔnɛʀ
free of charge, cost-free	**gratuit, sans frais**	gʀatɥi, sɑ̃ fʀɛ
free sample	**échantillon** *m* **publicitaire**	eʃɑ̃tijɔ̃ pyblisitɛʀ
freight, cargo, carriage	**fret** *m*, **transport** *m*, **cargaison** *f*	fʀɛ, tʀɑ̃spɔʀ, kaʀgɛzɔ̃
freight collect	**fret** *m* **contre remboursement**	fʀɛ kɔ̃tʀ(ə) ʀɑ̃buʀsəmɑ̃

freight included	frais *m pl* de transport compris	fʀɛ də tʀɑ̃spɔʀ kɔ̃pʀi
freight rate	tarif *m* du transport	taʀif dy tʀɑ̃spɔʀ
freight/forwarding charges	frais *m pl* de transport, tarif *m* des transports	fʀɛ də tʀɑ̃spɔʀ, taʀif de tʀɑ̃spɔʀ
fringe benefits	avantages *m pl* en espèces ou en nature, avantages de fonction	avɑ̃taʒ ɑ̃ ɛspɛs u ɑ̃ natyʀ, avɑ̃taʒ də fɔ̃ksjɔ̃
fulfilment of contract	exécution *f* d'un contrat	ɛgzekysjɔ̃ dœ̃ kɔ̃tʀa
full-time workers	main-d'œuvre *f* à plein temps	mɛ̃ dœvʀ(ə) a plɛ̃ tɑ̃
to furnish a customer with goods, to supply	livrer, fournir	livʀe, fuʀniʀ
general agency	agence *f* générale	aʒɑ̃s ʒeneʀal
general meeting of the shareholders	assemblée *f* générale	asɑ̃ble ʒeneʀal
giro account	compte *m* courant/de virement	kɔ̃t kuʀɑ̃, də viʀmɑ̃
to give in one's notice	donner sa démission	dɔne sa demisjɔ̃
to give notice (of redundancy, dismissal)	licencier	lisɑ̃sje
to go bankrupt	faire faillite *f*	fɛʀ fajit
goods, commodity, merchandise	marchandises *f pl*, produits *m pl*	maʀʃɑ̃diz, pʀɔdɥi
grade	sorte *f*, catégorie *f*	sɔʀt(ə), kategɔʀi
to grant an allowance	accorder une remise	akɔʀde yn ʀəmiz
to grant an extension	accorder un ajournement *m*/une prorogation *f* d'échéance	akɔʀde œ̃ aʒuʀnəmɑ̃/yn pʀɔʀɔgasjɔ̃ deʃeɑ̃s
to grant sole selling rights	accorder le droit *m* de vente exclusive	akɔʀde lə dʀwa də vɑ̃t ɛksklyziv
gross profit	bénéfice *m*, produit *m* brut	benefis, pʀɔdɥi bʀyt, bʀyt,
gross weight	poids *m* brut	pwa bʀyt
group, concern	groupe *m*	gʀup
guarantee, warrant	garantie *f*/contrat *m* de garantie	gaʀɑ̃ti, kɔ̃tʀa də gaʀɑ̃ti
hall plan	plan *m* des halls (d'exposition)	plɑ̃ deʒal (d'ɛksposisjɔ̃)

handbill	**tract** *m*	tʀɑkt
hard disk	**disque** *m* **dur**	disk dyʀ
haulage, bulk . . .	**transport** *m* **en vrac**	tʀɑ̃spɔʀ ɑ̃ vʀɑk
to have in stock	**avoir en stock**	avwɑʀ ɑ̃ stɔk
head office, headquarters	**siège** *m* **social**	sjɛʒ sɔsjal
hidden defect	**défaut** *m* **caché**	defo kaʃe
highly competitive market	**marché** *m* **très compétitif**	maʀʃe tʀɛ kɔ̃petitif
hire purchase	**achat** *m* **à crédit**	aʃa a kʀedi
holding/parent company	**société** *f* **mère**	sɔsjete mɛʀ
honest	**honnête, intègre**	ɔnɛt, ɛ̃tɛgʀə
hostess	**hôtesse** *f*	otɛs
immediate	**aussitôt, par retour, immédiat**	osito, paʀ ʀətuʀ, imedja
to import	**importer**	ɛ̃pɔʀte
import licence	**licence** *f* **d'importation**	lisɑ̃s d'ɛ̃pɔʀtasjɔ̃
importer	**importateur** *m*	ɛ̃pɔʀtatœʀ
in advance	**à l'avance, d'avance**	a l'avɑ̃s, d'avɑ̃s
in transit	**en transit**	ɑ̃ tʀɑ̃zit
included	**compris**	kɔ̃pʀi
income tax	**impôt** *m* **sur le revenu**	ɛ̃po syʀ lə ʀəvny
indebtedness	**endettement** *m*	ɑ̃dɛtmɑ̃
in-depth knowledge of the trade	**connaissances** *f pl* **approfondies dans un domaine**	kɔnɛsɑ̃s apʀəfɔ̃di dɑ̃z œ̃ dɔmɛn
industrial fair	**foire** *f* **industrielle**	fwa ɛ̃dystʀijɛl
industrial plant	**entreprise** *f* **industrielle, usine** *f*	ɑ̃tʀəpʀiz ɛ̃dystʀijɛl, yzin
industrial production	**production** *f* **industrielle**	pʀɔdyksjɔ̃ ɛ̃dystʀijɛl
industrial standard	**norme** *f* **industrielle**	nɔʀm ɛ̃dystʀijɛl
to inform	**informer**	ɛ̃fɔʀme
inheritance tax	**droits** *m pl* **de succession**	dʀwa də syksesjɔ̃
initial order	**première commande** *f*	pʀəmiɛʀ kɔmɑ̃d
ink-jet printer	**imprimante** *f* **à jet d'encre**	ɛ̃pʀimɑ̃t a ʒe d'ɑ̃kʀə
input	**entrée** *f*	ɑ̃tʀe
inquiry	**demande** *f* **(de renseignements)**	dəmɑ̃d (də ʀɑ̃sɛɲmɑ̃)
insolvency	**insolvabilité** *f*	ɛ̃sɔlvabilite
instalment	**versement** *m*, **partiel** *m*, **tempérament** *m*	vɛʀsəmɑ̃, paʀsjɛl, tɑ̃peʀamɑ̃

to instruct, to train	**former professionnellement**	fɔʀme pʀɔfɛsjɔnɛlmɑ̃
instructions, leaflet, pamphlet	**notice** f	nɔtis
insurance	**assurance** f	ɑsyʀɑ̃s
insurance against loss on the exchange rate	**assurance** f **sur les pertes au change**	ɑsyʀɑ̃s syʀ le pɛʀt o ʃɑʒ
insurance certificate	**certificat** m **d'assurance**	sɛʀtifikɑ d'ɑsyʀɑ̃s
insurance company	**compagnie** f **d'assurance**	kɔ̃paɲi d'ɑsyʀɑ̃s
insurance policy	**police** f **d'assurance**	pɔlis d'ɑsyʀɑ̃s
to intend	**avoir l'intention de**	avwaʀ l'ɛ̃tɑ̃sjɔ̃ də
interactive	**conversationnel**	kɔnvɛʀsasjɔnɛl
interest for default	**intérêts** m pl **de retard/ moratoires**	ɛ̃teʀɛ də ʀətaʀ/ mɔʀatwaʀ
interested, to be . . . in	**être intéressé(e) à**	ɛtʀ(ə) ɛ̃teʀese a
interests	**intérêts**	ɛ̃teʀɛ
interface	**interface** m	ɛ̃tɛʀfas
interview	**entretien** m, **entrevue** f	ɑ̃tʀətjɛ̃, ɑ̃tʀəvy
inventories	**stocks** m pl	stɔks
inventory	**inventaire** m	ɛ̃vɑ̃tɛʀ
to investigate	**faire des recherches** f pl, **examiner**	fɛʀ de ʀəʃɛʀʃ, ɛgzamine
investment	**investissement** m	ɛ̃vɛstismɑ̃
invoice	**facture** f	faktyʀ
to invoice, to bill	**facturer**	faktyʀe
invoice amount	**montant** m **de la facture**	mɔ̃tɑ̃ də la faktyʀ
invoice number	**numéro** m **de la facture**	nymeʀo də la faktyʀ
invoicing	**facturation** f	faktyʀasjɔ̃
issue (of a magazine)	**édition** f **(d'une revue)**	edisjɔ̃
to issue, to make out (a cheque)	**émettre**	emɛtʀ(ə)
item	**(marchandise) lot** m, **(compte) rubrique** f, **poste** m	(maʀʃɑ̃diz) lɔ, (kɔ̃t) ʀybʀik, pɔst(ə)
job, position	**emploi** m	ɑ̃plwa
to join a firm	**entrer dans une entreprise** f	ɑ̃tʀe dɑ̃z yn ɑ̃tʀəpʀiz
joint venture	**co-entreprise** f	kɔɑ̃tʀəpʀiz
to keep the minutes	**rédiger le compte-rendu** m	ʀediʒe lə kɔ̃təʀɑ̃dy
keyboard	**clavier** m, **pupitre** m	klavje, pypitʀ(ə)
label	**étiquette** f **(de marque)**	etikɛt
laser printer	**imprimante** f **à laser**	ɛ̃pʀimɑ̃t a lazɛʀ

latest catalogue	**le tout dernier catalogue** *m*	lə tu dɛʀnje katalɔg
lawsuit, litigation	**procès** *m*	pʀɔsɛ
lawyer	**homme** *m* **de loi, conseiller** *m* **juridique, avocat** *m*	ɔm də lwa, kɔ̃seje ʒyʀidik, avɔka
leaflet, instructions, pamphlet	**notice** *f*, **instructions** *f pl*	nɔtis, ɛ̃stʀyksjɔ̃ lwe
to lease	**louer**	lwe
ledger	**le grand livre** *m*	lə gʀɑ̃ livʀə
legal reserves	**réserves** *f pl* **légales**	ʀesɛʀv(ə) legal
legally protected	**protégé par la loi**	pʀɔteʒe paʀ la lwa
letter of credit (L/C)	**lettre** *f* **de crédit, accréditif** *m*	lɛtʀ(ə) də kʀedi, akʀeditif
letter of intent	**lettre** *f* **d'intention**	lɛtʀ(ə) d'ɛ̃tɑ̃sjɔ̃
liabilities	**dettes** *f pl*	dɛt
liability	**responsabilité** *f*	ʀɛspɔ̃sabilite
liable for tax	**imposable**	ɛ̃pozabl(ə)
liquid funds	**valeurs** *f pl*, **disponibles**	valœʀ dispɔnibl(ə)
liquidation, bankruptcy	**faillite** *f*	fajit
liquidity	**liquidité** *f*, **solvabilité** *f*	likidite, sɔlvabilite
list of exhibitors	**liste** *f* **des exposants**	list dez ɛkspozɑ̃
list of products	**liste** *f* **des produits**	list de pʀɔdɥi
list price	**prix-catalogue** *m*	pʀi katalɔg
listing	**listing** *m*	listiŋ
litigation, lawsuit	**procès** *m*	pʀɔsɛ
to load, to unload	**charger, décharger**	ʃaʀʒe, deʃaʀʒe
loan	**prêt** *m*, **crédit** *m*	pʀɛ, kʀedi
local taxes, rates	**impôts** *m pl* **locaux**	ɛ̃po lɔko
long hauls	**transport** *m* **de marchandises à longue distance**	tʀɑ̃spɔʀ də maʀʃɑ̃diz a lɔ̃g distɑ̃s
loss	**perte** *f*	pɛʀt(ə)
lot	**lot** *m*	lo
lump sum	**somme** *f* **globale forfaitaire**	sɔm glɔbal fɔʀfetɛʀ
machine shop	**atelier** *m*	atəlje
magnetic head	**tête** *f* **magnétique**	tɛt maɲetik
magnetic tape	**dérouleur** *m*	deʀulœʀ
mail circular, mailshot	**envoi** *m* **postal collectif**	ɑ̃vwa pɔstal kɔlɛktif
maintenance contract	**contrat** *m* **d'entretien**	kɔ̃tʀa d'ɑ̃tʀətjɛ̃
to make, to produce, to manufacture	**fabriquer, produire**	fabʀike, pʀɔdɥiʀ
to pay	**payer**	peje
to make out/to issue (a cheque)	**émettre (un chèque)**	emɛtʀə

to manage	diriger	diʀiʒe
management	direction f de l'entreprise	diʀɛksjɔ̃ də l'ɑ̃tʀəpʀiz
manager(ess)	directeur/directrice	diʀɛktœʀ/diʀɛktʀis
managing director	directeur m général	diʀɛktœʀ ʒeneʀal
manual	manuel m	manɥɛl
to manufacture, to produce	produire, fabriquer	pʀɔdɥiʀ, fabʀike
to manufacture under licence	fabriquer sous licence	fabʀike su lisɑ̃s
marginal costs	coût m marginal	ku maʀʒinal
market	marché m	maʀʃe
market analysis	analyse f de marché	analiz də maʀʃe
market research	analyse f/étude f de marché	analiz/etyd də maʀʃe
market situation	situation f du marché	sitɥasjɔ̃ dy maʀʃe
market survey	étude f de marché	etyd də maʀʃe
marketing	vente f, commercialisation f	vɑ̃t, kɔmɛʀsjalizasjɔ̃
marking	marquage m	maʀkaʒ
mask, picture	masque m	mask(ə)
mass production	fabrication f en série	fabʀikasjɔ̃ ɑ̃ seʀi
master	artisan m, patron m	aʀtizɑ̃, patʀɔ̃
master file	fichier m	fiʃje
maturity date of contract	date f de l'échéance d'un contrat	dat də l'eʃeɑ̃s d'œ̃ kɔ̃tʀa
meetings	séances f pl	seɑ̃s
memory	mémoire f	memwaʀ
memory protection	protection f de la mémoire	pʀɔtɛksjɔ̃ də la memwaʀ
merchandise, commodity, goods	marchandise f	maʀʃɑ̃diz
merchant, trader	négociant m	negɔsjɑ̃
to merge	fusionner	fyzjɔne
merger	fusion f	fyzjɔ̃
metal container	bidon m	bidɔ̃
minutes, to keep the . . .	faire le compte-rendu	fɛʀ lə kɔ̃t(ə)'ʀɑ̃dy
model, pattern, specimen	échantillon m, modèle m, spécimen m	eʃɑ̃tijɔ̃, mɔdɛl, spesimɛn
monitor	écran m, moniteur m	ekʀɑ̃, mɔnitœʀ,
monopoly	position f de monopole	pɔsisjɔ̃ də mɔnɔpɔl
mortgage	hypothèque f	ipɔtɛk
mouse	souris f	suʀi

280

English	French	Phonetic
to negotiate the conditions of a contract	débattre des conditions f pl d'un contrat	debatʀ(ə) de kɔ̃disjɔ̃ d'œ̃ kɔ̃tʀa
net cash	comptant m net	kɔ̃tɑ̃t nɛt
net weight	poids m net	pwa nɛt
network	réseau m	ʀezo
no hidden extras	aucun frais m supplémentaire caché	okœ̃ fʀɛ syplemɑ̃tɛʀ kaʃe
non-conformity with sample	non-conformité f à l'échantillon	nɔ̃'kɔ̃fɔʀmite a l'eʃɑ̃tijɔ̃
notes payable	dettes f pl représentées par des effets de commerce	dɛt ʀəpʀezɑ̃te paʀ dez efɛ də kɔmɛʀs(ə)
notification	avis m, notification f	avi, nɔtifikasjɔ̃
notification address	adresse f notifiée	adʀɛs nɔtifje
number, a limited . . . of	un choix m limité de	œ̃ ʃwa limite də
to object to something	protester	pʀɔteste
offer, proposal	offre f	ɔfʀ(ə)
to offer (make a firm offer)	offrir ferme	ɔfʀiʀ fɛʀm(ə)
to offer subject to confirmation	offrir sans engagement	ɔfʀiʀ sɑ̃z ɑ̃gaʒmɑ̃
office automation	bureautique f	byʀɔtik
official catalogue (exhibition)	catalogue m de l'exposition	katalɔg də l'ɛkspɔsisjɔ̃
official receiver	syndic m, administrateur m de faillite	sɛ̃dik, administʀatœʀ də fajit
one-off production	fabrication f hors série	fabʀikasjɔ̃ 'ɔʀ seʀi
on-the-job training	formation f sur le terrain	fɔʀmasjɔ̃ syʀ lə tɛʀɛ̃
to open a fair	ouvrir une foire f	uvʀiʀ yn fwaʀ
to open an account	ouvrir un compte m	uvʀiʀ œ̃ kɔ̃t
to open the meeting	ouvrir une séance f	uvʀiʀ yn seɑ̃s
opening, vacancy	poste m vacant	pɔst(ə) vakɑ̃
operating expenses and revenue	frais m pl et produit m d'exploitation	fʀɛ e pʀɔdɥi d'ɛksplwatasjɔ̃
operating instructions	mode m d'emploi	mɔd d'ɑ̃plwa
operating system	système m d'exploitation	sistɛm d'ɛksplwatasjɔ̃
order	commande f, ordre m	kɔmɑ̃d(ə), ɔʀdʀ(ə)
order book	carnet m de commandes	kaʀnɛ də kɔmɑ̃d(ə)
order form	bon m de commande	bɔ̃ də kɔmɑ̃d(ə)

order number	**numéro** *m* **de la commande**	nymeʀo də la kɔ̃mɑ̃d(ə)
orders on hand	**commandes** *f pl* **en carnet**	kɔmɑ̃d(ə) ɑ̃ kaʀnɛ
to organize a fair	**organiser une foire** *f*	ɔʀganize yn fwaʀ
organizer (of a fair)	**organisateur** *m* **de la foire**	ɔʀganizatœʀ də la fwaʀ
to outline	**donner une vue** *f* **d'ensemble**	done yn vy d'ɑ̃sɑ̃bl(ə)
output	**rendement** *m*, **sortie** *f*	ʀɑ̃dmɑ̃, sɔʀti
outstanding accounts	**créances** *f pl* **à recouvrir**	kʀeɑ̃s a ʀəkuvʀiʀ
outstanding quality	**qualité** *f* **supérieure**	kalite sypeʀjœʀ
overdraft credit	**découvert** *m* **de compte**	dekuvɛʀ də kɔ̃t
to overdraw an account	**mettre un compte à découvert**	mɛtʀ(ə) œ̃ kɔ̃t a dekuvɛʀ
overdue	**en retard, arriéré**	ɑ̃ ʀətaʀ, aʀjeʀe
overhead charges	**coefficient** *m* **de frais généraux**	kɔefisjɑ̃ də fʀɛ ʒeneʀo
overhead costs	**frais** *m pl* **indirects**	fʀɛ ɛ̃diʀɛkt
oversight	**erreur** *f*, **inadvertance** *f*	ɛʀœʀ, inadvɛʀtɑ̃s
package	**colis** *m*, **paquet** *m*, **progiciel** *m*	kɔli, pakɛ, pʀɔʒisjɛl
packaging	**conditionnement** *m*	kɔ̃disjɔnmɑ̃
packing	**emballage** *m*	ɑ̃balaʒ
packing at cost	**emballage** *m* **au prix de revient**	ɑ̃balaʒ o pʀi də ʀəvjɛ̃
packing list	**liste** *f* **des emballages**	list dez ɑ̃balaʒ
pallet	**palette** *f*	palet
pamphlet, instructions, leaflet	**notice** *f*, **brochure** *f*, **prospectus** *m*	nɔtis, bʀɔʃyʀ, pʀɔspektys
paper feed	**réserve** *f*/**avance** *f* **de papier**	ʀezɛʀv(ə), avɑ̃s də papje
parent/holding company	**société** *f* **mère**	sɔsjete mɛʀ
part payment	**paiement** *m* **partiel/ tempérament**	pɛmɑ̃ paʀsjɛl, tɑ̃peʀamɑ̃
part-time workers	**main-d'œuvre** *f* **à temps partiel**	mɛ̃'d'œvʀ a tɑ̃ paʀsjɛl
to participate in a fair	**participer à une foire** *f*	paʀtisipe a yn fwaʀ
password	**mot** *m* **de passe, mot** *m* **réservé**	mɔ də pas, mɔ ʀezɛʀve
patented	**breveté**	bʀəvte
pattern, model, specimen	**échantillon** *m*	eʃɑ̃tijɔ̃

to pay, to make payment	**payer, régler**	peje, ʀegle
to pay into an account	**verser de l'argent (sur un compte)**	vɛʀse də l'aʀʒɑ̃ (syʀ œ̃ kɔ̃t)
payee	**bénéficiaire** *m*	benefisjɛʀ
payment, settlement	**paiement** *m*, **règlement** *m*	pɛmɑ̃, ʀɛgləmɑ̃
payment against bank guarantee	**paiement** *m* **contre garantie bancaire**	pɛmɑ̃ kɔ̃tʀ(ə) gaʀɑ̃ti bɑ̃kɛʀ
payment by acceptance	**paiement** *m* **par traite acceptée**	pɛmɑ̃ paʀ tʀɛt aksɛpte
payment by cheque	**paiement** *m* **par chèque**	pɛmɑ̃ paʀ ʃɛk
payment by irrevocable confirmed documentary letter of credit (L/C)	**paiement** *m* **par accréditif irrévocable et confirmé**	pɛmɑ̃ paʀ akʀeditif iʀevɔkabl e kɔ̃fiʀme
payment by sight draft	**paiement** *m* **par traite**	pɛmɑ̃ paʀ tʀɛt
payment of the balance	**paiement** *m* **du solde**	pɛmɑ̃ dy sɔld(ə)
payment on account	**versement** *m* **à compte**	vɛʀsəmɑ̃ a kɔ̃t
payment on receipt of goods (ROG)	**paiement** *m* **à la réception de la marchandise**	pɛmɑ̃ a la ʀesɛpsjɔ̃ də la maʀʃɑ̃diz
penalties	**pénalités** *f pl*	penalite
pension fund, superannuation fund	**caisse** *f* **de retraite**	kɛs də ʀətʀɛt
percentage	**pourcentage** *m*	puʀsɑ̃taʒ
period of contract	**durée** *f* **du contrat (délai** *m* **de)**	dyʀe dy kɔ̃tʀa (dele də)
period of limitation	**prescription** *f*	pʀɛskʀipsjɔ̃
personal data sheet	**curriculum** *m* **vitae bref**	kyʀikylɔmvite bʀɛf
personal secretary	**secrétaire** *m/f* **de direction**	səkʀetɛʀ də diʀɛksjɔ̃
personnel, workforce, staff	**personnel** *m*	pɛʀsɔnɛl
personnel manager	**chef** *m* **du personnel**	ʃɛf dy pɛʀsɔnɛl
personnel matters	**affaires** *f pl* **du personnel**	afɛʀ dy pɛʀsɔnɛl
piggyback (combined road and rail) service	**trafic** *m* **combiné rail-route, service** *m* **de ferroutage**	tʀafik kɔ̃bine ʀajʀut, sɛʀvis də fɛʀutaʒ
to place an order	**passer une commande** *f*	pase yn kɔmɑ̃d
place of destination	**lieu** *m* **de destination**	ljø də dɛstinasjɔ̃
place of dispatch	**lieu** *m* **d'expédition**	ljø d'ɛkspedisjɔ̃
plant manager	**directeur** *m* **de l'usine**	diʀɛktœʀ də l'ysin
plotter	**table** *f* **traçante**	tabl(ə) tʀasɑ̃t
plug-compatible	**compatible de prise**	kɔ̃patibl(ə) də pʀiz
policy holder	**assuré** *m*	asyʀe

poor quality	mauvaise qualité f	movɛz kalite
position, job	position f	pozisjɔ̃
postage	port m, affranchissement m	pɔr, afrɑ̃ʃismɑ̃
poster	affiche f	afiʃ
power supply	alimentation f en énergie électrique	alimɑ̃tasjɔ̃ ɑ̃ enerʒi elɛktrik
premium	prime f	prim
pre-tax profit	bénéfice m avant impôts	benefis avɑ̃ ɛpo
price increase	augmentation f de prix	ɔgmɑ̃tasjɔ̃ də pri
price list	liste f des prix	list de pri
price maintenance	prix m pl imposés, imposition f des prix	pri ɛ̃poze, ɛ̃pozisjɔn de pri
price reduction	réduction f de prix, rabais m	redyksjɔ̃ də pri, rabɛ
prices	prix m pl	pri
printed letterhead	en-tête m imprimé	ɑ̃'tɛt ɛ̃prime
printer	imprimante f	ɛ̃primɑ̃t
prior sale	vente f en priorité	vɑ̃t ɑ̃ prijɔrite
private line	ligne f permanente	liɲ pɛrmanɑ̃t
probation period	période f d'essai	perjɔd d'ese
to produce, to manufacture	produire, fabriquer	prɔdɥir, fabrike
producer's price	prix m à la production	pri a la prɔdyksjɔ̃
product description	description f du produit	dɛskripsjɔ̃ dy prɔdɥi
product liability	responsabilité f du fabricant/de l'importateur	rɛspɔ̃sabilite dy fabrikɑ̃/də l'ɛ̃pɔrtatœr
production	production f	prɔdyksjɔ̃
production costs	frais m pl de production	frɛ də prɔdyksjɔ̃
production period	durée f de production	dyre də prɔdyksjɔ̃
production programme	programme m de production	prɔgram də prɔdyksjɔ̃
production schedule	plan m de production	plɑ̃ də prɔdyksjɔ̃
professional experience	expérience f professionnelle	ɛksperjɑ̃s prɔfesjɔnɛl
profit and loss account	compte m de pertes et profits	kɔ̃t də pɛrt e profi
profit margin	marge f bénéficiaire	marʒ(ə) benefisjɛr
profit sharing	participation f aux bénéfices	partisipasjɔ̃ o benefis
profitability	rentabilité f	rɑ̃tabilite
pro-forma invoice	facture f pro forma	faktyr prɔ fɔrma
programming language	langage m (de programmation)	lɑ̃gaʒ (də prɔgramasjɔ̃)

284

to prolong, to extend	prolonger	pʀɔlɔ̃ʒe
prolongation	prolongation f	pʀɔlɔ̃gasjɔ̃
promotion (professional)	promotion f	pʀɔmɔsjɔ̃
promotional letter	lettre f publicitaire	lɛtʀ pyblisitɛʀ
property	propriété f	pʀɔpʀijete
property tax	impôt m foncier	ɛ̃po fɔ̃sje
proposal, offer	offre f	ɔfʀ(ə)
prospectus, catalogue	prospectus m, catalogue m	pʀɔspɛktys, katalog
proxy	fondé(e) m/f de pouvoir/de procuration commerciale	fɔ̃de də puvwaʀ, də pʀɔkyʀasjɔ̃ kɔmɛʀsjal
public relations	relations f pl publiques	ʀəlasjɔ̃ pyblik
publicity agency	agence f publicitaire	aʒɑ̃s pyblisitɛʀ
publicity campaign	campagne f publicitaire	kɑ̃paɲ pyblisitɛʀ
publicity expenditure	frais m pl de publicité	fʀɛ də pyblisite
purchase	achat m	aʃa
to purchase, to buy	acheter	aʃte
purchase price	prix d'achat	pʀi d'aʃa
purchasing manager	responsable m/f des achats	ʀɛspɔ̃sabl(ə) dez aʃa
qualification	qualification f	kalifikasjɔ̃
quality	qualité f	kalite
quality control	contrôle m de la qualité	kɔ̃tʀol də la kalite
quantity	quantité f	kɑ̃tite
quantity discount	rabais m d'achat en grande quantité	ʀabɛ d'aʃa ɑ̃ gʀɑ̃d(ə) kɑ̃tite
questionnaire	questionnaire m	kɛstjɔnɛʀ
quotation	offre f avec indication f de prix m pl	ɔfʀ avɛk ɛ̃dikasjɔ̃ də pʀi
to quote prices	donner, fixer, établir les prix	dɔne, fikse, etabliʀ le pʀi
rail transport	transport m sur rail	tʀɑ̃spɔʀ syʀ ʀaj
railway consignment note	lettre f de voiture ferroviaire	letʀ də vwatyʀ fɛʀɔvjɛʀ
random-access memory (RAM)	mémoire f vive, RAM	memwaʀ viv
range, a wide . . . of	assortiment m/un grand choix m de	asɔʀtimɑ̃/œ̃ gʀɑ̃ ʃwa də
rate of interest	taux m d'intérêt	to d'ɛ̃teʀɛ
raw materials	matières f pl premières	matjɛʀ pʀəmjɛʀ
read-only memory (ROM)	mémoire f morte, ROM	memwaʀ mɔʀt(ə)

receipt	**reçu** m	ʀəsy
receipts	**recettes** f pl, **entrées** f pl	ʀəsɛt, ɑ̃tʀe
receivables	**créances** f pl	kʀeɑ̃s
receiving order	**décision** f d'ouverture de faillite	desisjɔ̃ d'uvɛʀtyʀ də fajit
recourse	**recours** m	ʀəkuʀ
to refer to	**s'adresser à**	s'adʀese a
(our/your) reference	**N/Ref.:, V/Ref.:**	
references	**références** f pl	ʀefeʀɑ̃s
to refund	**rembourser**	ʀɑ̃buʀse
refund of costs	**remboursement** m de frais	ʀɑ̃buʀsəmɑ̃ də fʀɛ
to refuse a claim	**refuser une réclamation**	ʀəfyze yn ʀeklamasjɔ̃
regarding, re.:	**objet:**	ɔbʒɛ
registered office	**siège** m social	sjeʒ sɔsjal
registered trade mark	**marque** f déposée	maʀk depoze
to regret	**regretter**	ʀəgʀete
to reject a motion	**rejeter une demande**	ʀəʒəte yn dəmɑ̃d
reliability	(person) **honnêteté** f, **sérieux** m, (thing) **fiabilité** f	ɔnɛte, seʀjø, fjabilite
reloading, transshipment	**transbordement** m	tʀɑ̃sbɔʀdəmɑ̃
reluctantly	**à contre cœur**	a kɔ̃tʀ kœʀ
to remind somebody of something	**rappeler quelque chose à quelqu'un**	ʀaple
to remit	**virer**	viʀe
remittance	**virement** m, **versement** m	viʀmɑ̃, vɛʀsmɑ̃
to rent	**louer**	lwe
repeat order	**commande** f supplémentaire	kɔmɑ̃d syplemɑ̃tɛʀ
replacement	**échange** m	eʃɑ̃ʒ
representative, agent	**représentant** m	ʀəpʀezɑ̃tɑ̃
representative on commission	**représentant** m à la commission/au percentage	ʀəpʀezɑ̃tɑ̃ a la kɔmisjɔ̃/o puʀsɑ̃taʒ
to request	**demander**	dəmɑ̃de
requirements	**exigences** f pl	ɛgziʒɑ̃s
reservation of title	**réserve** f de propriété	ʀezɛʀv(ə) də pʀɔpʀijete
result	**résultat** m	ʀezylta
retail price	**prix** m de détail (au détail)	pʀi də detaj
retailer	**détaillant** m, **commerçant** m	detajɑ̃, kɔmɛʀsɑ̃
return, yield	**rapport** m, **revenu** m	ʀapɔʀ, ʀəvny

returnable container	container *m* consigné	kɔ̃tɛnɛʀ kɔ̃siɲe
revenues	recettes *f pl*	ʀəsɛt
to revoke an offer	revenir sur une offre	ʀəvniʀ syʀ yn ɔfʀ(ə)
rise	augmentation *f* de salaire	ɔgmɑ̃tasjɔ̃ də salɛʀ
road transport	transport *m* sur route/routier	tʀɑ̃spɔʀ syʀ ʀut/ʀutje
roll-on/roll-off service	service *m* roulier	sɛʀvis ʀulje
royalty	droits *m pl* de licence, redevance *f* de brevet	dʀwa də lisɑ̃s, ʀədvɑ̃s də bʀəvɛ
to run a business	tenir une affaire *f*	təniʀ yn afɛʀ
sack, bag	sac *m*	sak
salary	salaire *m*	salɛʀ
sale	vente *f*	vɑ̃t
sale or return	vente *f* à l'essai	vɑ̃t a l'esɛ
sales	chiffre *m* d'affaires	ʃifʀ d'afɛʀ
sales letter, promotional letter	lettre *f* publicitaire	lɛtʀ pyblisitɛʀ
sales manager	chef *m* des ventes	ʃɛf de vɑ̃t
sales on commission	vente *f* à la commission	vɑ̃t a la kɔmisjɔ̃
sales potential	potentiel *m* de ventes *f pl*, débouchés *m pl*	pɔtɑ̃sjɛl də vɑ̃t, debuʃe
sales promotion	promotion *f* des ventes	pʀɔmɔsjɔ̃ de vɑ̃t
sales territory	secteur *m* de vente	sɛktœʀ
sample	échantillon *m*	eʃɑ̃tijɔ̃
sample collection	collection *f* d'échantillons	kɔlɛksjɔ̃ d'eʃɑ̃tijɔ̃
sample of no commercial value	échantillon *m* sans valeur	eʃɑ̃tijɔ̃ sɑ̃ valœʀ
savings/deposit account	compte *m* d'épargne	kɔ̃t d'epaʀɲə
scanner	scanner *m*, numériseur *m* d'images	skanɛʀ, nymeʀisœʀ d'imaʒ
school leaving certificate	diplôme *m* de fin de scolarité	diplom də fɛ̃ də skɔlaʀite
screen, monitor	écran *m*, moniteur *m*	ekʀɑ̃, mɔnitœʀ
seaworthy packing	emballage *m* maritime	ɑ̃balaʒ maʀitim
second-rate quality	deuxième choix *m*	døzjem ʃwa
secretary (to XY)	secrétaire *m/f* (de XY)	səkʀetɛʀ
security	sécurité *f*, nantissement *m*	sekyʀite, nɑ̃tisəmɑ̃
selection of samples	choix *m* d'échantillons	ʃwa d'eʃɑ̃tijɔ̃
to sell	vendre	vɑ̃dʀə
to sell as sole agent	avoir la représentation exclusive, vendre en tant que représentant exclusif	avwaʀ la ʀəpʀezɑ̃tasjɔ̃ ɛksklysiv/vɑ̃dʀə ɑ̃ tɑ̃ kə ʀəpʀezɑ̃tɑ̃ ɛksklysif

to sell goods on commission	vendre des marchandises f pl à la commission	vɑ̃drə de marʃɑ̃diz a la kɔmisjɔ̃
to sell off	solder, liquider	sɔlde, likide
seller	vendeur m	vɑ̃dœr
seller's warranties	garanties f pl du vendeur	garɑ̃ti dy vɑ̃dœr
selling conditions	conditions f pl de vente	kɔ̃disjɔ̃ də vɑ̃t(ə)
selling expenses	frais m pl de vente/de commercialisation	frɛ də vɑ̃t/də kɔmɛrsijal-izasjɔ̃
selling price	prix m de vente	pri də vɑ̃t
semi-finished goods	produits m pl demi-finis	prɔdɥi dəmi'fini
to send off, to ship, to forward, to dispatch	envoyer, expédier	ɑ̃vwaje, ɛkspedje
to serve an apprenticeship	faire un apprentissage m	fɛr œ̃ aprɑ̃tisaʒ
service	service m de maintenance	sɛrvis də mɛ̃tnɑ̃s
service manual	notice f d'entretien m	nɔtis d'ɑ̃trətjɛ̃
to set up a business	se mettre à son compte	sə mɛtr a sɔ̃ kɔ̃t
to set up a stand	monter un stand	mɔ̃te œ̃ stɑ̃d
to settle a claim	régler une déclaration de sinistre/une réclamation	regle yn deklarasjɔ̃ də sinistrə/yn rɛklamasjɔ̃
to settle an account	régler une facture	regle yn faktyr
settlement	règlement m d'une facture	regləmɑ̃ d'yn faktyr
share	action f	aksjɔ̃
shift key	touche f de changement de mode	tuʃ də ʃɑ̃ʒəmɑ̃ də mɔd
shift work	travail en équipes, les trois-huit	travaj ɑ̃ ekip, le trwa-'ɥi
to ship, to forward, to dispatch, to send off	envoyer, expédier	ɑ̃vwaje, ɛkspedje
shipment, consignment	envoi m de marchandises	ɑ̃vwa də marʃɑ̃diz
shipping documents	documents m pl d'expédition	dɔkymɑ̃ d'ɛkspedisjɔ̃
shipping marks	marquage m sur emballage d'expédition	markaʒ syr ɑ̃balaʒ d'ɛkspedisjɔ̃
short hauls	transport m de marchandises à courte distance	trɑ̃spɔr də marʃɑ̃diz a kurt distɑ̃s

288

shortage	**manquant** *m*, **quantité** *f* **en moins**	mãkã, kãtite ᴂ mwẽ
to show, to exhibit	**exposer (foire** *f*)	ɛkspoze
showroom	**salle** *f* **d'exposition**	sal d'ɛkspozisjɔ̃
signature	**signature** *f*	signatyʀ
single European market	**marché** *m* **européen**	maʀʃe øʀɔpeẽ
size	**taille** *f*	taj
skid (rollers)	**chariot** *m*, **traîneau** *m*	ʃaʀio, tʀɛno
skilled worker	**ouvrier** *m* **spécialisé, ouvrière** *f* **spécialisée**	uvʀije spesialize, uvʀijɛʀ spesialize
slot	**slot** *m*	slɔt
software	**logiciel** *m*	lɔʒisjɛl
software house	**SSII**	ssii
sole proprietorship	**entreprise** *f* **individuelle/en nom personnel**	ãtʀəpʀiz ẽdividyɛl/ã nɔ̃ pɛʀsɔnel
solicitor	**conseiller** *m* **juridique**	kɔ̃seje ʒyʀidik
solvency	**solvabilité** *f*	sɔlvabilite
to sort	**trier**	tʀije
sound	**sûr**	syʀ
source program	**programme** *m* **source**	pʀɔgʀam suʀs
space, blank	**blanc** *m*	blã
special design	**fabrication** *f* **spéciale/ hors série**	fabʀikasjɔ̃ spesjal/ 'ɔʀ seʀi
special discount	**escompte** *m* **spécial**	ɛskɔ̃t spesjal
special packing	**emballage** *m* **spécial**	ãbalaʒ spesjal
special price	**prix** *m* **spécial**	pʀi spesjal
specialized fair	**foire** *f* **spécialisée, salon** *m* **professionnel**	fwaʀ spesjalize, salɔ̃ pʀɔfesjɔnel
specification	**cahier** *m* **des charges**	kaje de ʃaʀʒ
to specify delivery route	**préciser la voie d'acheminement**	pʀesizeʀ la vwa d'aʃəminmã
specimen, pattern, model	**échantillon** *m*	eʃãtijɔn
spreadsheet	**tableau** *m*	tablo
staff, workforce, personnel	**personnel** *m*	pɛʀsɔnel
stand, stall, booth	**stand** *m* **de foire**	stãd də fwaʀ
stand rental	**redevance** *f* **pour un stand**	ʀədvãs puʀ ᴂ stãd
standard quality	**qualité** *f* **standard**	kalite stãdaʀ
standing order	**prélèvement** *m* **automatique**	pʀelɛvmã ɔtɔmatik
statement of account	**relevé** *m* **de compte**	ʀəlve də kɔ̃t

statement of earnings	compte *m* de pertes et profits	kɔ̃t də pɛʀt e pʀɔfi
statistics	statistiques *f pl*	statistik
stipulated	stipulé dans le contrat *m*	stipyle dɑ̃ lə kɔ̃tʀa
stock	stock *m*, stocks *m pl* disponibles	stɔk, stɔk dispɔnibl(ə)
to stock, to store	stocker, entreposer	stɔke, ɑ̃tʀəpoze
stock clerk	chef *m* magasinier	ʃef magaziɲe
stock control	contrôle *m* des stocks	kɔ̃tʀɔl de stɔk
stock rotation	rotation *f*, renouvellement *m* des stocks	ʀɔtasjɔ̃, ʀənuvɛlmɑ̃ de stɔk
storage	stockage *m*, tenue *f* des stocks	stɔkaʒ, təny de stɔk
to store, to stock	stocker	stɔke
to streamline (production)	rationaliser, moderniser	ʀasjɔnalize, mɔdɛʀnize
strictly confidential	strictement confidentiel	stʀiktəmɑ̃ kɔ̃fidɑ̃sjel
subcontractor	sous-traitant *m*	su'tʀɛtɑ̃
subject, re: (regarding)	objet: *m*	ɔbʒe
subject to payment on royalties	avec droits *m pl* de licence	avɛk dʀwa də lisɑ̃s
to submit an offer	soumettre une offre	sumɛtʀ(ə) yn ɔfʀ
subroutine	sousprogramme *m*	supʀɔgʀam
subscription price	prix *m* d'émission/de souscription	pʀi d'emisjɔ̃, də suskʀipsjɔ̃
subsidiary	filiale *f*	filjal
subsidy	subvention *f*	sybvɑ̃sjɔn
substitute	produit *m*/marchandise *f* de remplacement	pʀɔdɥi/maʀʃɑ̃diz də ʀɑ̃plasmɑ̃
superannuation fund, pension fund	caisse *f* de retraite	kɛs də ʀətʀɛtə
superior	supérieur *m* hiérarchique, chef *m*	sypeʀjœʀ jeʀaʀʃik, ʃef
supplier	fournisseur *m*	fuʀnisœʀ
suppliers, contractors	entreprise *f* de transport	ɑ̃tʀəpʀiz də tʀɑ̃spɔʀ
to supply, to furnish a customer with goods	livrer, fournir, approvisionner	livʀe, fuʀniʀ, apʀɔvizione
supply contract	contrat *m* de livraison	kɔ̃tʀa də livʀɛzɔ̃
surcharge	supplément *m* de prix	syplemɑ̃ də pʀi
surtax	surtaxe *f*, impôt *m* supplémentaire	syʀtaks, ẽpo syplemɑ̃tɛʀ

to take on, to employ, to engage	embaucher	ɑ̃boʃe
to take out insurance	contracter une assurance f	kɔ̃trakte yn asyrɑ̃s
to take stock	faire l'inventaire m	fɛr l'ɛ̃vɑ̃tɛr
to take the goods back	reprendre une marchandise f	rəprɑ̃drə yn marʃɑ̃diz
take-over	rachat m/reprise f d'une entreprise	raʃa/rəpriz d'yn ɑ̃trəpriz
tape unit, tape-station	unité f de la bande magnétique	ynite də la bɑ̃d maɲetik
tare	tare f	tar
tariff zone	zone f de tarif	zon də tarif
tax	taxe f, impôt m	taks, ɛ̃po
tax allowance	exonération f fiscale/ abattement m fiscal	ɛgzonerasjɔ̃ fiskal/ abatmɑ̃ fiskal
tax consultant	conseiller m fiscal	kɔ̃seje fiscal
tax exemption	abattement m à la base	abatma a la baz
tax-free	exempt d'impôt(s)	ɛgzɑ̃ d'ɛ̃po
teleprocessing	téléprocessing m	teleprɔsesiɲ
Teletex	Télétex m	teletɛks
telex	télex	telɛks
temporary staff	personnel m intérimaire	pɛrsonel ɛ̃terimɛr
tender	appel m d'offre	apel d'ɔfr
terms	conditions f pl	kɔ̃disjɔ̃
terms of contract	conditions f pl du contrat	kɔ̃disjɔ̃ dy kɔ̃tra
terms of payment	conditions f pl de paiement	kɔ̃disjɔ̃ də pɛmɑ̃
testimonial	certificat m de travail	sɛrtifika də travaj
third-party insurance	assurance f de responsabilité civile	asyrɑ̃s də rɛspɔ̃sabilite sivil
tool	outil m, outillage m	uti, utijaʒ
total (sum) amounting to FF . . .	montant m total de . . . FF	mɔ̃tɑ̃ total də
trade	commerce m	kɔmɛrs
to trade	faire du commerce	fɛr dy kɔmɛrs
trade custom	usages m pl dans le commerce	yzaʒ dɑ̃ lə kɔmɛrs
trade discount	rabais m négociant	rabɛ negɔsjɑ̃
trade fair	foire f commerciale	fwar kɔmɛrsjal
to trade in	donner en paiement	dɔne ɑ̃ pɛmɑ̃
trade margin, mark-up	marge f commerciale	marʒ kɔmɛrsjal
trade mark	marque f de fabrique	mark də fabrik
trade payables	dettes f pl sur achats et prestations de service	dɛt syr aʃa e prɛstasjɔ̃ də sɛrvis

trade relations	relations *f pl* commerciales	ʀəlasjɔ̃ kɔmɛʀsjal
trade union	syndicat *m*	sɛ̃dika
trader, dealer	commerçant *m*, négociant *m*	kɔmɛʀsɑ̃, negosjɑ̃
to train, to instruct	former professionnellement	fɔʀme pʀɔfesjɔnɛlmɑ̃
trainee	stagiaire *m/f*	staʒjɛʀ
training, education	formation *f*/éducation *f*	fɔʀmasjɔ̃/edykasjɔ̃
training courses for salespersons	cours *m pl* de formation pour vendeurs	kuʀ də fɔʀmasjɔ̃ puʀ vɑ̃dœʀ
to transfer	virer	viʀe
transfer of title for the purpose of securing a debt	remise *f* d'un bien en propriété à titre de garantie	ʀəmiz d'œ̃ bjɛ̃ ɑ̃ pʀɔpʀijete a titʀe də gaʀɑ̃ti
transit, in . . .	en transit	ɑ̃ tʀɑ̃si
transport	transport *m*	tʀɑ̃spɔʀ
transport insurance	assurance-transport f	asyʀɑ̃s tʀɑ̃spɔʀ
transshipment, reloading	transbordement *m*	tʀɑ̃sbɔʀdəmɑ̃
to treat	traiter	tʀɛte
trend	tendance *f*	tɑ̃dɑ̃s
trial sample	échantillon *m* d'essai	eʃɑ̃tijɔ̃ d'esɛ
trustee	syndic *m* administrateur de faillite	sɛ̃dik administʀatœʀ də fajit
turnover	chiffre *m* d'affaires	ʃifʀə d'afɛʀ
turnover tax	impôt *m* sur le chiffre d'affaires	ɛ̃po syʀ lə ʃifʀə d'afɛʀ
typist	dactylo *f*	daktilo
unanimous(ly)	unanime, à l'unanimité *f*	ynanim, a l'ynanimite
to undercut	vendre moins cher que, pratiquer le dumping	vɑ̃dʀə mwɛ̃ ʃɛʀ kə, pʀatike lə dœmpiŋ
under patent law	sous le droit des brevets	su lə dʀwa de bʀəvɛ
under reserve	sous réserve	su ʀezɛʀv
undermentioned	mentionné ci-dessous	mɑ̃sjone si'desu
to underwrite a risk	assurer un risque	asyʀe œ̃ ʀisk
underwriter	assureur *m*, souscripteur *m* de risque	asyʀœʀ, suskʀiptœʀ də ʀisk
unemployment	chômage *m*	ʃomaʒ
unit cost	coût *m* unitaire	ku(t) ynitɛʀ
unit price	prix *m* à l'unité	pʀi a l'ynite
to unload	décharger	deʃaʀʒe

English	French	Phonetic
unskilled worker	manœuvre *m/f*	manœvrə
update	mise *f* à jour	miz a ʒuʀ
user identification (user ID)	identification *f*	idãtifikasjɔ̃
utility (program)	utilitaire *f*	ytilitɛʀ
vacancy, opening	poste *m* vacant, offre *f* d'emploi	pɔst vakã, ɔfʀ(ə) d'ãmplwa
valid	valable	valabl(ə)
valuation	évaluation *f*, estimation *f*	evalyasjɔ̃, ɛstimasjɔ̃
variable costs	frais *m pl* variables	fʀɛ vaʀjabl(ə)
VAT (Value-Added Tax)	TVA (taxe sur la valeur ajoutée)	Te Ve A (taks a valœʀ aʒute)
venture capital	capital *m* spéculatif, capital-risques *m*	kapital spekylatif, kapital'risk
via (Dover)	voie (Douvres)	vwa
to visit a fair	visiter une foire	viʒite yn fwaʀ
visitor at a fair	visiteur *m*	visitœʀ
vocational training, on-the-job training	formation *f* professionnelle	fɔʀmasjɔ̃ pʀɔfesjɔnɛl
to vote for/against	voter pour/contre	vɔte puʀ (kɔ̃tʀ)
voucher	pièce *f* justificative, récépissé *m* reçu, quittance *f*	pijɛs ʒystfikatif, ʀesepise ʀəsy, kitãs
wage(s)	salaire(s) *m*	salɛʀ
wage tax	impôt *m* sur les salaires	ɛ̃po syʀ le salɛʀ
warehouse	entrepôt *m*	ãtʀəpo
warehouse company	société *f* d'entrepôts	sɔsiete d'ãntʀəpo
warrant, warranty, guarantee	garantie *f*	gaʀãti
water transport	transport *m* par eau	tʀãspɔʀ paʀ o
waybill, consignment note	feuille *f* de route	fœj də ʀut
wealth tax	impôt *m* sur la fortune	ɛ̃po syʀ la fɔʀtyn
well-founded complaint	réclamation *f* fondée	ʀeklamasjɔ̃ fɔ̃de
wholesale price	prix *m* de gros	pʀi də gʀo
wholesaler	grossiste *m*	gʀɔsist
without charge	sans frais *f pl*, non facturé	sã fʀɛ, nɔ̃ faktyʀe
without obligation	sans engagement *m*	sã ãgaʒmã
word processing	traitement *m* de texte	tʀɛtəmã də tɛkst
work in progress	produit *m* en cours de fabrication	pʀɔdɥi ã kuʀ də fabʀikasjɔ̃
to work overtime	faire des heures *f pl* supplémentaires	fɛʀ dez œʀ syplemãtɛʀ

workforce, staff, personnel	**personnel** m, **effectifs** m pl	pɛrsɔnɛl, efɛktif
working hours	**durée** f **du travail**	dyre dy travaj
working storage (computer term)	**mémoire** f **de travail**	memwar də travaj
works council member	**délégué** m/**membre** m **du comité d'entreprise**	delege, mɑ̃br dy kɔmite d'ɑ̃trəpriz
workshop	**atelier** m	atəlje
wrapping	**papier** m **d'emballage** m	papje d'ɑ̃balaʒ
to write off	**amortir**	amɔrtir
year under review	**année** f **sous revue**	ane su rəvy
yield, return	**rendement** m, **rapport** m	rɑ̃dəmɑ̃, rapɔr
zero-rated	**sans TVA**	sɑ̃ Te Ve A

5

French–English Index of Technical Vocabulary

f feminine
m masculine
pl plural

à contre cœur m	reluctantly
à l'attention f **de . . .**	for the attention of (att: . . .)
à l'avance f	in advance
à moitié prix m	at half price
à vos/nos frais m pl	at your/our expense
abattement m **à la base**	tax exemption
abattement m **fiscal**	tax allowance
accepter une offre	to accept an offer
accepter une réclamation	to allow a claim
accès m **direct**	direct memory access
accord m	accordance

accord *m*, convention *f*	agreement
accorder la représentation par une entreprise	to entrust a firm with the agency
accorder le droit *m* de vente exclusive	to grant sole selling rights
accorder un ajournement *m*, accorder une prorogation d'échéance	to grant an extension
accorder une remise	to grant an allowance
accusé *m* de réception de la commande	acknowledgement of order
achat *m*	purchase
achat *m* à crédit	hire purchase
acheter	to buy, to purchase
acheteur *m*	buyer
acompte *m*, arrhes *f pl*	down-payment
acquérir une licence	to acquire a licence
acquisition *f*	acquisition
actif *m*	assets
actif *m* immobilisé	fixed assets
actif *m* réalisable/de roulement	current assets
action *f*	share
activité *f* de développement *m*	development activity
adopter une résolution *f*	to carry a motion
adresse *f*	address
adresse *f* notifiée	notification address
s'adresser à	to refer to
affacturage *m*	factoring
affaires *f pl*, faire des . . .	to do business
affaires *f pl* du personnel	personnel matters
affiche *f*	poster
affranchissement *m*	postage
agence *f* d'encaissement	collection agency
agence *f* générale	general agency
agence *f* publicitaire	publicity agency
agent de maîtrise	foreman
ajuster les prix *m pl*	to adjust prices
alimentation *f* en énergie électrique	power supply
amorce *f*	bootstrap (computer term)
amortir	to write off
amortissements *m pl*	depreciations
analyse *f*/étude *f* de marché	market analysis, market research
année *f* sous revue	year under review
annonce *f* publicitaire	advertisement
annuler	to cancel
annuler un contrat *m*	to cancel a contract
appel *m* d'offre	tender
apprenti(e) *m/f*	apprentice
apprentissage *m*, faire un . . .	to serve an apprenticeship

approvisionner	to supply to deliver
d'après la facture *f*	as per invoice
d'après le contrat *m*	as per contract
d'après votre commande *f*	as per your order, in accordance with your order
argent *m* **au jour le jour**	call-money
arrêter un compte *m*	to close an account
arriéré *m*	amount overdue
arriérés *m pl*	arrears
artisan *m*, **patron** *m*	master
assemblée *f* **générale ordinaire**	general meeting of the shareholders
assortiment *m*	range
assurance *f*	insurance
assurance *f* **de responsabilité civile**	third-party insurance
assurance *f* **sur les pertes au change**	insurance against loss on the exchange rate
assurance-crédit *f*	credit insurance
assurance-transport *f*	transport insurance
assuré *m*	policy holder
assurer un risque	to underwrite a risk
assureur *m*	underwriter
atelier *m*	machine shop, workshop
atteindre le quorum	to constitute a quorum
attester	to certify
au prix *m* **coûtant, au prix** *m* **de revient**	at cost
au sujet de	concerning
aux bons soins *m pl* **de (abs)**	c/o (care of)
aucun frais *m* **supplémentaire caché**	no hidden extras
augmentation *f* **de prix**	price increase
augmentation *f* **de salaire**	rise
aussitôt, par retour	immediate
assitôt que possible	at your earliest convenience
avantages *m pl* **en espèces, avantages en nature**	fringe benefits
avec droits *m pl* **de licence**	subject to payment of royalties
avis *m* **de crédit**	credit note
avis *m* **d'expédition**	dispatch note
avocat *m*	lawyer
banque *f* **de données**	databank
base *f* **de données**	database
bénéfice *m* **avant impôts**	pre-tax profit
bénéfice *m*/**produit** *m* **brut**	gross profit
bénéfices *m pl* **après impôts**	net profit
bénéficiaire *m*	beneficiary, payee
bidon *m*	can, metal container

biens *m pl* **de consommation**	consumer goods
biens *m pl* **d'investissement**	capital goods
bilan *m*	balance sheet
bilan *m* **annuel**	annual financial statement
blanc *m*	blank, space
boîte *f*	cardboard box, carton
boîte *f* **aux lettres électronique**	electronic mailbox
bon *m* **de commande**	order form
bordereau *m* **de débit**	debit note
branchement *m*	cable connection
breveté	patented
brochure *f*	brochure, leaflet
bulletin *m* **de livraison**	delivery note
bureautique *f*	office automation
cadeau *m* **publicitaire**	advertising gimmick
cadre *m* **supérieur**	executive
cageot *m*	crate
cahier *m* **des charges**	specification
caisse *f*	case
caisse *f* **de retraite**	pension fund
calcul *m* **(du prix de revient)**	calculation
calculer	to calculate
campagne *f* **publicitaire**	publicity campaign
candidature *f*	application
capital *m* **extérieur**	borrowed capital
capital *m* **propre**	equity capital
capital-risques, capital *m* **spéculatif**	venture capital
carnet *m* **de commandes**	order book
carte *f* **de la foire**	fair pass
carte-réponse *f*	business reply card
cash flow *m*	cash flow
catalogue *m*	catalogue
catalogue *m*, **le tout dernier . . .**	latest catalogue
catalogue *m* **de l'exposition**	official (exhibition) catalogue
catégorie *f*	grade
certificat *m* **d'assurance**	insurance certificate
certificat *m* **de travail**	testimonial
certifier	to certify
certifier un contrat *m*	to certify, ratify a contract
cession *f* **d'une créance**	assignment of a debt
chaîne *f*	assembly line
charger	to load
charges *f pl* **à payer**	accruals
charges *f pl* **fixes**	fixed costs
chariot *m*	skid (rollers)
chef *m* **des ventes**	sales manager

chef *m* du personnel	personnel manager
chef *m* du service financier	financial controller
chef magasinier *m*	stock clerk
chiffre *m* d'affaires	sales, turnover
chiffre *m* d'affaires estimé	estimated annual turnover
choix *m*, un grand . . . de	a wide range of
choix *m*, un . . . limité de	a limited number of
choix *m* d'échantillons	selection of samples
chômage *m*	unemployment
ci-joint	attached
circulaire *f*	circular
classifications *f pl*	classifications
clause *f* du contrat	contract clause
clavier *m*	keyboard
client *m*	customer
clore une réunion *f*	to close the meeting
coefficient *m* de frais généraux	overhead charges
co-entreprise *f*	joint venture
colis *m*	package
collaboration *f*	co-operation
collection *f* d'échantillons	sample collection
commande *f*	order
commande *f* d'avance	advance order
commande *f* supplémentaire	repeat order
commandes *f pl* en carnet	orders on hand
commerce *m*	trade
commerce, faire de . . .	to trade
commerçant *m*	trader, dealer
commerçant *m* en franchise	franchised dealer
commission *f*	commission
commissionnaire *m*	commission agent
compagnie *f* d'assurances	insurance company
compatible de prise	plug-compatible
complaisance *f*	courtesy
compris	included
compromis *m*	compromise
comptabilité *f*	accounting, bookkeeping
comptable *m*	accountant, bookkeeper
comptant *m* contre documents	cash against documents (CAD)
comptant *m* net	cash
compte *m*	account
compte *m* courant/de virement	giro account, current account
compte *m* d'épargne	deposit, savings account
compte *m* de pertes et profits	profit and loss account, statement of earnings
compte-rendu *m*, faire de . . .	to keep the minutes
compter	to bill, to invoice

compter, débiter	to charge
conception *f* technique	engineering
concession *f*	franchise
concessionnaire *m*	franchised dealer
conclure un contrat *m*	to contract, to enter into a contract
concordat *m*	composition
concurrence *f*	competition
concurrence *f*, être en . . .	to compete
concurrent *m*	competitor
conditionnement *m*	packaging
conditions *f pl*	conditions, terms
conditions *f pl* d'achat	buying conditions
conditions *f pl* de paiement	terms of payment
conditions *f pl* de participation	conditions of participation
conditions *f pl* de vente	selling conditions
conditions *f pl* du contrat	terms of contract
conditions *f pl* imprévisibles	circumstances beyond our control
conférence *f*	conference
conflit *m*	dispute
connaissances *f pl* approfondies dans un domaine	in-depth knowledge of the trade
connaissement *m*	Bill of Lading (B/L)
conseiller *m* fiscal	tax consultant
conseiller *m* juridique	solicitor, lawyer
conseiller *m* publicitaire	advertising consultant
consortium *m*	consortium
container *m*	container
container *m* consigné	returnable container
contracter une assurance *f*	to take out insurance
contrat *m* d'entretien	maintenance contract
contrat *m* de livraison	supply contract
contrat *m* de travail	contract of employment
contrat *m* de vente	contract of sale
contrat *m* est nul et avenu	the contract is null and void
contrat *m* expire	the contract expires
contre-maître *m*	foreman
contrôle *m*	audit
contrôle *m* de la qualité	quality control
contrôle *m* des stocks	stock control
contrôler, surveiller	to control
convention *f*	agreement
conversationnel	interactive
cours *m pl* de formation pour vendeurs	training courses for salespersons
courtier *m*	commission agent
couverture *f*	cover
couvrant les frais *m pl*	cost-covering

couvrir un risque *m*	to cover a risk
coût *m* marginal	peripheral costs
coût *m* total	all-in costs
coût *m* unitaire	unit cost
coûts *m pl*, frais *m pl*	costs
créance *f*	debt, claim
créance *f* douteuse	doubtful debt
créance *f* irrécouvrable	bad debt
créances *f pl* (balance sheet)	receivables
créances *f pl* à recouvrir	outstanding accounts
créancier *m*	creditor
crédit *m*	loan
crédit *m* à court/moyen/long terme	short-/medium-/long-term credit
créditer	to credit
curriculum *m* vitae	curriculum vitae
curriculum *m* vitae bref	personal data sheet
dactylo *f*	typist
date *f* de la facture	date of invoice
date *f* de l'échéance d'un contrat	maturity date of contract
date *f* d'expédition	date of shipment
dates *f pl* limites	deadlines
débattre des conditions *f pl* d'un contrat	to negotiate the conditions of a contract
débiter, compter	to charge
débiteur *m*	debtor
décharger	to unload
décider d'une requête *f*	to decide on a motion
décision *f* d'ouverture de faillite	receiving order
déclaration *f* de sinistre	claim
déclaration *f* sur l'honneur, affidavit *m*	affidavit
déclarer faillite *f*	to file for bankruptcy
découvert *m* de compte	overdraft credit
dédommagement *m*	compensation
dédommager	to compensate
défaut *m*	defect, fault
défaut *m* caché	hidden defect
délai *m*, supplémentaire *m*	additional period of time
délai *m* de prescription *f*	period of limitation
délais *m pl*	deadlines
délégué *m* (membre *m* du comité d'entreprise)	works council member
demande *f*	demand, inquiry
demande *f* de renseignements commerciaux	inquiry
demande *f* d'indemnisation	claim, debt

demander	to request
démonstration f	demonstration
démonter un stand	to remove a stand
densité f	density
dépenses f pl	expenditure, expenses
déposer un brevet m	to apply for the patent
dérouleur m	magnetic tape
description f du produit	product description
destinataire m/f	consignee
détaillant m	retailer
dettes f pl	liabilities
dettes f pl représentées par des effets de commerce	notes payable
dettes f pl sur achats et prestations	trade payables
deuxième choix m	second-rate quality
développement m des affaires	business development, growth
développement m prévu	anticipated growth
devis m	estimate
différend m	dispute
diplôme m de fin de scolarité	school leaving certificate
directeur/directrice	manager(ess)
directeur m de l'usine	plant manager
directeur m général	chairman, managing director
direction f de la foire	fair management
direction f de l'entreprise	management
diriger	to manage
disque m, disquette f	disk
disque m dur	hard disk
disque m souple	floppy disk
dividende m	dividend
documents m pl contre acceptation	documents against acceptance
documents m pl contre paiement	documents against payment
documents m pl d'expédition	shipping documents
dommage m	damage
donner en paiement	to trade in
donner les prix	to quote prices
donner une vue f d'ensemble	to outline
droits m pl de licence	royalties
droits m pl de succession	inheritance tax
duplicata m/double m du bulletin de livraison	duplicate consignment note
durée f de production	production period
durée f du contrat	period of contract
durée f du travail	working hours
échange m	replacement
échanger une marchandise f	to exchange the goods

échantillon *m*	pattern, model, specimen
échantillon *m* d'essai	trial sample
échantillon *m* publicitaire	free sample
échantillon *m* sans valeur	sample of no commercial value
échéance *f*/date *f* d'échéance	due date
écran *m*	display, screen, monitor
édition *f* (d'une revue)	issue (of a magazine)
éducation *f*	education, training
effacer	to erase
effecteur une livraison *f*	to effect delivery
effet *m* en souffrance	overdue bill
emballage *m*	packing
emballage *m* au prix de revient	packing at cost
emballage *m* d'export	export packing
emballage *m* maritime	seaworthy packing
emballage *m* spécial	special packing
embaucher	to employ, to engage, to take on
émettre (un chèque)	to make out, to issue
emploi *m*	job, position
employé(e) *m/f*	employee
employé(e) *m/f* de commerce	clerk
employeur *m*	employer
en ce qui concerne	concerning
en retard, arriéré	overdue
en transit	in transit
en-tête *m* imprimé	printed letterhead
endettement *m*	indebtedness
enregistrer une commande	to book, to enter an order
entrée *f*	entry, input
entrées *f pl*	receipts
entreposer	to store
entrepôt *m*	warehouse
entreprise *f*	business, company, firm
entreprise *f* individuelle	sole proprietorship
entreprise *f* industrielle	industrial plant
entrer dans une entreprise *f*	to join a firm
entretien *m*, entrevue *f*	interview
envoi *m* de marchandise	consignment, shipment
envoi *m* postal collectif	mail circular/mail-shot
envoyer	to dispatch, to ship, to forward
équilibrer un compte *m*	to balance an account
erreur *f*	error, oversight
escompte *m*	discount
escompte *m* au comptant	cash discount
escompte *m* spécial	special discount
estimation *f*	valuation
établir les prix	to quote prices

étiquette f (**de marque**)	label
être sans provision	to bounce
étude f **de marché**	market survey
évaluation f, **estimation** f	valuation
exécuter un ordre	to execute an order
exécution f **d'un contrat**	fulfilment of contract
exempt d'impôt(s)	tax-free
exigences f pl	requirements
exiger des dommages et intérêts m pl	to demand compensation
exiger le paiement m	to demand payment
exonération f **fiscale**	tax allowance
expédier	to ship
expéditeur m	consignor, shipper
expérience f **professionnelle**	professional experience
expert m	expert
expert m **comptable**	chartered accountant
exploiter un brevet m	to exploit a patent
exportateur m	exporter
exporter m	to export
exposant m	exhibitor
exposer	to exhibit, to show
exposer (foire f**)**	to show, to exhibit
exposer clairement son point de vue	to clarify a position
exposition f	exhibition
fabrication f **en série**	mass production
fabrication f **hors série**	one-off production, customized production
fabrication f **spéciale**	special design
fabriquer	to manufacture
fabriquer sous licence	to manufacture under licence
facturation f	invoicing
facture f	invoice
facture f **commerciale**	commercial invoice
facture f **consulaire**	consular invoice
facture f **pro forma**	pro-forma invoice
facturer	to invoice, to bill
faillite f	bankruptcy, liquidation
faillite f, **faire . . .**	to go bankrupt
se faire représenter par une entreprise	to entrust a firm with the agency
faux frais m pl	extras
fermer un compte m	to close an account
feuille f **de route**	waybill, consignment note
fiabilité f	reliability
fichier m	file

filiale *f*	subsidiary
film *m* **publicitaire**	commercial
fixer les prix	to quote prices
foire *f*	fair
foire *f* **commerciale**	trade fair
foire *f* **industrielle**	industrial fair
foire *f* **spécialisée**	specialized fair
fonder	to establish, to found
fondé(e) *m/f* **de pouvoir/de procuration commerciale**	proxy
formation *f*	training, education
formation *f* **professionnelle**	on-the-job training, vocational training
former professionnellement	to train, to instruct
fournir	to deliver, to supply
fournisseur *m*	supplier, contractor
frais *m pl* **d'administration**	administration expenses
frais *m pl* **de production**	production costs
frais *m pl* **de publicité**	publicity expenditure
frais *m pl* **de transport**	forwarding/freight charges
frais *m pl* **de transport compris**	freight included
frais *m pl* **de vente/de commercialisation**	selling expenses
frais *m pl* **et produit** *m* **d'exploitation**	operating expenses and income
frais *m pl* **indirects**	overhead costs
frais *m pl* **supplémentaires**	extras
frais *m pl* **variables**	variable costs
franchise *f*	franchise
fret *m*	cargo, carriage, freight
fret *m* **aérien**	aircargo, airfreight
fret *m* **contre remboursement**	freight collect
fusion *f*	merger
fusionner	to merge
garantie *f***/contrat** *m* **de garantie**	guarantee, warrant
garanties *f pl* **du vendeur**	seller's warranties
gratuit	cost-free, free of charge
grossiste *m*	wholesale dealer
groupe *m*	group, concern
heures *f pl*, **faire des . . . supplémentaires**	to work overtime
homme *m* **de loi**	lawyer
honnête	honest
honnêteté *f*	reliability
horaire *m* **aménagé (travail** *m* **à la carte)**	flexible working hours, flexitime

hôtesse f	hostess
hypothèque f	mortgage
identification f	user identification (user ID)
importateur m	importer
importer	to import
imposable	liable for tax
impôt m	tax
impôt m **foncier**	property tax
impôt m **supplémentaire**	surtax
impôt m **sur la consommation**	excise tax
impôt m **sur la fortune**	wealth tax
impôt m **sur le chiffre d'affaires**	turnover tax
impôt m **sur le revenu**	income tax
impôt m **sur les salaires**	wage tax
impôt m **sur les sociétés**	corporation tax
impôts m pl **locaux**	local taxes, rates
imprimante f	printer
imprimante f **à jet d'encre**	ink-jet printer
imprimante f **à laser**	laser printer
imprimante f **à marguerite**	daisy wheel printer
imprimante f **matricielle**	dot-matrix printer
inadvertance f	oversight
informations f pl **détaillées sur**	detailed information about
informer	to inform
inscription f	application
s'inscrire à (une foire)	to apply for space
insolvabilité f	insolvency
intègre	honest
intention, avoir l'. . . de	to intend
intéressé(e), être . . . à	to be interested in
intérêts m pl	interests
intérêts m pl **composés**	compound interest
intérêts m pl **de retard/moratoires**	interest for default
interface m	interface
inventaire m	inventory
inventaire m, **faire l'** . . .	to take stock
investissement m	investment
langage m **(de programmation)**	programming language
lecteur m	drive
lettre f **commerciale**	business letter
lettre f **de change**	Bill of Exchange
lettre f **de crédit, accréditif** m	letter of credit (L/C)
lettre f **de rappel**	dunning letter, reminder letter
lettre f **de transport aérien**	air waybill
lettre f **de voiture ferroviaire**	railway consignment note

lettre *f* **d'intention**	letter of intent
lettre *f* **publicitaire**	promotional letter
lettre *f* **publicitaire de relance**	follow-up letter
licence *f* **d'importation**	import licence
licenciement *m*	dismissal
licencier	to give notice (of redundancy, dismissal)
lieu *m* **de destination**	place of destination
lieu *m* **d'expédition**	place of dispatch
ligne *f* **permanante**	private line
liquidité *f*	liquidity
liste *f* **des emballages**	packing list
liste *f* **des exposants**	list of exhibitors
liste *f* **des prix**	price list
liste *f* **des produits**	product list
listing *m*	listing
litige *m*	dispute
livraison *f*	delivery
livrer dans les délais de livraison	to deliver within the specified time
livrer, fournir, approvisionner	to supply, to deliver
logiciel *m*	software
logiciel *m* **d'application**	application software
lot *m* **(marchandise)**	item
louer	to lease, to rent
louer une surface *f* **d'exposition**	to book exhibition space
machine *f* **à calculer (de poche)**	calculator
mailing *m*	electronic mail/E-mail
main-d'œuvre *f* **à plein temps**	full-time workers
main-d'œuvre *f* **à temps partiel**	part-time workers
manœuvre *m/f*	unskilled worker
manquant *m*	shortage
manuel *m*	manual
marchander	to bargain
marchandise *f* **défectueuse**	defective goods
marchandises *f pl*	goods, commodity, merchandise
marchandises *f pl* **en vrac**	bulk goods
marché *m*	market
marché *m* **commun**	common market
marché *m* **européen**	single market
marché *m* **intérieur**	domestic market
marché *m* **très compétitif**	highly competitive market
marge *f* **bénéficiaire**	profit margin
marge *f* **commerciale**	trade margin
marquage *m*	marking
marquage *m* **sur emballage d'expédition**	shipping marks

marque *f*	brand
marque *f* déposée	registered trade mark
masque *m*	mask, picture
matériaux *m* défectueux	faulty material
matériel *m* de fabrication	direct material
matériel *m* d'exposition	display material
matières *f pl* premières	raw materials
mauvaise qualité *f*	poor quality
mentionné ci-dessous	undermentioned
se mettre à son compte	to set up a business
mettre un compte à découvert	to overdraw an account
mélange *m*	blend (tea, coffee)
mémoire *f*	memory
mémoire *m* à disque magnétique	disk storage
mémoire *f* de travail	working storage
mémoire *m* morte, ROM	read-only memory (ROM)
mémoire *f* vive, RAM	random access memory (RAM)
mise *f* à jour	update
mode *m* d'emploi	operating instructions
modifier un contrat *m*	to amend a contract
moniteur *m*	monitor
monnaie *f* étrangère	foreign currency
montage *m*	assembly
montant *m* de la facture	invoice amount
montant *m* total de . . . FF	total (sum) amounting to FF . . .
monter un stand *m*	to install a stand
mot *m* de passe, mot *m* réservé	password
N/REF.:	our reference
nantissement *m*	security
négociant *m*	dealer, trader
non facturé	without charges
non-conformité *f* à l'échantillon	non-conformity with sample
norme *f* industrielle	industrial standard
notice *f*	instructions
notice *f* de montage	assembly instructions
notice *f* d'entretien	service manual
notification *f*	notification
notoriété *f*	business reputation
numérique	digital
numéro *m* de la commande	order number
numéro *m* de la facture	invoice number
objet *m*	subject, regarding
obliger	to compel
offre *f*	offer, proposal
offre *f* avec indication *f* de prix	quote

offrir ferme	to make a firm offer
offrir sans engagement	to offer subject to confirmation
ordre *m*	order
ordre *m* **du jour**	agenda
organigramme *m*	flowchart
organisateur *m* **de la foire**	organizer (of a fair)
organiser une foire *f*	to organize a fair
outil *m*, **outillage** *m*	tool
ouvrier *m* **spécialisé, ouvrière** *f* **spécialisée**	skilled worker
ouvrir un compte *m*	to open an account
ouvrir une foire *f*	to open a fair
ouvrir une séance *f*	to open a meeting
paiement *m*	payment
paiement *m* **à la livraison**	cash on delivery
paiement *m* **à la réception de la marchandise**	payment on receipt of goods
paiement *m* **contre garantie bancaire**	payment against bank guarantee
paiement *m* **d'avance**	advance payment
paiement *m* **du solde**	payment of the balance
paiement *m* **par accréditif irrévocable et confirmé**	payment by irrevocable confirmed documentary letter of credit
paiement *m* **par chèque**	payment by cheque
paiement *m* **par traite**	payment by sight draft
paiement *m* **par traite acceptée**	payment by acceptance
paiement *m* **partiel/tempérament**	part payment
palette *f*	pallet
papier *m* **d'emballage** *m*	wrapping
paquet *m*	package
parc *m* **des expositions**	exhibition centre
participation *f* **aux bénéfices**	profit sharing
participations *f pl*	partnerships
participer à une foire *f*	to be a participant at a fair
partiel *m*	instalment
parties *f pl* **contractantes**	contracting parties
passer un contrat *m*	to enter into a contract
passer une commande *f*	to place an order
passerelle *f*	communication line
patron *m*	boss, master
payable à la commande *f*	cash with order
payer	to pay
pays *m* **de destination**	country of destination
pénalités *f pl*	penalties
période *f* **d'essai**	probation period
personnel *m*	personnel, workforce, staff
personnel *m* **intérimaire**	temporary staff

perte *f*	loss
pièce *f* d'exposition	exhibit
pièce *f* jointe	enclosure
pièce *f* justificative	voucher
se plaindre de	to complain about
plan *m* de production	production schedule
plan *m* d'ensemble (de la foire)	floor plan
plan *m* des halls (d'exposition)	hall plan
planning *m* budgétaire	budgetary accounting
plus-values *f pl* en capital	capital gains tax
poids *m* brut	gross weight
poids *m* net	net weight
police *f* d'assurances	insurance policy
port *m*	postage
porter plainte contre . . .	to bring an action against . . .
position *f*	position, job
position *f* de monopole	monopoly
poste *m* (compte)	item
poste *m* vacant	opening, vacancy
potentiel *m* de ventes *f pl*	sales potential
pourcentage *m*	percentage
pratiquer le dumping *m*	to undercut
préciser la voie d'acheminement	to specify delivery route
prélever	to draw money from an account
prélèvement *m* automatique	standing order
première commande *f*	initial order
prendre note d'une commande *f*	to enter, to book an order
prendre part à une conférence *f*	to attend a conference
présenter une demande *f*/une requête *f*	to bring forward a motion
se présenter à	to apply for
président *m*	chairperson
prêt *m*	loan
prime *f*	premium
prise *f*	point (electrical)
prix *m pl*	prices
prix *m* à l'unité	unit price
prix *m* à la consommation	consumer price
prix *m* à la production	producer's price, factory gate price
prix *m* avantageux	favourable price
prix *m* concurrentiel	competitive price
prix *m* d'achat	purchase price
prix *d* de détail (au détail)	retail price
prix *m* de gros	wholesale price
prix *m* de revient	cost price
prix *m* de vente	selling price
prix *m* d'émission, de souscription	subscription price

prix *m* **fixe**	fixed price
prix *m* *pl* **imposés**	price maintenance
prix *m* **raisonnable**	fair price
prix *m* **spécial**	special price
prix *m* **tout compris**	all-in price
prix-catalogue *m*	list price
procès *m*	lawsuit, ligitation
production *f*	production
production *f* **industrielle**	industrial production
produire	to produce
produit *m* **brut**	gross profit
produit *m* **de remplacement**	substitute
produit *m* **en cours de fabrication**	work in progress
produits *m* *pl* **demi-finis**	semi-finished goods
produits *m* *pl* **finis**	finished goods
progiciel *m*	package
programme *m* **de production**	production programme
programme *m* **source**	source program
prolongation *f*	prolongation
prolongation *f* **d'un crédit**	extension
prolonger	to prolong, to extend
prolonger un contrat *m*	to extend a contract
promotion *f*	promotion (professional)
promotion *f* **des ventes**	sales promotion
propriété *f*	property
prospectus *m*	prospectus, catalogue
protection *f* **de la mémoire**	memory protection
protection *f* **du fichier**	file protection, write-lock
protégé par la loi	legally protected
protester	to object to something
publicité *f*	advertising
pupitre *m*	keyboard
qualification *f*	qualification
qualité *f*	quality
qualité *f* **de première classe**	first-class quality
qualité *f* **d'usage**	commercial quality
qualité *f* **moyenne**	fair average quality (faq)
qualité *f* **standard**	standard quality
qualité *f* **supérieure**	outstanding quality
quantité *f*	quantity
quantité *f* **en moins**	shortage
questionnaire *m*	questionnaire
quittance *f*	receipt
rabais *m* **d'achat en grande quantité**	quantity discount
rappeler quelque chose à quelqu'un	to remind somebody of something

rapport *m* annuel	annual report
rapport *m*, revenu *m*	return, yield
recettes *f pl*	revenues, receipts
recherches *f pl*, faire des . . .	to investigate
réclamation *f*	complaint, claim
réclamation *f* fondée	well-founded complaint
recours *m*	recourse
reçu *m*	receipt
redevance *f* de brevet	royalty
redevance *f* pour un stand	stand rental
rédiger le compte-rendu *m*	to keep the minutes
réduction *f* de prix, rabais *m*	price reduction
références *f pl*	references
refuser une réclamation	to refuse a claim
règlement *m* de la foire	exhibition regulations
règlement *m* des réclamations	adjustment
règlement *m* d'un litige, règlement *m* d'une facture	commercial settlement of a settlement
régler une déclaration *f* de sinistre	to settle a claim
régler une facture *f*	to settle an account
regretter	to regret
rejeter une demande	to reject a motion
relations *f pl* commerciales	trade relations
relations *f pl* publiques	public relations
relevé *m* de compte	statement of account
remboursement *m* de frais	refund of costs
rembourser	to refund
remise *f*	discount
remise *f* d'un bien en propriété à titre de garantie	transfer of title for the purpose of securing a debt
rendement *m*	yield, return
rendement *m*, sortie *f*	output
renommée *f* commerciale, notoriété *f*	business reputation
rentabilité *f*	profitability
rentrée *f* des commandes	bookings
report *m*	carry-over, brought forward
reprendre une marchandise *f*	to take the goods back
représentant *m*	agent, representative
représentant *m* à la commission	representative on commission
représentation, avoir la . . . exclusive	to sell as sole agent
reprise *f* d'une entreprise	take-over
réseau *m*	network
réseau *m* de distribution	distribution network
réserve *f*/avance *f* de papier	paper feed
réserve *f* de propriété	reservation of title
réserves *f pl* légales	legal reserves
responsabilité *f*	liability

responsabilité *f* **du fabricant ou de l'importateur**	product liability
responsable *m/f* **des achats**	purchasing manager
résultat *m*	(trading) result
retard *m*	delay
retirer	to draw money from an account
revenir sur une offre	to revoke an offer
revenu *m*	return, yield
ristourne *f*	discount
rotation *f* **des stocks**	stock rotation
rubrique *f* **(compte)**	item
sac *m*	bag, sack
saisie *f*	attachment (seizure of goods)
saisie *f* **de données**	data acquisition
salaire(s) *m*	wage(s), salary
salaires *m pl* **directs**	direct labour
salle *f* **d'exposition**	show room
salon *m* **professionnel**	specialized fair
sans engagement *m*	without obligation
sans frais *m pl*	without charge
sans TVA	zero-rated
sauf erreur	E & OE (errors and omissions excepted)
sauvegarde *f*	back-up saving
savoir apprécier	to appreciate
scanner *m* **(numérisseur** *m* **d'images)**	scanner
secrétaire *m/f* **(de XY)**	secretary (to XY)
secrétaire *f* **bilingue/trilingue/ multilingue**	foreign language secretary
secrétaire *m/f* **de direction**	personal secretary
secteur *m* **de vente**	sales territory
service *m* **après-vente**	after-sales/customer service
service *m* **de ferroutage**	piggyback (combined road and rail) service
service *m* **de maintenance**	service contract
service *m* **des devises**	foreign exchange department
service *m* **d'expédition**	dispatch department
service *m* **roulier**	roll-on/roll-off service
séances *f pl*	meetings
sécurité *f*	security
sérieux *m*	reliability
siège *m* **social**	head office, registered office
signature *f*	signature
situation *f* **du marché**	market situation
situation *f* **économique**	economic position
situation *f* **financière**	financial standing

slot *m*	slot
société *f* d'entrepôts	warehouse company
société *f* mère	holding/parent company
solde *m*	balance
solder	to sell off
solder un compte *m*	to balance an account
solliciter un emploi	to apply for a job
solvabilité *f*	solvency, liquidity
somme *f* globale forfaitaire	lump sum
sorte *f*	grade
soumettre une offre	to submit an offer
souris *f*	mouse
souscripteur *m* de risques	underwriter
sous le droit des brevets	under patent law
sous réserve *f*	under reserve
sous-traitant *m*	subcontractor
sousprogramme *m*	subroutine
spot *m* publicitaire	commercial
SSII	software house
stagiaire *m/f*	trainee
stand *m* de foire	stand
statistiques *f pl*	statistics
stipulé dans le contrat *m*	stipulated in the contract
stock *m*, stocks *m pl*	stock
stock *m*, avoir en . . .	to have in stock
stockage *m*	storage
stocker	to store, to stock
stocks *m pl*	inventories
strictement confidentiel	strictly confidential
structure *f* des capitaux	capital structure
subvention *f*	subsidy
succursale *f*	branch (office, shop)
suivre des cours *m pl* du soir	to attend an evening course
supérieur *m* hiérarchique	superior
supplément *m* de prix	surcharge
sûr	sound
surface *f* d'exposition	floor space
surtaxe *f*	surtax
surveiller	to control
syndic *m*/administrateur *m* de faillite	trustee, official receiver
syndicat *m*	trade union
système *m* d'expédition en commun	Community Transport Procedure (CTP)
système *m* d'exploitation	operating system
système *m* d'exploitation disque	disc operating system (DOS)
table *f* traçante	plotter

tableau *m*	spreadsheet
taille *f*	size
tampon *m*	buffer
tare *f*	tare
tarif *m* **du transport**	freight rate
taux *m* **d'escompte**	discount rate
taux *m* **d'intérêt**	rate of interest
taux *m* **uniforme**	flat rate
taxe *f*	charge, fee, tax
taxe *f* **professionnelle**	business licence tax
télex	telex
télécopie *f*	fax
téléprocessing *m*	teleprocessing
Télétex *m*	teletex
tempérament *m*	instalment
tendance *f*	trend
tenir une affaire *f*	to run a business
tête *f* **magnétique**	magnetic head
tirer un chèque	to draw a cheque
tomber à échéance *f*	to fall due
tonneau *m*	barrel
touche *f* **de changement de mode**	shift key
tract *m*	handbill
trafic *m* **combiné rail-route**	piggyback (combined road and rail) service
traîneau *m*	skid (rollers)
traite *f*	draft
traite *f* **non honorée**	overdue bill
traitement *m* **de l'informatique**	data transfer
traitement *m* **de texte**	word-processing
traitement *m* **électronique de l'information/informatique** *f*	electronic data processing
traiter	to treat
tranche *f* **d'amortissement**	amortization instalment
transbordement *m*	reloading, transshipment
transit, en ...	in transit
transport *m*	transport, carriage
transport *m* **aérien**	air transport
transport *m* **de marchandises à courte distance**	short hauls
transport *m* **de marchandises à longue distance**	long hauls
transport *m* **en vrac**	bulk haulage
transport *m* **par eau**	water transport
transport *m* **sur rail**	rail transport
transport *m* **sur route/routier**	road transport
transporteur *m*	carrier, forwarder

travail *m* en équipes, travail *m* les trois-huit	shift work
trier	to sort
TVA (taxe à valeur ajoutée)	VAT (value-added tax)
unanime, à l'unanimité *f*	unanimous(ly)
unité *f* centrale	central processing unit (CPU)
unité *f* de la bande magnétique	tape unit, tape-station
d'usage *m* courant, d'usage *m* dans le commerce *m*	accepted in the trade
usages *m pl* dans le commerce	trade custom
usine *f*	industrial plant, factory
utilitaire *m*	utility (computer program)
V/REF.:	your reference
valable	valid
valeur *f* comptable	book value
valeurs *f pl* disponibles	liquid funds
vendeur *m*	seller
vendre	to sell
vendre des marchandises *f pl* à la commission	to sell goods on commission
vendre en tant que représentant exclusif	to sell as sole agent
vente *f*	sale
vente *f* à la commission	sales on commission
vente *f* à l'essai	sale or return
vente *f* en priorité	prior sale
vente *f* forcée	compulsory sale
versement *m*	remittance
versement *m* à compte	payment on account
versement *m*	instalment
verser de l'argent (sur un compte)	to pay into an account
virement *m*	remittance
virer	to remit, to transfer
visiter une foire	to attend a fair
visiteur *m*	visitor to a fair
voie (Douvres)	via (Dover)
voies *f pl* de transmission	transmission channels
voter pour (contre)	to vote for (against)
zone *f* de tarif	tariff zone

6

Index